Critical literacy in the classroom

In a number of classrooms recently, in Australia and elsewhere, English teachers have been redefining their teaching and inventing new ways of 'doing' it. This is no longer a matter of drilling students in grammatical skills, instructing them in turning out a five-paragraph essay, responding appreciatively to novels, plays and poems or creating their own in a like manner. Instead, teachers are finding ways to help their students understand and act on critical literacy theories.

According to these ideas, English in all its forms and uses can never be a matter of neutral communication of factual information or fictional truths. Critical literacy investigates how forms of knowledge, and the power they bring, are created in language and taken up by those who use such texts. It asks how language might be put to different, more equitable uses, and how texts might be re-created in a way that would tell a different story.

Critical literacy is increasingly emphasised in syllabuses, government reports and the like and advocated by literacy theorists. This book is unusual in offering a carefully documented and critically analysed account of its implementation in ordinary classrooms. It:

- bridges the gap between academics' theorising and teachers' work
- describes how secondary teachers have planned and implemented critical literacy curricula on a range of topics, from Shakespeare to the workplace
- listens to teachers reflecting on their teaching and analyses classroom talk
- extrapolates from present practice to a future critical literacy in a digitised, hypermedia world.

Teachers and students of education, critical literacy advocates and theorists of literacy and schooling can learn much from this book, which shows how critical literacy teachers, and their students, are contributing to the ongoing reinvention of English education as critical literacy.

Wendy Morgan is Senior Lecturer in Language and Literacy Education at Queensland University of Technology, Australia. She has taught secondary English for many years, and published several books on critical literacy education.

Critical literacy in the classroom

The art of the possible

Wendy Morgan

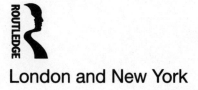

London and New York

First published 1997
by Routledge
11 New Fetter Lane, London EC4P 4EE

Simultaneously published in the USA and Canada
by Routledge
29 West 35th Street, New York, NY 10001

Typeset in Palatino by M Rules

Printed and bound in Great Britain by
T. J. International Ltd, Padstow, Cornwall

British Library Cataloguing in Publication Data
A catalogue record for this book is available from the British Library

Library of Congress Cataloging in Publication Data
Morgan, Wendy, 1944–
    Critical literacy in the classroom: the art of the possible/Wendy Morgan.
       p. cm.
    Includes bibliographical references and index.
    1. Language arts (secondary)—Australia. 2. Critical pedagogy—
    Australia. 3. Discourse analysis—Australia. I. Title.
    LB1631.M66 1997
    428′.0071′2—dc200   96-46525 CIP

ISBN 0-415-14247-4 (hbk)
    0-415-14248-2 (pbk)

to Alithea and Stephanie

whom I taught in class and out of class
and who continue to teach me much
about the possibilities of living and learning
of which they make an art

Contents

Preface   viii
Acknowledgements   x

1 Mapping the terrain of critical literacy: language,
  society and schooling   1

2 Reading curricula   29

3 School writing and textual selves   57

4 Between authority and freedom: teachers negotiating
  the discourses of English   79

5 Classroom talk: business as usual   106

6 'A Daniel come to judgement'   141

7 Postmodern classrooms on the borders?   167

  Coda   204
  Bibliography   207
  Index   215

Preface

> [P]ractice, not theory, is the larger notion, . . . while theory and knowledge can help us criticise and develop practice, they must always be criticised finally in terms of practice.
>
> (Warnock 1996: 31)

In much talk about education and educational research a chasm has been created between theory and practice. This book refuses to accept such a binary. Practices – of teaching and learning, reading and listening, writing and speaking – are always already theorised by those who carry them out, even if the theories are of the 'folk'. And theory is always acts of theorising: a practice of intellectual work.

But books about critical literacy or critical pedagogy have so far had more to say about theory-for-practice (the state of society, the nature of literacy, the institutions and practices of schooling, a vision for another, more just order) than they have about theory-in-practice – the mundane, often muddied interactions among critical literacy teachers and students in schools. Most teachers, however knowledgeable, would be dismayed to be told, for example, that 'the [all-purpose] teacher must call on recent discussions of discourse analysis to develop a terminology adequate to the complexity of signifying systems' (Berlin 1993: 264). Much more – or less – is needed than a sophisticated, esoteric terminology. Just how can teaching for learning be effected in critical literacy classrooms?

This book attempts to redress the balance between theory and practice and to address that question. It looks closely at the work of a number of secondary school teachers who aim to implement a critical literacy in their classrooms: at their planning of curricula and the principles that inform it; at the conversations that go on in lessons; and at their framing of assessment tasks and responses to student papers. It follows them in their conversations and those of students, as they engage with the concepts of critical literacy and the issues that arise when these are 'translated' into teaching practice. Here is 'the art of the possible'.

This book is inevitably of its time and place and may be none the worse for that. The place: Australia, in suburban schools. The time: a period when critical literacy is no longer simply an imported subversive alternative to 'business as usual' in English classrooms; in some education policy documents, professional development materials and the like it is becoming a matter of interest and some familiarity to English teachers. At this point, then, at a time and place that a version of critical literacy is becoming endorsed and even at risk of becoming an orthodoxy, some instances of that present practice repay scrutiny.

Any such practice will take on particular, even peculiar, forms as it adapts to its ecological niche. To focus on this is in keeping with critical literacy, which attends closely to the contexts of culture, society and history in order to understand (and critique) the ways we read and write and speak – hence think and are. Critics and theorists cannot read off universally applicable principles from a reading of local ways in classroom locales. But neither are these practices so idiosyncratic that they cannot speak, *mutatis mutandis*, to other teachers and educationists in other contexts. So it is too with the public syllabi, school curricula, texts and activities: while they are specific to their contexts, this does not mean that there is no relevance in stories about them: about the choices critical literacy teachers make, their negotiations with older practices of schooling, the constraints that contain the possibilities for the practice they invent on the spot. That is, this book is not urging an export drive in either the raw materials of texts or the technologies of teaching: no prefabs here, only perhaps a scaffolding of principles, and a few working drawings for adaptation in other climates.

In this book is a two-way trade, between one kind of expert (writers, academics) and another (teachers). The critical literacy teachers described here are contributing to the endless (re)construction of the field as they negotiate a theory for their practice. Their concerns, and the adjustments they make in their theorising and theorised practice, have much to say to those writers who have claimed their place in the vanguard of educational reform for social reconstruction. Classrooms are also sociocultural sites for a different practice, and critical literacy, like charity, begins at home.

'The possible' in the book's subtitle is meant to convey two meanings. One will have resonance for those familiar with the writing of critical pedagogues like Giroux and McLaren, who talk of a 'language of possibility' which is to complement the 'language of critique' characteristic of critical theory. They would speak of (and so conjure up, at least in imagination) possibilities for a more just and equitable, more tolerant and ethically responsible world. The other sense of 'the possible' sets limits to the first – but also realises it. This is the world where every utopia remains just that, but where it is possible to nudge reality – uncertainly, and never permanently – in that direction.

'The art' lies in the work of teachers, who are crafty artisans and also creative performance artists: choreographers, conductors, scriptwriters and actors. In their skill is the practice of critical literacy in classrooms.

Acknowledgements

My grateful thanks to the teachers at Park Ridge State High School, Brisbane, particularly Vicki Bothwell, Spiro Jovic and Ivy Monteiro for admitting me into their confidence, and above all to Lindsay Williams, a respected colleague, friend and friendly critic. To the Year 10, 11 and 12 English students of Park Ridge High in 1993–5 my thanks also, for their tolerance of my intrusions into their classrooms and conversations. So too I recall with affection the students who taught me much in our English lessons at The Geelong College, Victoria, and The Wilderness School, South Australia.

The hypertextual form of chapter seven was developed with Storyspace software.

The investigations reported in this book were made possible by a number of research grants: from the Education Faculty of Queensland University of Technology; the National Languages and Literacy Institute of Australia; and the Australian Association for the Teaching of English.

I have learned much from several colleagues in their responses to my first ideas: Ray Misson, Colin Lankshear, Peter Adams, Bill Corcoran and Michele Knobel. They are not of course responsible for my stubborn attachment to any dubious ideas that still appear in these pages.

Chapter 1

Mapping the terrain of critical literacy
Language, society and schooling

DISCOURSES OF ENGLISH: A GEOGRAPHY

A history is a story that purports to be true. But 'the' history of English as a school subject, and of critical literacy within that discipline, cannot so easily be told. For there are always competing histories, trundling a barrow or taking the lead with a band wagon, coming from somewhere and going to somewhere. So I would situate my account in this chapter within another discipline, of geography. Not that one can evade history – mine and others' pervade these pages. And not that a particular form of knowledge can claim to be the only bearer of ultimate truth. Different disciplines of knowledge offer different ways of 'reading' the world. Nonetheless, to talk of a 'geography of English' and a 'map of critical literacy' is to make the metaphor more salient: to remind us that this account offers viewpoints from various topographical sites rather than 'the' historical overview. (For sometimes controversial and always partial histories see for example Dixon 1967, Meek and Miller 1984, Hunter 1988, Doyle 1989, Elbow 1990, Goodson and Medway 1990, Willinsky 1990, B. Green 1993, B. Green and Beavis 1996.)

Here then is a first quick 'mud map' of the terrain, as I see it, to be critiqued and redrawn, with greater detail, in this and subsequent chapters.

Critical theories of literacy derive from critical social theory and its interest in matters of class, gender and ethnicity. Both share the view that society is in a constant state of conflict, for the possession of knowledge (hence power), status and material resources is always open to contest. Struggles to define the world and claim its goods are carried out by unequally matched contestants, for certain social groups have historically controlled the ideologies, institutions and practices of their society, thereby maintaining their dominant position. But since these are socially and historically constructed, they can be reconstructed. One of the chief means of such re/construction is language. Therefore critical literacy critics and teachers focus on the cultural and ideological assumptions that underwrite texts, they investigate the politics of representation, and they interrogate the inequitable, cultural positioning of speakers and readers within discourses. They ask who constructs the texts whose representations are dominant in a particular culture at a particular time; how readers come to be complicit with the persuasive ideologies of texts; whose interests are served by such representations and such readings; and when such texts and readings are inequitable in their effects, how these could be constructed otherwise. They seek to promote the conditions for a different textual practice and therefore different political relations than present social, economic and political inequalities as these are generated and preserved by literacy practices within and beyond formal education. (For more comprehensive accounts of critical literacy see Gee 1990, Fairclough 1989, 1992a, 1992b, Lankshear 1994, Lankshear and McLaren 1993, A. Luke 1993.)

Critical literacy, as practised in schools in Australia and elsewhere, is sometimes represented as being one of a number of competing or complementary versions of English teaching (e.g. Christie *et al.* 1991). Thus before filling in some of the features of this sketch and drawing a larger map of the areas that border it, we need to consider that notion of 'models'. This familiar term is flawed if it suggests a normative, even exemplary schema for English education and a predetermined form of practice, both of which exist apart from the person who teaches according to that 'model'. A preferable term is *discourse*, with its suggestions of interactive, negotiated conversations – those characteristic ways of talking and writing, hence thinking and being which are common to members of a particular socio-cultural group. These convey ideologies and thus enable members of the discourse group to make a particular sense of their experience and the world. Within any broad discursive field, such as that of English education, there will be a number of related discourses. These include those which advocate teaching the cultural heritage or functional literacy and so on. (The implications and applications of this theory of discourse will be taken up more fully in chapter three.)

A number of poststructuralist and sociolinguistic writers (e.g. Foucault 1972, 1980, Macdonell 1986, Gee 1990, Fairclough 1992b, Lemke 1995, Weedon 1987) have given the term 'discourse' a broader scope than the linguistic: they argue that the ways of talking which are characteristic of a social or cultural group have a bearing on more than just the language dimensions of people's lives. Particular uses of language (as discourses) do not just arise out of an ideology or social practice but help to constitute it. Thus people's thinking (both their ideologies and their argumentation), their social actions and attitudes and even their very sense of self are shaped by discourses. With some simplification, though it will serve present purposes, 'discourse' in this extended sense can be summed up in four points, each of which has bearing on English education and critical literacy.

First, discourses constitute and are constituted by social practices and institutions. In compulsory public education, for example, a dominant or 'commonsense' discourse about schooling in literacy and literature inheres in the official channels of policy directives, syllabi, curricula and assessment instruments; through preservice and inservice training; through the lore of the staffroom and the example of teachers at work. This and other discourses and hence practices of English convey a sense of what teachers value, how they act, what knowledge and competence are most important in teachers and students and how these can be measured.Through these means certain kinds of students and teachers are formed. Each discourse of English teaching has a coherence in the language, beliefs and practice of its proponents; but there are also incoherences. Indeed, any teacher – like any of us – is also internally inconsistent, since each of us participates in a number of discourses. In a certain context one discourse may be to the fore which is not congruent with another which in turn may shape our actions in a different situation.

Second, therefore: discourses 'converse' or 'argue' with one another. Any discourse tends to work in relation to others and in distinction from them, offering alternatives to what other discourses offer. Within the field of English, for example, the discourse of a humanist, progressive education (these days most often encompassed by the Whole Language Movement) promotes one kind of reading practice to 'develop' and 'encourage' one kind of reader, whereas in the discourse of critical literacy the aim of teaching is to 'produce' a different kind of reading and reader. But, as just noted, no teacher is circumscribed entirely by one discourse. Not only are there seepages between analogous discourses of English, but also we all have various political and religious and ethnic affiliations, belong to different interest groups and the like. Hence no one exemplifies a discourse in a 'pure' form, for no such purity exists in practice. Some of those conversations or arguments may take place within as well as between individuals and groups; the friction between them is what makes possible a meta-level understanding and the possibility of changing the balance of our affiliations to this discourse or that.

My third point is that discourses do political work. Any ideology organises the knowledge, beliefs and desires, the conscious and unconscious thoughts and attitudes of a group in such a way as to shape and maintain certain social and cultural arrangements. Therefore a discourse is always involved in circulating and promoting a certain ideology in preference to another, hence advancing the interests of a particular social group. It may do so all the more effectively if the knowledge and form of life so promoted are taken for granted as commonsense, having become so natural as to be invisible. For instance, it has been argued that a progressive education, so 'natural' to middle-class teachers, has profited the middle-class children who found its practices most congenial, most comfortably at one with home language and literacy practices:

With its stress on ownership and voice, its preoccupation with children selecting their own topics, its reluctance to intervene positively and constructively during conferencing, and its complete mystification of what has to be learned for children to reproduce effective written products, it is currently promoting a situation in which only the brightest middle class children can possibly learn what is needed. Conferencing is used not to teach but to obscure. This kind of refusal to teach helps reinforce the success of ruling-class children in education; through an insidious benevolence other children are supportively encouraged to fail.

(Martin 1985: 61)

This argument is quoted not so much as a self-evident truth – though it may hold some – as evidence of the politics at work in a discourse about the political nature of discourses in English education. If this view wins out, the power of its proponents to direct funding its way, establish preservice and inservice training programmes and the like is greatly enhanced. That is, the political work of any discourses in promoting an ideology is bound up with the differential and inequitable access which different social groups have to social status and material goods.

Finally, discourses help constitute not only the objects spoken and written about but also the speaking, writing subjects and their sense of self – their subjectivity (for we are subject to, and subject ourselves to, the discourses to which we give our affiliation). Discursive practices have a purchase on us which extends deeper than official institutions and the making of knowledge 'out there' in the world. As Weedon puts it (1987: 108): 'Discourses are more than ways of thinking and producing meaning. They constitute the "nature" of the body, unconscious and conscious mind and emotional life [of people subject to them]'. Even if not all that shapes us is accessible to our conscious scrutiny, we may see traces at work in and between people. For example, suppose I as a teacher adopt the discourse of life as a moral journey. This would provide me with an interpretative framework for my own experiences and those of others – students, characters in texts – and hence for my customary attitude and actions in the world. It would help mobilise my desires as a reader: I will want to participate in the challenges of fictional characters. It could even help sculpt my teaching and my relationships with my student readers. I would not of course be alone in this view; I am not a self-sufficient individual whose ideas and views originate with myself. I would be participating in a dialogue about moral development in humanist progressive teaching; I would be 'spoken into being' by the ways I am spoken or written about within such a discourse and thus the ways I speak and think about myself. And by such means I would be given an identity. It could be said that discourses about texts, reading, teaching and educational outcomes were having a conversation with each other through me. But by participation in that discourse I may also help to reshape it, particularly if I have access to other related or opposing discourses. And so I may be an agent of change in education, as well as subject to its discourses. For both of these aspects – subjectivity and agency – are crucial to critical literacy.

THE BORDER LANDS OF CRITICAL PEDAGOGY

As well as gesturing towards my geographical metaphor, the title of this section alludes to expressions favoured among advocates of radical pedagogy. Consider two book titles: *Between Borders* (Giroux and McLaren 1994) and *Border Crossings* (Giroux 1992). In others there is talk of 'border narratives' (McLaren 1995) and 'border pedagogy' (Aronowitz and Giroux 1991). Following postcolonial and postmodern emphases on difference, they define their term thus:

> Borders signal in the metaphorical and literal sense how power is inscribed differently on the body, culture, history, space, land, and psyche. When literacy is defined in monolithic terms, from the centre, within a linear logic that erases uncertainty, it only recognises the borders of privilege and domination.
>
> (Giroux 1991: x)

The expression might also suggest that they roam the frontiers in their educational work, that they are pioneers and scouts in advance of the main party in penetrating new terrain, and that they find themselves in company there with those who are deemed 'other' and consigned to the margins of the dominant socioeconomic and cultural order. This is one of a number of terms which the mostly American proponents of this discourse use to differentiate themselves from the mainstream of education – terms such as 'radical', 'critical', 'Freirean', 'liberation' or 'postcolonial' pedagogy.

These border lands are watered by other tributaries than those emanating from North and Latin America; still waters that run deep with perhaps less eclat. These arise in the springs of British and Australian cultural studies and in the critical sociolinguistic approaches of Norman Fairclough (1989, 1992a, 1992b), Gee (1990) and others.

The legacy of Freire

First to the New World and the innovative work of Paulo Freire in Brazil, as reported in his *Pedagogy of the Oppressed* (1970). Freire, teaching literacy to peasants there, came to condemn the 'banking' model of education, which consisted of 'depositing' tokens of learning in the vaults of passive students' minds. Instead, he advocated a collectivist, student-centred method in which learning emerges out of a joint negotiation of needs and interests, and blooms in a critical consciousness. This pedagogy has two

aspects: first, students learn to perceive social, economic and political contradictions in what they know and what they are told. Second, they learn
to take action against the oppressive and dominant elements within those
contradictory situations.

Following Freire's lead, North American advocates such as Shor (1980,
1987), Giroux (1983, 1988), Aronowitz and Giroux (1985, 1991) and
McLaren (1995) have taken up and developed its key concepts and projects
in a number of works (cf. also Lankshear and McLaren 1993). The abbre-
viated account of critical literacy which follows here might therefore seem
redundant, but I have two purposes. First, I want to indicate that this too
is an evolving discourse in its dynamic relations with other discourses
and practices. Second, by representing the ideal of critical pedagogy we
shall be in a better position to see how its realisation in Australian curricular and classroom practice fits that ideal: what is taken up, what is
modified, what ignored.

In brief, then, the advocates of critical pedagogy define it as a theorised
practice of teaching that opposes the dominant ideologies, institutions and
material conditions of society which maintain socioeconomic inequality.
Within education this radical movement aims to develop students' critical
awareness of those oppressive social forces, including school structures
and knowledges. So enlightened, students will be empowered and will
demonstrate their emancipation by practising an active citizenship to help
right society's wrongs. Thus individual selves and society at large will be
transformed through this language of critique and possibility and through
social action. As Lankshear and McLaren put it,

> In addressing *critical* literacy we are concerned with the extent to which,
> and the ways in which, actual and possible social practices and concep-
> tions of reading and writing enable human subjects to understand and
> engage the politics of daily life in the quest for a more truly democratic
> social order. Among other things, critical literacy makes possible a more
> adequate and accurate 'reading' of the world, on the basis of which, as
> Freire and others put it, people can enter into 'rewriting' the world into
> a formation in which their interests, identities and legitimate aspira-
> tions are more fully present and are present more equally.
>
> (Lankshear and McLaren 1993: xviii)

Such an emancipatory pedagogy did not have its sole fount in Freire. It is
better described metaphorically as a river with tributaries from various discourses: the 'new' sociology of education, and radical neo-Marxist
(Gramscian) and more recently feminist and postcolonial arguments for
the disempowered and hence for the reconstitution of society. The founding concepts held in common by these positions are sociological. First:
knowledge, meaning and truth are not 'out there' in some metaphysical
realm but are forged in the fires of history. Second: individuals are not

bounded and autonomous; rather, they too are formed within the ideologies and practices of society. Third: present societal arrangements are profoundly and systematically inequitable. And finally, such conditions can be changed when people come to understand the causes of those inequities. The influx of another stream, of poststructuralism (or postmodernism: the terms are sometimes used interchangeably), has more recently muddied the waters somewhat in its suspicion of the clarity of a single river of history (Lyotard 1984); but it is confluent with those earlier streams in its emphasis on the sociolinguistic production of meaning and selves.

A schooling for society

There has been disagreement over how far the structures of a society, including its educational systems, determine and reproduce the class, socioeconomic affiliations, culture and subjectivities of its members (e.g. Althusser 1971, Bowles and Gintis 1976, Bourdieu and Passeron 1977), and how far people also produce their culture and may thus transform aspects of it. Certainly writers on critical pedagogy have gone beyond analysis of such systems and structures and beyond resistance to them – from a 'language of critique' to a 'language of possibility', 'centred on hope, liberation, and equality. Agency and (raised) consciousness were reinstated on centre stage, albeit this time with structural constraints acknowledged' (C. Luke 1992: 26).

High among those constraints, according to this discourse of critical pedagogy, is education, which has a massive commitment to maintaining 'business as usual'. As noted, Freire argued that passive, authoritarian and alienating forms of traditional instruction function to reproduce the material inequities of a hierarchical society. Critical pedagogy writers in the United States have developed a similar argument about the paradoxically dehumanising and antidemocratic effects of a humanist, cultural heritage education and the dysfunctionality of a functionalist literacy programme. Schools stand in urgent need of reform, and they offer therefore an unparalleled opportunity for interrupting repressive ideologies and intervening against the inequalities they bring.

Such repressions and inequalities are not brought about for the most part by coercion in modern societies, according to this view. Education, like other institutions, is one means among many by which the dominant groups in society almost invisibly, almost unconsciously, maintain their hegemony and those who are socioeconomically disadvantaged are persuaded to consent to their inequality. Among the means by which such consensus is achieved are the stories and representations of society circulated in hegemonic ideologies. Accepting this story in broad outline, critical pedagogy theorists take as the focus of their critique not so much the forms of representation as the politics that inform such representations.

While such critique is not the whole of their agenda, which is ultimately to transform the sociopolitical order, it is a necessary step towards that end, since 'all texts are involved in politics and power, all tacitly endorsing certain platforms of action' (Berlin 1993: 260). There are two broad ways of understanding how such texts make meaning. A structuralist view of language and other sign systems argues that meaning is guaranteed in accordance with the codes and the values assigned them within a particular cultural context. By contrast poststructuralists argue that meaning is not given but is achieved provisionally through the struggles among a number of potential meanings and signifying practices. Each of these two views leads to a very different pedagogy. Certainly the latter view underpins the theorising of radical pedagogy writers. However, a more structuralist view of 'cracking the code' – uncovering the ideological meanings hidden in texts – seems at times closer to teachers' practice of deconstructing texts (as such teaching is described or as I have directly observed it) . The authority for this latter approach lies in that older structuralist Marxist conception of ideology as 'false consciousness', as well as in the discourses of English from Leavis onwards which also aim to liberate students from the snares of mass mediated popular culture. (This is a point to which we shall return.)

Pedagogy for praxis

If ideological *mis*representation leads to false or 'naive' consciousness, it must be possible for people to recognise its falsity and so attain to a (more) 'true' or critically clearsighted consciousness and a (more) accurate representation of their world. As mentioned, the development of such 'critical consciousness' in students is at the heart of Freire's educational 'praxis'. Teachers through their strategies bring students to the point where they can 'name their world' according to their experience of it and not according to the ideologies, institutions and discourses that declare it to be otherwise (Freire 1970). But such analysis and critique are the beginning, not the end, of education. For Freire's concept of praxis brings together knowledge and action. Unlike traditional education, which consists of a transference of knowledge from knowing teacher to ignorant, passive student, a liberating education '*is an act* of knowledge' and consciousness is '"intention" toward the world' (Freire 1985: 114; italics added). Thus the critique of existing sociopolitical conditions leads to the possibility of changing them. And so, through acting upon the world to reshape it more equitably people also reshape – transform – themselves. As Lankshear and McLaren sum up praxis,

> Praxis aims at enabling social groups to find the origins of their collective misunderstandings in ideology. In the grip of ideological distortions, social groups misunderstand their true situation and accept representations of reality that impede their recognition and pursuit of the interests

and goals they have in common. At the same time, ideological views of reality and the situation of social groups are not entirely false. The ideas and beliefs humans have of the world, and their place and circumstances within it, 'contain some indication of the real aims and interests of individuals and thereby imply some alternative self-conception based on their true meaning.' Praxis is to make explicit the genuine self-conceptions implicit in ideological views, and to indicate how contradictions and inadequacies contained in existing 'knowledge' and self-understanding can be overcome.

(Lankshear and McLaren 1993: 41)

How is such praxis to be carried out? In Freire's account (1970) he and his teams of literacy workers acted first as ethnographers of the people, observing their language and perceptions. They then selected a number of the people's key words to be used in developing their literacy and 'codified' each by a drawing or photograph. The next stage was crucial: problem-posing discussion of the situation so depicted, in order to explore this aspect of the learners' known reality. In this process of 'conscientisation',

They would stand back from it, relate to it existentially, and, with assistance from the coordinator, move to understand it more critically and to scrutinise their own initial understandings of it, thereby engaging in a critique of their own ideologically mediated perceptions of the situation in question, sorting out the 'truth' and 'distortions' in their self-conceptions.

(Lankshear and McLaren 1993: 44)

There is no denying the significance of the social revolutions brought about in part by such literacy campaigns among the illiterate and economically oppressed in various countries of Latin America and elsewhere. There is less agreement about how well such a radical pedagogy 'translates' into 'first world' schooling and whether the gains can be as far reaching with students who may be economically the 'oppressor'. In the postindustrial contexts of this world, the older revolutionary rhetoric still evident in the writing of Giroux, Aronowitz, McLaren and others might need to be replaced by a less melodramatic agenda for social equality, 'in the pragmatic terms of stubborn advocacy, continuing conversation, and small gains' (Knoblauch and Brannon 1993: 23). Nonetheless, much that is useful in Freire's educational praxis has been taken up by teachers in the literate nations of the West and North, as for example Ira Shor (1980) did in working with less privileged open admissions students at the City University of New York. In the course of codifying their forms of life he turned their attention to that most naturalised and ubiquitous feature of American life, the hamburger. The processes of discussion led students to research its nutrition, culture, politics and economics and to work in committee to change the decision-making structures of the student cafeteria and its menu so that its patrons could buy a cheap nutritious meal. To take the common burger as the text of the classroom is indeed to construct an object lesson in order to read a world in a word.

CRITIQUING THE CRITICAL

Radical pedagogy has not evaded criticism, on several grounds. The critiques have come mainly from poststructuralists and feminists, but it should not be thought that they have had the 'last word'; in recent years their slings and arrows have spurred critical pedagogy theorists to reconfigure their theory and practice. Discourses learn from as well as competing with one another.

What is truth?

One criticism has to do with the authority of the truth arrived at by such Freirean conscientisation as Shor has demonstrated. Some poststructuralists for example are profoundly sceptical of the view cited above (Lankshear and McLaren 1993: 41; italics added) of the 'ideological *distortions*' which lead people to '*misunderstand* their *true* situation'. These critics argue that it is simply not possible to get beyond or behind representation to some unconstructed truth or unmediated reality: 'it would make little sense, therefore, to speak of "mis"representation as though it were a political manipulation, an ideological cover for the truth' (Knoblauch and Brannon 1993: 172). But to concede that truth is constructed in texts, and that there are many candidates for the status of truth, entails fundamental challenges to a 'traditional' critical pedagogy. It means recognising that its 'truth' too is one discourse among many: that critical pedagogy is itself an ideology, located in the politics of its time and place, and can therefore lay no special claims to superior status and authority as the truth. For 'what the argument supposes to be true about dominant ideology – that it's a concealment of interestedness within an assertion of superiority – it must also either concede about itself or else suspend on its own behalf by appeal to a transcendental rationality' (Knoblauch and Brannon 1993: 163). Under the pressure of such arguments critical pedagogues concede the point:

> Educators need to be sceptical regarding any notion of reason that purports to reveal the truth by denying its own historical construction and ideological principles. Reason is not innocent, and any viable notion of critical pedagogy cannot exercise forms of authority that emulate totalising forms of reason that appear to be beyond criticism and dialogue.
> (Giroux 1992: 77)

But to grant the force of this argument about the systems of knowledge which are also systems of power and which thereby produce a 'regime of truth' (Foucault 1980: 131) might seem to subvert the whole rationale for critical pedagogy. That is, if all representations are always and only that, and there is no escape to some realm beyond, there would seem little point in conducting a critical inquiry into their truth or falsity. And thus the basis for moral indignation, the ground for launching political action, would become shifting sand.

Radical pedagogy theorists have countered such pessimistic scepticism by several means. One is to argue that modernist ideals of justice and equality can still be pursued by means of modernist tools of rational analysis, since modern rational analysis is capable of recognising also 'the limits of its own historical tradition' (Giroux 1992: 40). Another argument is to accept that any truth is indeed constructed within a social and historical context, to assert that this 'provides the politics of representation and a basis for social struggle' and to argue with Laclau that 'the lack of ultimate meaning radicalises the possibilities for human agency and democratic politics' (Giroux 1992: 52–3). That is, the terrain of reason and truth is the arena for struggle about whose views of the world will prevail; all the more reason then to engage in that struggle. Yet another, related, tactic is to claim a 'standpoint epistemology' of partiality on behalf of the oppressed. Rejecting the idea of a metaphysical truth or universal laws for conduct, the proponents of this epistemology take their stand on a commitment – without firm foundations in ultimate principles – to an ethics of social justice (Lankshear and McLaren 1993). Rather illogically perhaps this epistemology adheres to the belief that 'rational argument will ultimately prevail and that truth rather than power will adjudicate over claims to valid knowledge' (Usher and Edwards 1994: 23). But rationality and logic are in any case not the whole of the matter: the language of critique is to be complemented with a language of possibility which serves as a 'precondition for nourishing convictions that summon up the courage to imagine a different and more just world and struggle for it' (Giroux 1992: 78). The ethics and politics of this agenda still however depend on the persuasiveness of reason.

The project of enlightenment: a vanguard politics

Here lies another problem, if the radical pedagogy theorists trust to reason as the engine that will drive social change, while couching their reasoning in heavily academic discourse. To make this criticism is not to argue for a naive empiricism. But it is to recognise the problem with any view of critical consciousness as 'a higher state of grace into which the elect are received' (Buckingham and Sefton-Green 1994: 208) – for a (teacher's) esoteric discourse may have limited power to dissolve the ideological scales on others' (students') eyes. As an additional problem, these higher reaches of critical consciousness may ironically be one step on the slippery downward path to vanguardism. This is a politics founded on a belief that those few who are in advance of the footslogging cohorts have greater clarity of vision and therefore the right to point out the way. Such charges might be levelled also at this present discussion; however, there is legitimate work of analysis and discrimination to be done – it is after all the basis of the 'critical' – given several provisos: that the critique is not identified as the work of social change itself; that it also turns its scrutiny on itself and reflects on its constructedness; and that other ideologies are recognised as having credibility and legitimacy for those who live within them, even when we dispute their morality.

The case for rationality, founded on confidence that truth and meaning can be fully accessible to our conscious minds, has been the object of further poststructuralist critique. They have demoted to the status of myths not only the universality or transcendence of propositions but also the very ideal of the rational person, the autonomous 'sovereign' subject celebrated by humanists. These critics point out that not all our mental operations are available to us for analysis, and not all of them are logical. The inchoate and contradictory workings of our unconscious, our emotions, our desires, must be factored into any accounts of human thought and action – and into any pedagogy. And even then we will not have the whole story. A critical pedagogy is the more limited, they argue, to the extent that it works exclusively in the realm of the rational and enforces the rules of reason in the classroom (Ellsworth 1989) – and assumes a coherence, consistency and unity of a self that is essentially the same in all situations. For example, among Shor's students engaging in rational deconstruction of the hamburger, were there none who harboured still a desire for the food? Were there none whose sense of self did not still embrace the fast food lifestyle and derive pleasure from it in other social contexts? A critical pedagogy which aims to be effective in its transformational work needs to take into account the diverse, complex ways in which people negotiate their culture (Giroux 1992: 77).

When education is conceived as rational demystification and the teacher as a transformative evangelist-hero,

> much of what students are expected to 'discover' in such teaching is predetermined, and much of what passes for 'analysis' is simply a sophisticated exercise in guessing what's in the teacher's mind. Meanwhile, the possibility that students might *resist* what they perceive as an attack on their pleasures and preferences, as yet another attempt by teachers to impose their values and beliefs, seems to have been ignored.
> (Buckingham and Sefton-Green 1994: 129–30)

Freire and Macedo, among others, have denied such a tendency to coopt students to their own views: 'one has to respect the levels of understanding that those becoming educated have of their own reality. To impose on them one's own understanding in the name of their liberation is to accept authoritarian solutions as ways to freedom' (Freire and Macedo 1987: 41). Nonetheless the question remains as to when a project of enlightenment is education of and for the free and when it is imposition on those who are to be freed despite themselves. One example from a self-styled 'confrontational pedagogue' may exemplify these problems. Strickland (1991: 116) argues that any student's 'ignorance' is 'an active form of resistance to knowledge . . . analogous to the repression of the unconscious' and is founded in a desire to reproduce dominant neo-conservative ideologies.

> The point at which the student's 'ignorance' manifests itself, the point at which the student 'desires to ignore' the knowledge proffered by the teacher, is precisely the point at which any real learning has to take place. It is the point at which minds are changed. The difficulty comes in *flushing out this resistance and confronting it in the classroom.*
>
> (Strickland 1991: 17, italics added)

Here the 'ignorant' are seen in psychoanalytic terms; to other critical pedagogy writers who follow Freire their lack of understanding is attributed to a kind of simplicity or innocence toward the true nature of their oppression. Whether such ignorance is supposedly motivated or not, a similar problem inheres in these views concerning 'not only the rightness of liberatory action but also the appropriateness of ignoring the resistance it occasions' (Knoblauch and Brannon 1993: 166).

Empowerment

It is a truism of poststructuralism that the 'oppressed' or 'marginalised' are not 'natural', given groupings. Instead, when they are named as such they are made a group, and made therefore into subjects of the discourse of radical pedagogy. As we have seen, such acts of naming and knowing also give the 'knowers' an identity: they become 'transformative intellectuals' authorised to liberate those groups they have defined as subjects. But such teachers also become subjects of this discourse, even as this legitimises their actions and identity. It is a temptation for any 'liberatory' pedagogues to conceive of themselves as the 'empowerers' with the knowledge to name the nature of the domination which oppresses others and therefore the power to liberate those so oppressed from their oppressors. That is to fall into the 'us and them' trap of thinking in terms of mutually exclusive binary opposites and focusing only on 'them' as objects of concern and change. Giroux (1992: 15) does argue that teachers as transformative intellectuals 'offer their belief to others in a framework that always makes it debatable and open to critical inquiry'. Nonetheless, he goes on to talk of their being able to 'exercise power' unproblematically in translating their theoretical convictions into teaching practice – but does not acknowledge how debatable his own convictions are.

Paradoxically then the agenda of emancipation may entail regulation, when it categorises the oppressed and the liberators and governs the roles and potentialities of each. This may make it the harder to recognise that

> emancipation is only possible within power-knowledge formations within which there are also immanent forms of oppression. Emancipation and oppression are not transcendental states, but are themselves practices situated within power-knowledge formations.
>
> (Usher and Edwards 1994: 98)

In the complex and dynamic sociopolitical practices of education, the best intentioned educators may sometimes be oppressive in their practices. And the 'oppressed' may already be aware of their 'oppression' (even if they do not use that term), and may be exercising some power. This might take the form of resisting emancipation or negotiating an identity within the dominant culture and its discourses.

This issue is likely to be particularly pressing for teachers of first world students, whether 'working class' or 'middle class', whose forms of life are very different from those of the illiterate and dispossessed in Latin America or elsewhere. A project to enlighten the former may be self-defeating if it does not take into account not only their subordination to the teacher's authority within the school but also their complex productive relation-ships within their culture. For while their teachers may aim to 'emancipate' them from their thraldom to mass mediated culture and capitalist con-sumerism, such students may accumulate rather a kind of cultural capital, consisting of a capacity to play the intellectual game and mimic the terms and gestures of their teachers. Granted, all thought is learned and pro-duced within a shaping, constraining context; nonetheless the risk remains that members of a 'school of thought' may be merely thinkers similarly schooled.

As we have seen, the aim of such schooling is to 'empower' students, not only to do the work of critique but consequently to become agents for democratic renewal, since 'social betterment must be the necessary conse-quence of individual flourishing' (Giroux 1992: 11). Particular concepts of power have been implicit in much of the foregoing discussion. The very word and idea of 'empowerment' have unfortunately become banal in much recent educational talk. Indeed, the whole notion is problematic if power is understood to be a possession which can be given by one person who has it to another who does not. Those who are powerless are defined as such in relation to a power which is conceived of as oppressive; but those who empower are defined in relation to an enabling conception of power.

We have seen already the risk of arrogance when the teachers are author-ised as agents of empowerment and emancipation. There is also a risk of overestimating their influence. Students may not share their teacher's belief that his or her ideologies are visibly powerful and self-evidently persuasive. They may not therefore want to appropriate their teacher's knowledge, beliefs and practices. (For the classic exploration of such dilemmas see Ellsworth 1989.) By contrast to this view of power as property is the poststructuralist view of power as produced in and by social relationships and therefore producing certain roles and identities in people. If power has no simple substance which one empowering person can transmit to another, then the desired goal of empowerment may also dissolve in uncertainty – unless the means and ends of teaching can be thought of in very different terms as relative, productive and negotiated power relations. (Hence the focus of this book on the momentary, mundane minutiae of classroom practice.)

Dialogue: voices speaking differently

As we have seen, Freirean emancipation is to be effected not simply or solely by the teacher's demonstrations of analysis and critique of oppressive conditions but through teacher–student dialogue. Here students learn to raise their voices in naming those conditions as they know them to be, not as they have been told these must be. For those who have been silenced this act may itself be empowering. And it leads to further action as students and teacher engage in dialectic with the texts, ideologies and institutions which have a vested interest in maintaining that silence.

The goal of such dialogue, to American advocates of critical pedagogy, is a reinvigorated democracy. Freedom of speech (within limits) is of course a cornerstone of democracy, in which various groups may tell their own story their way and be given the courtesy of a fair hearing. Hence the citizens of such an ideal democracy will accept their and others' forms of life in their diversity. At the same time these active and responsible citizens will critique business, government, the media and other aspects of public life. Such tolerance and eternal vigilance are in the cause of a better world society and environment, now and in the future, for themselves and their fellows.

Returning to this less than ideal present, however, there are tensions and contradictions in the imperative to speak out of one's experience, to speak of one's oppression. The unproblematic celebration of students' different voices, Giroux concedes, 'has increasingly been reduced to a pedagogical process that is as reactionary as it is inward looking' (1992: 80; cf. Orner 1992). That is, such dialogue among students is designed to give expression to a range of knowledges and viewpoints and so to permit a dialogue across those differences. However, this may take the form of a polite *conversazione* in which differences are politely accommodated and identities are confirmed. Or it may silence some even in the attempt to speak for all members of a group. Or it may erupt as a confrontationist 'talking back' that is 'constructed within communities of resistance and is a condition of survival' (Ellsworth 1989). While any such speech is a kind of social action, it may serve to maintain partisan politics and inequities.

Somewhat different problems with the politics of voice become visible in this admirable but difficult advice by Sholle and Denski (1993: 308):

> Such a pedagogy must allow students to speak from their own experience at the same time that it encourages them to identify and unravel the codes of popular culture that may work to construct subject relations that serve to silence and disempower them.

For a start there is the problem of 'experience'. This is presented as unproblematically authentic and coherent: something we can know and sum up in words. But what if experience is already constructed like ourselves through discourse? (This issue is addressed further in chapter three.) And when such confessions occur in the sound shell of the classroom further difficulties arise, of voyeuristic pleasure or surveillance and critique from less duped teacher and peers. But students are not so easily fooled into articulating their identity and experiences in terms which are to be publicly critiqued as 'disempowering'.

The question remains then of how effective such voicing and such a language of critique may be as a means of enabling people to be agents in transforming their lives and society. Certainly the desire to encourage such speech and dialogue is admirable; but naïvety about the power relations involved may undermine any effectiveness.

Praxis: agency for social change

Any form of education aims to bring about changes in students. It must therefore have in view both what an educated person should be and the ideal society to whose realisation they will contribute. More humanist discourses of education, conservative or liberal, have focused on the individual as their goal. Such educated individuals will presumably contribute to the betterment of their society insofar as adjustments to the status quo are desirable. This of course falls far short of the more radically utopian ideal of critical pedagogy. In this wider sociopolitical agenda schools are a key site of struggle. In one stage of this struggle students are to be developed as fully conscious, rational individuals with a meta-level understanding of language and politics and their roles as subjects. Next they are then to be mobilised as agents, active citizens committed to democratic action for the sociopolitical reconstruction of society. What remains rather hazy in a number of accounts of critical teaching is how student subjects of discourses become such agents. This is part of a larger debate about how far ideologies and discourses determine our thoughts and actions. More recently writers on critical pedagogy (e.g. Lankshear and McLaren

1993) have acknowledged how impossible it is to disentangle subjectivity from agency, given the complexity of subject positions – multiple, shifting, constructed and reconstructed – and agency always in process of achievement, always constrained. So too there are no tidy formulations about how the ethical (the relation to or disposition of oneself, the governance of the self) works with, for, alongside or against the political (the relations among people and the governance of groups). Since our understanding is so provisional, so incomplete, a kind of humility is needed in undertaking the work of critical literacy.

FOUR ENGLISHES IN AUSTRALIA

This next section briefly sketches more of the features of four sometimes overlapping, sometimes competing, discourses of English. These are variously current in the English-speaking world, so although the focus here is on the Australian context, readers elsewhere may well be reminded of features familiar in their local terrain. The purpose of this geography is to locate one of those discourses, critical literacy, in relation to neighbouring features of the educational landscape. By this means we may more easily define its contours – remembering the cautions at the beginning of this chapter, that this too is a partial and interested account.

Such accounts in Australia (e.g. the *Statement on English*, see Australian Education Council and Curriculum Corporation 1994b) and elsewhere (e.g. in Britain the 'Cox Report' 1989: see Cox 1991) often categorise certain 'models'. With some variation these have become so familiar they have taken on the status of unquestionable reality, as distinct and consistent forms of English teaching. Of course, such discourses about English education have a purpose. This may be to make a space for an emergent rival by showing the inadequacies of all other claims to define the 'proper' business of English (see Christie *et al.* 1991). Or it may be to make a case for a policy document by showing how it embraces all approaches in a tolerant synthesis (e.g. the Queensland Syllabus: Department of Education 1994b).

While critical literacy, like charity, begins at home and may need to unsettle the comforts of these certainties, there is enough rough correspondence between these categories and the practices of English teachers for us to proceed – with caution, remembering from discussion earlier in this chapter how hybrid such discourse-practices may be.

In my story there are four sometimes overlapping groupings, founded on different concerns: aesthetic, ethical, rhetorical or political. The aesthetic takes an often conservative approach to a bookish cultural heritage; the ethical concerns itself with the personal and literary development of readers and writers; the rhetorical has a functional emphasis on appropriate or correct expression and use of genres; and the political centres on the effects of power in texts and society. Any of these discourses can and does make authoritative claims for its truth and value according to its own founding principles, and it is indeed productive for the teachers and students who find themselves within it.

In Australia the discourse of 'the' cultural heritage is not currrently in the ascendant among educators and is certainly less evident in Australia than in the conservative restorations of Britain and the United States – though occasionally vociferous teachers, academics and members of the public wage rearguard action. Residual traces of this discourse exist unevenly in two mutually confirming spheres: in some school and university syllabi, book lists, textbooks, teaching and examinations; and in aspects of the institutions of publishing, bookselling, arts funding, prizes and the like. Its proponents have a vision of culture as the persons and products of an educated sensibility. Those so educated are offered a particular subjectivity: attuned to nuances of language, keenly alert to excellence in artistry, ever refining their moral vision through the explorations of literature. This admirable aspiration needs to be taken seriously, as do the arguments of its opponents: that this hierarchy of tastes, institutions and practices is dubious in its judgements and exclusive in its claims to superiority; and that its attachment to universal aesthetic and moral values and literary standards covertly carries an oligarchic politics. That is, these standards are often assimilated to the maintenance of civilisation as 'we' know it and nostalgia for an imaginary golden age of a shared past. And thus it shores up the privileged position of the 'cultured' class.

The discourse that promotes students' growth as responsive, expressive individuals had wide currency in Australia in the 1970s and 1980s. It met little head-on resistance from cultural heritage teachers, partly perhaps because its sway was always greatest in primary and lower secondary English teaching and it could be seen as a juvenile developmental phase preparatory to the more rigorous academic work of pre-university English. This discourse has also been underpinned by educational and other sociocultural institutions and practices. These include the academic disciplines of developmental psychology, reader response theories and pedagogies, and institutionalised educational movements like process writing or Whole Language with their professional development programmes. Traces of the discourse are now most visible in syllabus imperatives to teachers and stated outcomes for students (in Profiles, Performance Standards and the like) that writers should undergo the orthodox, sometimes lock-step, stages of planning, drafting, conferencing, revising and publishing.

This discourse is founded in a nostalgia different from the historical gaze of the cultural heritage; here it is for childhood as a time of unfettered exploration of self and environment and more generally for an individuality which is autonomous – the source of its own thoughts and feelings. It offers students a subjectivity as creative selves and teachers as those who foster such subjects in their free development as writers and readers. The ethical sincerity of such teachers is evident in their desire to acknowledge the creativity of their students and their right to freely encounter authentic literature, in contrast to the decontextualised grammar drills and comprehension exercises of a more traditional practice. However, critics of this progressive discourse find it inadequate when it construes literacy practices as personal and not – as they are – profoundly social and political in character.

Contestation among competing discourses became much more public later in the 1980s when such progressive teachers confronted advocates of genre teaching and functional grammar (see Reid 1987; *English in Australia* 90: 1989). The latter group argue that genres themselves are institutionalised cultural practices for accomplishing social purposes. Their explicit teaching is promoted particularly in the Queensland English Syllabus (Department of Education, Queensland 1994b), but it has also become an article of faith among a number of educators across Australia, notably TESOL (teaching English to speakers of other languages) teachers. This rhetorical discourse has two strands, originally inseparable in the work of teachers and grammarians like Martin, Rothery and Christie who derived their theories from Michael Halliday's functional systemic grammar. One strand, which focuses on explicit instruction in generic structures and features, is more commonly practised among English teachers and is often problematically isolated from the second strand, which uses a Hallidayan grammar. Indeed, in a number of secondary English course books the features of genres may be presented alongside the elements of a classificatory grammar taught through decontextualised drills. However, unlike that older discourse of functional literacy (sometimes denigrated as 'skills and drills'), this newer English makes broader claims. Its recognition that any society has characteristic ways of carrying out various functions through language has become linked with a politics of social justice. Its proponents argue that students, particularly those not from the dominant culture, need to be given instruction in the 'powerful genres' of public life; to have these at command may enable those formerly excluded from social and political power to lay claim to it. So knowledge of language functions can bring wider 'empowerment'.

Critics claim that this rhetorical discourse may instead be underpinned by a more traditional, authoritarian ideology that inducts students into given forms of writing and enforces submission to them. Certainly the subjectivity offered to teachers is of coaches and masters; students are offered the corresponding role of apprentices. Genre advocates say almost nothing about the personal moral, aesthetic or even ethical formation of student-subjects. Their focus is on a more public competence and on the social benefits for the disempowered who understand the workings of genres. (In this form the discourse has been unclear about how the self-interest of the privileged and their linguistic competence was also to be harnessed to work towards a more socially just society. This is perhaps one reason why more recently advocates of grammar and genre have sought a rapprochement with critical literacy.)

The fourth discourse is more radically political. An earlier stream from the 1970s, of cultural and comunications studies, has now for the most part converged with the turbulent waters of critical literacy. While radical pedagogy is opposed to the present hegemony of institutions like public education, in Australia critical literacy has paradoxically become inserted, sometimes contradictorily, in state syllabus documents (e.g. the *Senior Syllabus in English*, Queensland Board of Senior Secondary School Studies 1996) and in government-funded professional development seminars and programmes (e.g. Morgan *et al.* 1996). The ideal subject position this discourse offers teachers is, as we have seen, of sociopolitical critic and agent of enlightenment; and students are offered a subjectivity as enlightened critic and liberated agent of sociopolitical reform.

Like the accounts of other discourses above this simplified overview of critical literacy is manifestly unsatisfactory in suggesting a single realisation in a 'pure' form. Therefore before we discuss it more adequately there are points to be made about the 'conversations' or 'arguments' among these four discourses.

For example, cultural heritage and growth discourses emphasise in different ways the educational – moral, affective and expressive – benefit to private individuals and are founded, more or less overtly, on assumptions about the shared cultural values which underpin such aesthetic-cum-moral approaches. Their ethics is one of care and government of the self. By contrast both genre and critical literacy advocates argue for an English whose ethics address the politics of differentially advantaged groups. The latter discourse however is more radically utopian in seeking nothing less than the renovation of society, while a discourse of functional grammar is compatible with a realistic accommodation to present sociopolitical arrangements. For these two any utopia is still to be achieved. For the cultural heritage a past utopia is to be reinstituted; and for a growth discourse a utopia is perhaps first to be achieved within any individual, the benefits flowing outwards in greater tolerance towards others in a society organised as at present.

Students' capabilities as instructed readers are the focus of two very different discourses, of cultural heritage and critical literacy. For despite the emphasis of the former on literary canonical texts and the attention of the latter to non-literary texts, both tend to take a defensive approach of 'inoculation' against popular culture (Buckingham and Sefton-Green 1994). Students' reading practices are regarded with more tolerance in growth and genre discourses. The former depends on a personalist and expressivist reader-response pedagogy and therefore aims to give student readers opportunities to do what comes 'naturally'. Their competence is demonstrated in responses which centre on the reader's sensibility rather than simply on textual knowledge. By contrast the focus of genre teachers' reading instruction has been to identify generic structures and features in order that students may reproduce them. However, advocates of genre teaching who also have knowledge of functional systemic linguistics will use the resources of the grammar to analyse the meanings that are 'realised' in written texts.

Different kinds of writing are privileged within different discourses: essays of literary criticism or argumentation; writer-centred, more confessional explorations of personal understanding; the production of texts which adhere to the structures – and strictures – of a generic model; or writing which supplements and challenges the sufficiency of a given model in form or substance. In each case the kind of writing required of students follows from, confirms and demonstrates the particular kind of reading competence promoted almost as much as it does their writing capabilities.

The point to be made from this schematic overview is that such discourses of English education are not entirely distinct from one another. They may be informed by somewhat similar ideologies. None is fixed and stable; through their conversations and even arguments over time they may assimilate compatible aspects of others or change by accommodating criticism from other discourses. Ultimately all are alike founded on principles of modernist education. That is, they take for granted that the deliberate interventions of education aim at the improvement of students and society, however differently each conceives of those goals. They assume that the effectiveness of teachers' professional work can be measured in the products and persons of students. And each discourse has faith that there are proper objects of study, whether these be academic disciplines or the culture at large, and that these can be adequately engaged with by rational inquiry into the meaning 'in' any text, practice and institution. (We shall see subsequently how critical literacy has attempted to engage with the radical challenges poststructuralism and postmodernism present to this educational endeavour.)

CRITICAL LITERACY IN AUSTRALIA: A NEW ORTHODOXY?

Like any discourse, critical literacy in Australia has been holding conversations not only with the competing discourses of cultural heritage and the like in Australia but also with its siblings and cousins in the United States and Britain. Like any discourse, its characteristics derive partly from those inheritances and conversations; and like any, as it ages it can develop hardening of the categories with the risk of cardiac arrest.

The sketch of the peculiarly Australian version of critical literacy that follows delineates just a few characteristic lines, as I see them. Any such sketch risks being a caricature. However, the remaining chapters will I hope in their close examination of specifics correct any overgeneralisations here about what after all is a multiplicity of practices, shifting over time, that claim affiliation within the discourse of critical literacy.

This does not pretend to be a history of its development within Australian English schooling. I mention only two points, which I believe have been crucial in facilitating its acceptance here. One is the prevalence since the 1970s and 1980s of school and classroom-based curriculum development and implementation within the generous parameters of states' generally liberal and open-textured syllabi. Even the public examination systems of postcompulsory schooling have a significant component of school-based assessment. Since the mid-1970s therefore Australian secondary English classrooms have been a smorgasbord assembled by teachers in accordance with a diverse range of discourses. This has led to a sometimes uneasy mix of ingredients; however, it has also permitted the comparison, evaluation and judiciously selective synthesis among discourses and the development of new practices formed in and for local conditions. Australian teachers have consequently sought out textbooks and resource books to help them in their curriculum initiatives, often adapting such resources for their own purposes rather than adhering to them submissively. And through such reinvented practices teachers can develop an experiential and reflective understanding of theory, including of critical literacy.

The autonomy and professionalism of English teachers (both cause and effect of such developments) has not so far been overturned by conservative forces of the right. This leads to a second facilitating factor: the official endorsement or at least tolerance of critical literacy at state and federal levels of educational policy. One factor in this uptake is the advocacy of critical literacy by educators who have credibility and influence among bureaucrats and policy makers. The corresponding factor is the continuity of a federal Labor Government for thirteen years from the mid-1980s. This period has been characterised by increasing federalist intervention in matters formerly the prerogative of states (including schooling) and an encouragement of nation-wide coherence in educational provision. The important point here is that however far it has veered from left to centre, and however much it has flirted with economic rationalism, Labor has maintained its avowed commitment to multiculturalism and a social justice agenda. Advocates of critical literacy could therefore aver to educational bureaucrats that this form of English education was educating the nation's citizens against discrimination based on race, class and gender. So, for example, a socially and culturally critical examination of texts appears in the national *English: A Curriculum Profile* and *Statement on English* (Australian Education Council and Curriculum Corporation 1994a, 1994b) in the 'contextual understanding' strand organiser.

At the heart of an Australian critical literacy is a view of language and text as always operating within and on, for or against, the inequitable sociopolitical arrangements of society. Central to its work therefore is the scrutiny of the linguistic and visual forms of representation and the implicit or explicit struggle over meaning within the available signifying systems. There have been three connected strands in this Australian emphasis. One has been the feminist and political or 'resistant' poststructuralist work carried out by Annette Patterson, Bronwyn Mellor and others in their Chalkface Press publications. Such titles as *Changing Stories* (Mellor *et al.* 1984), *Reading Fictions* (Mellor *et al.* 1991), *Gendered Fictions* (Martino with Mellor 1995) and the like are workbooks for students, but possibly their greatest influence has been to give teachers a language and a practice through which to learn concepts and theory of critical literacy (Morgan 1993b). (I align my *Ned Kelly Reconstructed* (Morgan 1994d) with this cluster of resources: see chapter two.) With similar views but working in somewhat different ways teacher educators like Colin Lankshear, Pam Gilbert, Allan Luke, Bronwyn Davies, Ray Misson, Bill Corcoran and Jack Thomson have popularised sociopolitical views of language and texts by their accessible writing and presentations at English teachers' conferences.

The second and closely entwined strand is cultural studies. In Australia again it has often filtered through to teachers' practice by means of imported resource- and workbooks: those of the ILEA (Inner London Education Authority) English Centre, for instance. The Birmingham Centre for Contemporary Cultural Studies has also been influential in the Australian Studies work of Graeme Turner and others, which in turn has been communicated to teachers more recently educated at university. So too media and film studies teachers, themselves shaped by the work of British colleagues, have contributed in various ways to English teachers' attention to media texts.

The third contributing strand has been the sociolinguistic work of the likes of Gunther Kress (1985), Terry Thredgold (1987) and Barbara Kamler and Claire Woods (1987). As functional linguists they declare allegiance to Hallidayan grammar, but in their analyses of the textual representations of ideology they stand at least as close to the work of the British critical sociolinguist, Norman Fairclough (1989, 1992a, 1992b). In many respects Fairclough's Critical Language Awareness project, as translated into teaching practice by such writers and teachers as Catherine Wallace (1992) in England and Hilary Janks (1993a, 1993b) in South Africa, is highly congenial to an Australian critical literacy.

Indeed, a socioculturally critical analysis of language and image in texts seems to define almost the whole of the teachers' and students' work in the version of critical literacy most often advocated in Australian policy documents and curricular materials. For example, the Queensland English Syllabus states that 'critical literacy approaches are based on the belief that effective use of language requires people to explore the assumptions and the perspectives, both stated and hidden, on which texts are constructed'; and 'a critical literacy framework brings conscious understanding of how words and grammatical structures shape images of the world and relationships within it' (*A Guide to Using English Syllabus Materials*, Department of Education, Queensland 1994a: 2). That is, the historical and material systems of socioeconomic and political oppression tend to be bracketed off from direct sustained inquiry, hence the follow-through of direct action to redress such oppression is almost nowhere visible. For example, the author of one sample of curriculum materials in a state English teachers' journal asserted that his approach would encourage the implementation of critical literacy 'by showing them [teachers] that it requires only slight changes to their usual practice' (Thorburn 1995: 51). This is perhaps why teachers and education systems are so ready to take up critical literacy, when the discourse claims as a selling point that it will not shift teachers from their present comfort zone.

Another reason for this de-emphasis on praxis is perhaps the uneven circulation of ideas. Australian secondary teachers involved in literacy education have in general little direct knowledge of the work and ideas of Freire, and the writings of Giroux, Aronowitz and McLaren which popularise and develop his pedagogy would certainly not be 'hot gospel' among teachers here. Australian critical literacy teachers are generally a third generation, twice removed from the first, having developed their ideas and practice through contact with the writing and professional development work of the 'second generation' of Australian educators such as Gilbert, Lankshear, Luke and others. I am not suggesting that such a line of inheritance condemns teachers in this country to a degenerate or attenuated version of the original purity of practice; rather, I acknowledge that this, like any discourse-practice, adapts to its ecological niche through forms of specialisation. It may be that the utopian vision and the hortatory rhetoric of the Americans is not congenial to a more laconic, less idealistic Australian mode of scepticism. Teachers here might admit to being 'critical', but not to being 'transformative', and certainly not to being 'transformative intellectuals'. While they may suffer from a limited sense of what the 'vocation' of critical literacy entails, they may also thereby be saved from a besetting arrogance.

There may be a further reason for the underplaying of praxis in an Australian critical literacy. As the history of relations between church and state remind us, the closer the ties the more accommodations are made – and not always or equally in both directions. So too with education, which is after all a state responsibility. It would be naive to expect that the state would endorse a pedagogy which proclaims its intention to undermine the economic status quo and the legitimacy of the present practice of government.

As Foucault appositely remarked, 'every educational system is a political means of maintaining or modifying the apppropriation of discourse, with the knowledge and powers it carries with it' (1972: 227). In Australia the systematic means of maintaining a modified, deradicalised critical literacy is through a complex ensemble of social discourses, institutions and practices. This ensemble includes government policies as realised in national Statements, state curricula and the like; systems of preservice and inservice teacher training; disciplines of school and university knowledges; a purposeful pedagogy of orthodox and circumscribed inquiry and critique; and a body of 'officials' to service the discourse (professional development providers, educational bureaucrats and so on). Inserted thus into the structures of official governmentality critical literacy in Australia can become not so much an oppositional practice as one utilised to carry out a government agenda of social justice. A more dedicatedly oppositional pedagogy might take issue with the officially endorsed version of 'social justice' and question its sufficiency for radical social change. In Australia currently we are more likely to see an official critical literacy translating into classroom instruction policies which have already been established. Reification is always a risk when any discourse of education gets taken as an orthodoxy by officialdom. (We shall explore this further in chapter five as we listen to teachers talk about their work.)

In this account I do not mean to argue that 'crit lit' teachers have sold out, abandoning the pure vision of the Early Fathers for complicity with the grubby forces of Caesar. As I have already indicated, such binaries are inappropriate if they suggest that each is a distinct and opposed force; rather, both are to some degree continually made over through their reciprocal relations. And critical literacy is still (always) being renegotiated, as the rest of this book suggests.

A POSTMODERN CRITICAL LITERACY: THE POSSIBILITIES OF A (SUB)VERSION

For however fixed in its orthodoxy any educational discourse may seem, that stability is merely apparent and always liable to change. So it is with this Australian 'commonsense' version of critical literacy. There are several connected ways in which certainty may yield to a differently productive uncertainty – which is not a simple 'advance', since there will always be contradictions, tensions, contingencies and internal resistances to complicate matters. One way is to re-examine Freirean pedagogy in order to critique the containment of this current Australian version (see further chapter two). This does not mean simply reinstating an apostolic tradition (no practices are absolutely correct); it might mean drawing selectively on its instructional techniques for different strategic purposes in new contexts. A second method is to move between conceptions of critical literacy and attempts to put it into practice – and to scrutinise the results self-reflectively. This is not to make 'authentic' experience the touchstone of theory, but to provide a mutually corrective friction. (Something of this will be attempted in the following chapters.) The third is to take into account those critiques of radical pedagogy outlined above in order to develop a postmodern critical literacy, or what Lather calls a 'post-critical pedagogy' (1992). (The final chapter attempts to move in this direction.)

As we have seen, their central target is the positivism and its consequences manifest in various aspects of the theory. If, as poststructuralists argue, truth is less certain, if definitions and hierarchies will not hold firm, if structures of knowledge turn out to be a shifting ensemble of power-ful discourses and practices, then there can be no given meaning hidden in a text to be uncovered by rational analysis, nor can ideology be conceived of as misrepresentation of truth and reality. Hence the simple opposition between 'false' and 'true' or 'critical' consciousness blurs. People cannot therefore be led unproblematically out of their demystification into a state of rational enlightenment. For not only is reason more unreliable than has been assumed, but we too are not entirely rational, coherent fully conscious and self-conscious knowers. That is one reason why the superior knowledge and therefore authority of the teacher as emancipator of the oppressed is cast into doubt; the other is the possibility of regulatory and oppressive effects in what are intentionally benevolent actions.

If we accept these counter-arguments (critically, of course), what are the consequences for a postmodern critical literacy classroom practice? First, the matter of those oppositions between dominance and subordination and between power and powerlessness. If we abandon the binaries of 'us' and 'them' as uniform, readily categorisable groups or fixed identities, we may be more ready to understand the workings of multiple, shifting differences within each of us and among group members as well as between groups. That will entail developing a different teaching practice, one that is able to engage more flexibly with those provisional groupings and affiliations – in ways that are less monologically authoritative. There is no simple opponent, no single possessor of power, no simple villain or hero, not even us.

This leads on to the question of subjectivity. If we concede that we are not always the same, and not always consciously captains of our fates and masters of our souls, but are mobilised also by (maybe unconscious) desire and pleasure according to the various discourses that speak to us, two consequences follow for a postmodern critical literacy. First, if we – teachers and students – are able to understand something of the complex productive shaping of 'individuals' by ideologies, discourses and practices, we may develop a different view of how people may act, provisionally, at a particular time and within particular conditions, as agents with more modest capacities. (Curricular units which attempt to engage with these matters of subjectivity and individuality are described in chapters two and three.) Second, we may develop a different classroom practice, which attempts to engage with the pleasure and desire of teachers and students, not in order to frown on those affects as irrational but to explore how and why they may be powerful, productive and legitimised, and how and why they might be otherwise. (See chapter two for further discussion and examples of such practice.)

These shifts of emphasis entail further changes. If we find unsatisfactory the orthodox critique of ideology, what more postmodern kinds of deconstruction can we utilise and to what rather different ends? Some commentators follow Ebert (1991) in distinguishing a postmodernism of resistance from a 'ludic' postmodernism. They approve of the former – a more Foucauldian critique of the effects of history and power on knowledge – because of its focus on the contestation of meanings. And they disapprove of the latter – a Derridean demonstration of the instability of textual meanings – because of its apolitical scepticism, absence of moral vision, and self-referential playfulness. But the strategic use of such ludic antics in irony, parody and self-conscious mockery of solemn certainties has a place in a postmodern critical literacy classroom. In such play we can defamiliarise the 'normal' and 'natural' and destabilise the universality of truths, the givenness of meaning and the solemnity of our authority. Through these means, as well as by the linguistic play of metaphor and punning, we may come closer to working with and not just away from the affective, the irrational, the unconscious. (And so too we may deconstruct those binaries.) This is a practice of disequilibrium in knowledge and in knowers – a state not easily maintained amidst all the positivities of modernist education. But the practice of scepticism, within an ethics of care for others, can also be a form of praxis.

So to the matter of critical enlightenment. It is argued that postmodern critical literacy teachers may still maintain a commitment to transformation of selves and society through education, but it will be conceived of and pursued very differently from before:

> The age-old question of whether education is merely to reproduce the social order or is to be the vehicle for social change could no longer be answered definitively either way. Indeed, such a discourse would have no work to do, since the determinism and predictability upon which it is premised would no longer be present.
>
> (Usher and Edwards 1994: 211)

If we accept that emancipation and oppression are alike situated within discourses and practices in which knowledge is inseparable from power, then 'emancipation' will be understood as a shifting, limited, incomplete process towards ends we can never be certain are in all ways beneficial. If this makes for more humility in our goals, more provisionality and tentativeness in our agendas and more diversity in our curricula, then more might be gained from less. (The dilemmas of emancipatory and oppressive work are discussed in chapters four and six.)

The exhortations and generalities of critical pedagogy need to be complicated by the particulars of practice, the 'musts' and 'shoulds' modified by the 'is'es of each moment's teaching work. This book attempts to provide such a dialectic. It puts at the centre of discussion the nature of the daily work of teachers, including myself. It seeks to understand something of the institutions, discourses and practices which shape critical literacy teachers and which they also shape. In several of the chapters one such teacher is followed in his daily work, to see how he, like others perhaps, is already reshaping critical literacy – sometimes in the direction of a postmodern practice. The descriptions and critiques of this teaching are intended to engage with that mundane messiness, rather than to provide tidy answers where none are to be found.

For in all of this there are advantages in giving up the impossible pursuit of certainty. If critical literacy, as a discourse, does not aspire to realise an ideal state (of being and society) but recognises that it is already a particular form of *social practice*, then this is what we as critical literacy teachers aspire to for ourselves and our students: to practise that practice within specific social contexts and relationships located in time and space. It will inevitably be an impure practice, shot through with contradictions and tensions, contingencies, self-sabotage and resistances from within and from other discourses, as well as by modest if uncertain changes in our students and ourselves.

Chapter 2

Reading curricula

> The issue is representation, the practices by which people name and
> rename the world, negotiate the substance of social reality, and contest
> prior namings in favour of new or different ones.
>
> (Knoblauch and Brannon 1993: 3)

In educational textbooks, teacher training courses and narratives about
teaching, curriculum planning has been presented as a science, governed
by rationality in planning and outcomes, or as an art which depends on a
teacher's creativity, flair and intuition. It may rather be practised as something less noble: the craftwork of stitching together a pragmatic patchwork
of scraps lying to hand (texts, worksheets, classroom activities, assignments) re-purposed for the immediate occasion. But in these acts too the
teacher-worker's skill may entail both art and the logic of a reasoned
purpose.

This chapter explores something of these processes and products, in
examining the making of three critical literacy units. While designed for
secondary English classrooms, they are multidisciplinary in nature, encompassing texts and issues found also in history and geography and media
and cultural studies. By 'texts' is understood whatever in our social environment can be read as a text: whatever constructs a meaning through
shared codes and conventions, signs and icons. Indeed, critical literacy
inevitably entails a cultural studies approach to texts in refusing to confine
its examination to words-on-the-page. As we saw in chapter one, it argues
that texts, as representations of the world, in their circulation and uses
help to constitute the practices and possibilities of that world.

In the developing orthodoxies of secondary English critical literacy practice, a number of hand-me-down curricular units are available in course
and resource books (e.g. Morgan *et al.* 1995). They too can be read as texts:
as defining the nature of the terrain to be raked over critically, the stance to
be taken by teachers, the work to be carried out by them and their students.
Many of them concern that almost too familiar triad of race, class and
gender. (I hear the yawns and groans of my teacher education students
when lecturers or fellow students present yet another unit on 'Images of

Women in the Media' or 'Ethnic Stereotypes in Advertising'. All the more need then to reframe what can no longer be heard because it has been overplayed.) Into the units described in this chapter are also interwoven such matters of linguistic and cultural diversity, socioeconomic class, gender relations and sexuality, but usually in overlapping and somewhat reconfigured ways.

For the categories themselves are problematic, especially if each is conceived of in some pure form. People's diverse grasp of them depends on their histories and subjectivities, which are shared with others (cobbled together out of various ideologies and discourses) and individual, peculiar in being so intimately woven into the fibres of our 'own' being. And that of course sets a limit to the work that can be done to analyse discriminatory practices and to change our own and others'. This is not to say that the work should not be attempted: it most certainly should, but in the knowledge that there are often very intimate, invisible, emotional attachments to our present lives and selves.

In presenting my curricular units here, as texts, I have also re-read them and found them wanting in various ways. And indeed they do not pretend to provide a total curriculum package. The gaps here are not meant to suggest that issues – say of gender – which are not given full frontal treatment here are not centrally important. (They are woven throughout other chapters of this book.) Despite inevitable gaps and imperfections, there is much here for students and teachers to learn, when less than immaculate critical literacy activities are given life by a teacher's skills. But the critique does remind us that there is no pedagogical Mecca to be attained through pre-specified teaching techniques. Self-scrutiny is a practice in learning.

THE PEDAGOGICAL IMPERATIVE

In a call that bears the marks of classic critical literacy, Giroux (1991) hails teachers to reframe the literacy curriculum and reinvent pedagogy:

> the crisis of literacy in this country must be framed as part of a politics of difference that provides students with the opportunity to engage in a deeper understanding of the importance of democratic culture, while developing classroom relations that prioritise the importance of diversity, equality, and social justice. . . . This means organising curricula in ways that enable students to make judgements about how society is historically and socially constructed, how existing social practices are implicated in relations of equality and justice, as well as how they structure inequalities and racism, sexism, and other forms of oppression. It also means offering students the possibilities for being able to make judgements about what society might be, and what is possible or desirable outside existing configurations of power.
>
> (Giroux 1991: xiv)

But what this might be in practice he does not specify: descriptions of the enactment of those messier realities he leaves almost entirely to others. As suggested in chapter one, such calls to radical pedagogy may ironically substitute for an engagement with teaching. It is a pedagogy of wishful thinking which does not specify and interrogate actual practice. The rhetoric however may derive from a worthy desire to rescue pedagogy from being identified with 'instruction' as techniques: formulae, rituals, gestures practised mechanically. It may come from a hope to elevate 'pedagogy' into something more socially significant and transformative. The claim for pedagogy as part of a critical cultural practice underlines the assertion of Morton and Zavarzadeh (1991: vii) that pedagogy is to be understood as 'the act of producing and disseminating knowledge in culture, a process of which classroom practices are only one instance.' Of course, if pedagogy is a form of cultural practice, cultural studies as a practice and discipline is also a form of pedagogy: 'the deepest impulse [informing cultural studies] was the desire to make learning part of the process of social change itself' (R. Williams 1989: 158). Indeed, some critics argue that cultural practices are also forms of pedagogy (cf. Dyson 1994 on Michael Jordan as a teacher and example of desire for youth).

The following examples of curricular units which explore such acts of 'producing and disseminating knowledge in culture' should however be read with an awareness that this 'one instance', secondary classroom teaching practice, has particularities which condition the work that can be done there. The grand alliance of the cultural and pedagogical does not excuse teachers from asking (and finding, if tentatively) answers to the questions Simon (1992: 55) poses as inherent in pedagogy, 'a term which signals the practical synthesis of the question "what should be taught and why?" with considerations as to how that teaching should take place.' Peculiar such practices may be, and worthy of examination themselves, as they are in later chapters, but they cannot be glossed over: they are techniques that have evolved specifically for school environments. They have long been effective in producing knowledge and knowers – in ways we might want to challenge; but we have to find ways to work within, with and on as well as against such institutionally entrenched practices.

When we teachers deny the 'pedagogical imperative', the necessity to enact teaching for learning, it is often from worthy motives of the kinds touched on in chapter one. (As the pages below indicate, I too have not always been able to resist the temptation.) We want to 'give' our students the knowledge and insights we have made our own. We would rush them quickly – too quickly – up the mountain to the peak of enlightenment. In this desire for learning as an attained position, equivalent to 'having been taught', we forget that we too as learners were not born fully armed with insight, like wise Athena from Zeus' head; rather, we have (r)evolved by twists and turns in the generation of our present, always unfinished selves.

So too students need time and experience, with the guidance of many teachers in and beyond school, and through curricula in which theory is experienced as activities, later reflected on, rather than handed on as a body of knowledge known by others.

Such de-emphasis on teaching-for-learning is the more likely when teachers define their students as duped by culture, even if not cultural dopes, who stand in urgent need of reorientation and repositioning if they are to resist the lures of a 'predatory culture' (McLaren 1995). Such defensiveness about popular culture may not encourage teachers on the Right or on the Left to ask how their students use popular texts and what social functions these serve (Buckingham and Sefton-Green 1994). As noted in chapter one, we may begin with the assumption that our students are wrong – benighted, bemused, bewitched by dominant ideologies. We may assume that we understand contemporary western popular culture, its ideologies and discourses, and our students' position within it, better than our students do, and that our job is to help them reach our understanding and thus be 'empowered' to renegotiate their position. (See Grossberg 1994: 18–20 on the problems of assuming that students are not already asking questions, negotiating and enacting 'answers' of a kind – their kind.) We might rather begin by asking how our students, who have learned how to live within fast capitalism and postmodern culture, are *right*. If we do not attend closely to what students already know and think about culture and language, power and possibility; if we cannot imaginatively sense how they 'perform' or produce themselves in that culture – then we are not likely to work to make bridges of learning between their understanding and ours. And then we may not be able to work with their knowledge and desires, the investments they have made in the culture of their world, towards helping make them even more 'right'. (What might be involved in working with students' desires and subjectivities is taken up in the third example of this chapter.)

CRITICAL LITERACY CURRICULUM: (RE)FRAMING THE WORLD

The focus of critical literacy curricula may range from the macroscopic (social practices including literacies themselves) to the microscopic (particular texts within sociocultural contexts). Several such foci are briefly described here, before we examine in greater detail some sample curricular units. These are not in competition as 'the' pure form of critical literacy: when we choose one as a primary focus for a particular pedagogical purpose, the other dimensions are inevitably entailed.

The first, most broadly encompassing, has usually occurred within the context of adult literacy education. Here teacher and students begin with current social practices. Within this it is the students who have the right and responsibility to identify a social problem which then becomes the curriculum to be investigated by teacher and students in company. Such an invitation goes beyond simply asking students what the questions are. As Grossberg argues, 'We need . . . to discover what the questions *can be* in the everyday lives of our students, and what political possibilities such questions open up' (1994: 20, italics added). That is, while any topic broached will have broad social and political parameters, students' knowledge of them is likely to take the form of personal experience. But in ranging across such collected experiences in classroom interactions, it may be possible to trace some common threads. This may prompt teacher and students to try to account for them in ways that supplement more personal orders of explanation. (Chapter three offers one means of finding these threads and orders, through auto/biographical work.) In the course of such investigations, texts will surface which warrant close scrutiny for the ways they (sometimes simultaneously) sustain or undermine such practices.

One such 'text', very close to the person, is the cotton shirt. For a US garment-makers union literacy programme, Maureen LaMar and Emily Schnee (1991) devised a workshop for ESL (English as a second language) learners within a programme called 'The Global Factory'. Adult students began by exchanging information in answer to the questions (not however defined initially by the students) 'Where was your shirt made?' and 'Who made your shirt?' Having discovered how much manufacture occurred offshore in the third world, students then researched, discussed and compared working conditions for garment workers in various countries (place and hours of work, working and living conditions, hourly wage, union membership and the like). This led to examination of which individuals and groups bear the costs or reap the profits in the global factory system. And so, through information sharing, reading and further research, the students came to explore twentieth-century changes in the international structure of the garment industry – in the course of their learning literacy (Knoblauch and Brannon 1993: 149–50; for a similar curriculum for secondary students on aspects of their involvement in a global market of teen commodities see L. Williams 1995). This is of course in line with the Freirean approach through generative words and themes described in chapter one, and like it is framed within a revolutionary agenda to liberate proletarian workers from unconscious complicity within the toils of capitalism.

Other similarly broad social practices in everyday life are rock and roll (Grossberg 1986), the blues (Merod 1992) and pop music (Buckingham and Sefton-Green 1994). These forms of music have in origin at least oppositional tendencies that already do some of the work of critical literacy. But this can bring unexpected difficulties that did not apparently arise among the garment workers, as Grossberg (1986) makes clear when he describes how he attempted to teach rock and roll as a cultural phenomenon:

> If I positioned myself as a scholar and cultural critic, I lost my credibility as a 'fan' and the students in my class became suspicious and

sceptical. . . . But to speak with the voice of the fan was to relinquish my position as a critic and professor. . . .

The students . . . jealously guarded their music, claiming that, in the very attempt to dismantle and interpret its significance, I not only demonstrated my lack of understanding but also betrayed the music by contributing to rock and roll's unwanted legitimation. . . . I . . . felt that my students were mounting a valid challenge to my interpretive apparatus. Their voices might ultimately be closer to the voices of the music itself. Increasingly, I turned my attention to the significance of this double bind, attempting to read rock and roll in terms of the demands which its culture placed upon my own critical discourses.

(Grossberg 1986: 179)

The reciprocity of such a curriculum, which begins with students' interests, practices and problems, may confront us teachers with more than we bargained for. Pop music, with its densely overlaid system of symbols and codes of meaning, can be used by adolescents as a way of locating themselves within a social order. All the more difficult, then, to bring popular culture into the classroom without seeming to incorporate it into the framework of 'our' adult disciplines of knowledge.

Of course such a 'luxury', however complicated, of following our students' lead in determining the curriculum focus is not available to all teachers in secondary schools. But where the frameworks are already determined by others, even such unlikely-seeming topics as 'Poetry: the Art of Self Expression' or texts like *Pride and Prejudice* may still allow teachers to give students the opportunity to identify and investigate a social issue connected with that topic which is of interest to them.

In a second kind of curriculum, the focus may be on the circulation of verbal-visual texts and their uses by students and other community members. Critical scrutiny is directed at how knowledge is formed and presented as text, how it is disseminated and how it attains authority as knowledge that matters – and how these matters often have material consequences. A curriculum unit in which students investigated literacy and material practice is described in chapter three. In another example, Catherine Wallace (1992) describes the investigations she and her adult ESL students carried out into reading and writing as social practices by exploring the following questions:

1 What reading practices are characteristic of particular social groups, for example, what kind of reading behaviour typifies a particular family or community setting?

2 How is reading material produced in a particular society, that is how do texts such as newspapers, advertisements, leaflets and public information material come to us in the form they do, who produces them, and how do they come to have the salience they do?

3   What influences the process of interpreting texts in particular contexts?

Through such questions teachers can lead students to explore something of the intimately entwined relations between language and experience. And so they may come to see something of the struggles for meaning in and about their lives.

Other projects similarly en-role students as critical 'ethnographers' – researchers of language use in particular social contexts. (See Anderson and Irvine 1993 for the conjunction of critical literacy with ethnography.) Shirley Brice Heath's work has pioneered such co-research with primary students in the United States, as an outcome of her long-term study of community literacy practices in *Ways with Words* (1983; see also Brice Heath and Mangiola 1991). Conversely, not schooling but absence from school – 'truancy' – is the subject of a curriculum project described by Michael Garbutcheon Singh (1989). Here students from language back-grounds other than English in a working-class suburb of Geelong, Victoria, researched this 'problem' among their fellows, wrote autobiographical accounts of their experiences, conducted surveys and interviews, and wrote up reports of their findings on schools. At this point ethnographic research has gone beyond investigating social practices involving literacy; for the student researchers and their audiences it has lead to the production of 'new knowledge through collaboration with others in a socially signi-ficant task' (Singh 1989: 37). In such ways then these curricula also begin with students' experiences and knowledge. They work outwards from the person and the particular literacy or educational practice to more general sociocultural practices without losing sight of those individuals who are affected by those practices.

But what is a teacher to do who is compelled to teach a text not of her choosing? (That was the origin of the first of the curriculum units described below.) In such a case, the movement of the unit may take students from the single text to others juxtaposed with it and so outwards to the social, cultural and political contexts which have conditioned them, rather than working from lived experience out to its sociopolitical framing, or from the broadly cultural down to the textual. There is valuable work to be done here, in developing critical perspectives on particular texts, provided that the critique also encompasses the sociocultural. The units examined in the next section cover all of these levels as they range variously across texts, cultural practices and issues of language and representation.

THE CASE OF NED KELLY

In the light of what has just been argued about the need for connecting with students' own cultures, it may seem odd to take as a topic the story of an Australian bushranger hanged more than a century ago. The simple truth is that as a teacher I was stuck with a class set of three Australian plays, in which Douglas Stewart's verse play, *Ned Kelly* (1943), seemed the least dreary. The less simple truth is that I saw here opportunities to work with a great array of materials from the 1870s to the present day, from poems to beer coasters, films to postage stamps, cartoons to editorials and police records – which bear testimony to the perennial Australian interest in this most famous postcolonial legend. I knew too that there was enormous diversity in the opinions held about the figure. Some texts argue that Kelly was an innate criminal and callous murderer. In others he epitomises the suffering, fighting, always game underdog, an un-vanquished victim of official ineptitude and corruption whose example 'in a perverse way, put the seal of manhood on our young Australian nation' (Brown 1948: 9).

I saw that with this diversity of materials and viewpoints my Year 10 students (aged about fifteen) and I could explore something of the ways texts work: their content (what they include and therefore what they leave out, what they emphasise and what they underplay); their use of language, codes and conventions (the generic features that suggest how a text is to be read); the role of readers in their interactions with the text; the various ways in which texts relate to one another; and the historical and cultural factors which affect the possible meanings of a text. All of these texts in their contexts construct and deconstruct a single 'truth'. Some speak with the weight of historical (police, legal and bureaucratic) officialdom. Others speak out of the discourse of the English-oriented middle class whose social control and respectability were challenged by this larrikin descended of Irish convicts. Yet others drawing on discourses of heroism elevate him into a Robin Hood or Christ figure.

The picture composed of these mosaic fragments is enormously complicated, beyond what I can convey here, and I do not wish to suggest that it can tell a simple story (or conglomerate of stories) of haves and have nots, English and Irish, selectors and squatters. For this unit therefore I came to take as my epigraph the provocative statement by a leading Australian historian that 'There was no such person as Ned Kelly. Indeed, there is no such thing as a human being, in some ways. There is only what he thinks of himself at different periods of time, and what other people think of him at different periods of time' (Manning Clark in Cave 1968: 23). That is, any attempt to recover the person from the texts is a futile project. It is impossible that Ned Kelly could ever be present to us; instead, there are endless possibilities for representing that figure. (An account of the teaching of this unit, with samples of students' work, is given in Morgan 1992b; for the English/history course book with texts and activities see Morgan 1994d. And for a similar treatment of another historical legend, that of Eliza Fraser, a woman shipwrecked off the coast of Queensland in the 1830s who lived with Aboriginal people until her rescue by an escaped convict, see Morgan 1994e.)

To treat that range of texts as historical is also of course to treat them as cultural. Most of them do not emanate from the students' lived culture, but as they were presented I do not believe they were lifeless to the students: some at least of the stories and debates spoke to them across the years. And various dimensions of a changing and (dis)continuous postcolonial culture in the making can be traced into the present. This kind of historical, cultural and textual work has several potential benefits. It may help students to relativise their own culture's preoccupations and provide them with a sense of history. For the postmodern culture they inhabit appropriates bits and pieces of the past as images for consumption: elements of an everpresent, everchanging style of fashion.

But how can teachers help students gain access to historical and cultural knowledge that is not already available to them? One suggestion, through performative activities, is taken up in the final section of this chapter. My approach at the time of teaching was to set one text alongside another, and to let the texts by their disjunctions or 'arguments' dramatise the historical and cultural partiality of each. Though I no longer regard this as sufficient to do all the work of critical literacy, I believe there is still value in this kind of cross-disciplinary, close-focused intertextual work.

Before spelling out the principles on which this intertextual work was founded, I turn to another unit which also clusters diverse texts. This comes closer to home in time if it goes further in place, being aligned with geography rather than history. (See 'The World's Your Oyster: Holidays that Don't Cost the Earth' in Morgan *et al.* 1995; for its critical literacy framing see Morgan 1994b; for further work on the discourses of tourism developed out of this unit see Lankshear and Williams 1996; and for a somewhat different approach to tourism see chapter seven.)

THE LEISURE INDUSTRY

'When the going gets tough, the tough take a holiday' (tee shirt message).

This unit attempts to make some of those connections between the familiar and the strange, the homely and the exotic, by focusing on the global phenomenon of tourism – fast becoming the world's largest industry.

My point of departure was that students are rather like tourists, their bags packed with ideas and beliefs shaped by the language and texts which variously represent the world. In this unit they were encouraged to examine a sample of texts about tourism and perhaps therefore to know a world different from those presented in the glossy travel brochures or their present imaginings. This world is the home of 'third world' indigenous peoples to which wealthy first world tourists come. Despite this wealth, it does not follow that the main beneficiaries will be the local people, their culture and environment. For the holidaymakers bring business on a large scale, often provided by multinational developers. As a result of these

incursions original peoples may be displaced to make way for tourist com-
plexes; often fragile environments are degraded under the pressure of
greater numbers of people who are greedy in their use of resources like
water; and local culture is subjected to pressures of various kinds. We in
the West have created these conditions: what is to be done about them?

To explore these problems and some possible responses, the unit took
two popular destinations as sites for exploration. The first was the Pacific
Islands, the shortest hop overseas for many Australians and a site of many
Westerners' myths and yearnings. The second was Phuket, an island off the
coast of Thailand, as a case study in the challenges to place and culture
brought by large-scale tourism, and the answering challenges mounted by
the local people. 'Ecotourism' was investigated as a possible answer to
such problems via two case studies. The second of these returns to
Australia and the site of a proposed Club Med development, to bring the
issues home to us.

Part of the purpose of the unit was to implode any pure categories of 'us'
and 'them': to deconstruct the binaries and essentialisms of the 'Other':
Pacific Islanders who are inevitably smiling and easy-going, Japanese who
are industrious, inscrutable and herd-like – and so on. These racist identities are enfolded with another contradiction in oppositional terms: the
'leisure industry' of tourism. Westerners earn their spending money in
their home place of work, in the first world. Many of them then travel overseas as tourists, to the third world, where they can play, experience their
pleasures and live out their dreams of paradise – at least if those contradictions do not surface. In the unit however, students were asked to
examine the ways in which language sets up such oppositions; to deconstruct each text's version of reality with its beliefs and values; and to
understand the consequences of the reading position from which that text,
that version of the world made an obvious, though always questionable,
sense. Through such work it was intended that the students should be
able to identify the contradictions, challenge and break down some of the
oppositions; to relativise viewpoints (for instance, to stand for a while in
the position of developers, not only those to be 'developed'), while also
asking what the consequences may be for all the interested parties, including ourselves. And so it was hoped that they would be able to respect and
approach those who are different from them – and therefore know their
own difference differently.

That was the intention. In its textual work, it closely resembled
approaches to the Ned Kelly materials. Both units work with texts that
cover a similar transmedia range, including merchandise that commodifies
images and meanings. In both students were to examine the contradictions
and gaps in texts, chart oppositions, analyse arguments and compose dia-
logues, stage a town meeting to give voice to various groups,
imaginatively take on various roles, and so on. And in both I tried to avoid

'pure' categories of otherness or disadvantage, weaving together matters of ethnicity and gender, economic and social grouping and so on. And I now see that both perhaps overemphasised an analytical approach – while this still has uses, as I argue in the following section.

READING BETWEEN TEXTS, BETWEEN LINES

My planning of the units was founded on four principal ideas. Oversimple though they may be here in all their clarity, they were still useful to focus activities and students' learning. Indeed, the wording of the points presented here was negotiated with my Year 10 students as we reflected, at the end of the Ned Kelly unit, on what they had come to understand. These were the formulations they felt comfortable with.

1   Any text is made in a particular society at a particular time. This influences the form it takes and the ideas it represents.

When texts on the same topic but from different contexts are juxtaposed, students need no longer see any writer as utterly inventive and original, but rather as one of a number of workers in a particular field of discourse. For instance, the meaning of motherhood is given very different valuation across a range of texts that concern Ellen, the mother of Ned Kelly. In an interview she gave to a newspaper, and in a television series, *The Last Outlaw* (1980), she appears as an epitome of caring and selfless motherhood. Yet to one historian, George Farwell (1970: 116–17), she is 'shrewish, domineering, slatternly', a woman who 'emotionally castrated' her son. Other historians have suggested that traditional Irish Catholic respect for womanhood and motherhood underlay Ned's vendetta against the police when they harassed his sisters violently and imprisoned his mother. Yet again in children's picture-books Ellen Kelly has become transformed into a comic or menacing harridan. There is no unchallengeable truth about the nature or meaning of motherhood in these texts; and anyone who reads them from, say, a feminist position will question these versions and ask whose views of women are promoted in these ways – and what the consequences might be for women and men in society then and are for readers now.

When texts with conflicting meanings are juxtaposed, this calls into question the sufficiency and authority of any one textual version. So instead of asking my students those too familiar teacherly questions, 'What is the meaning of this story?' or 'What is the author trying to say?', I have in effect been asking, 'How does this mean?' – 'How are the meanings assigned to a certain figure or events constructed in any text, how does it attempt to get readers to accept its construct?'

One of the ways in which meaning is assigned is through the discourses that make up the warp and woof of any text. Take as an example discourses about 'sustainable' tourism. Different groups may seek to appropriate the approval given these days to ecotourism, or ecologically sensitive tourism, by defining it in terms that permit certain consequences. For instance, to Seree Wangpaichitr, Deputy Governor of the Tourism Authority of Thailand:

> Sustainable tourism means viewing tourism with long term goals in sight. When developing tourism in a certain area we cannot avoid affecting the environment. But as long as we can keep the quality of the environment in that area acceptable, tourism is sustainable.
>
> (Plumarom 1993: 16–17)

How sustainable? Acceptable to whom? And who stands to profit by such a definition?

> Thailand's last natural frontiers, the national parks, are no longer safe from large-scale tourism development. . . . Though [the parks are] protected by the law, developers, backed by influential politicians, military officers and corrupt government officials, have constantly committed encroachments and other illegalities without serious persecution. In the name of ecotourism, new attempts have been made to legalise private investments and to establish tourism zones in thirteen national parks of the country.
>
> (Plumarom 1993: 16–17)

A further advantage of juxtaposing of texts is this: different genres, different media, can help students see something of the characteristic features and functions of each, and how a text may exploit the conventions of a genre. The television drama, *The Trial of Ned Kelly* (Simpson 1977), through camera angles, flashbacks, close ups and the like, encodes the scenes of the shooting of four policemen at Stringybark Creek as 'documentary realism'. This presentation encourages viewers to accept this version as the truth – which only we are privileged to share with Ned Kelly, and can draw on in the face (literally) of police perjury. But the codes and conventions of this version can be made more salient when set alongside an indignant newspaper editorial from the time of the trial, a pro-Kelly ballad, or a recent editorial account – for in each the genre conditions what is presented and how, and the particular rhetoric each uses to persuade.

2 Any text gives you a particular version (or part of) a story: it emphasises certain things; and it has gaps and is silent about certain things.

The juxtaposing of texts which offer different, perhaps discrepant versions makes it easier for students to see what has been emphasised, and what suppressed, in each case, and therefore to see what meaning they are being asked to accede to. For example, Douglas Stewart's play ends with Ned as 'one man against all the world' in wild, heroic defiance against the authorities, assailed and brought down but not ultimately bested. That is not the inevitable conclusion that can be drawn – as becomes clear when it is set against other dramatised versions. A silent film from 1923 had as its final card, 'The wages of sin is death' (Seal 1980). And *The Last Outlaw* had Ned's voice-over as his body is wheeled away after the hanging saying what he told a reporter shortly before: 'If my lips teach the public that men are made mad by bad treatment, and if the police are taught that they may exasperate to madness men they persecute and ill treat, my life will not be entirely thrown away.' This is followed by superimposed words on the screen which tell how a Royal Commission was shortly afterwards set up to investigate the role of the police in the outbreak, and that 'the reforms which followed created a tradition of public accountability and self-exam-ination which endures to this day.' Thus, when Stewart's play represents Ned as a doomed solitary, it underplays the issue of political action. For instance, it says nothing about the widespread grassroots movement of support for the Kelly 'rebellion' among small selectors and Kelly's plan to establish an (Irish) republic of North-west Victoria. But this does enable us to say something about the containment of more recent movements for political self-determination.

Or take another example, of a recent advertisement for Polynesian Airlines in the magazine *Pacific Island Paradises* (1994: 5). 'Beachcomb by Boeing', it announces, and offers a pretty pastel sketch of shells arranged in the pattern of the islands. 'Pack a towel and sunglasses and plan your island-hopping itinerary. Where you go is up to you.' The advertisement ends with the slogan, 'We call it home. You'll call it Paradise.' What is absent from this depiction of tourism is given satirical treatment in a story by Morris Lurie called 'The Larder' (reprinted in Morgan 1994c). This tells of a group of forty tourists who have just returned to their tropical island from an excursion to its reef, where they have gathered about a hundred beautiful shells, each housing a one-clawed shellfish. One tourist, who has gathered nine, laughs, 'Don't know what the hell I'm going to do with them, but there they were, free for the taking, you can't pass up a chance like that. Damn rare. Chance of a lifetime.' He justifies his action on the grounds that the sea is the 'larder of the earth. Man's richest feeding ground. There's plenty more where this came from. . . . Pity they're not edible though.' The story ends as this boatload of tourists leaves – taking only about twenty shells, and another arrives. Meanwhile, after the depar-ture of the first group, 'the unwanted shells were pushed into a pile and thrown away, like the unwanted shells of the week before, and the week before that, and the week before that.' Silences in the advertisement about the nature of the 'beachcombing' are certainly set to speak sardonically here.

3 Texts don't contain one fixed, definite meaning put there by the author. Different kinds of readers in different societies and times can produce different meanings for the same text because of what they bring to it.

When diverse texts are set alongside one another, readers can see that reading a further text alters the way we reread a previous one. For instance, a number of ballads circulated in the 1880s celebrating the gang's deeds. But when an enterprising publisher and member of the Legislative Assembly of Victoria called Hall collected them, he felt it advisable to frame them by a moralising introduction which denigrated 'the larrikin class . . . the youth in various large centres of population', and he justified the publication as merely offering 'samples of the pernicious stuff that is provided to poison the ear' (Meredith and Scott 1980: 91–2). Reading these words from a member of the establishment, one can no longer read the ballads innocently: class conflict is being enacted here, in the struggles over the legitimacy of popular songs. (Plus ça change. . . .)

4 Any text offers you a way of seeing and valuing things and invites you to accept its version as the truth, the way things are meant to be. What comes to be accepted as the truth, as knowledge, comes to serve someone's interests.

As the previous examples indicate, when text is juxtaposed with discrepant text, it is easier for students to explore the discourses these texts participate in, and thus their ideological base. This teaching work can be carried out in a number of ways: by problematising inconsistencies and suppressions; by analysing pairs of oppositions to see how each is constructed and one is privileged; by pressing metaphors to yield an unintended meaning. Ideologies may be more salient in older texts or those which do not speak according to our discourses. In these cases we do not read from within the same framework of beliefs and values, do not share the same repressions, do not take for granted the same silences. For example, my girl students drew out of Stewart's play the metaphors that constructed 'true' masculinity as physically active, aggressive and even macho. This of course is familiar also to those who know those cigarette advertisements which present the myth of Marlboro Country. Real men, like the Kellys, continue to ride the country – though they might now be called in for questioning by students of critical literacy.

Among the texts about tourism too are conflicting discourses – about places and peoples of the South Pacific. One such is an editorial in a magazine entitled *Pacific Island Paradises* (1994; reproduced in Morgan *et al.* 1995). Interrogate the way it constructs 'us' and 'them' and some questionable representations surface. For example, to ask 'What kind of a world is presented here, and what are its inhabitants like?' enables us to see that this is offered as a dream world that is nevertheless tactile, real – yet a world that excludes unhappiness and dissensions. It is presented as a world without fences and borders (ignoring a history of colonisation and national self-determination) – yet the rest of the magazine is organised according to geographical regions and nation states. The editorial asserts that there is a pervasive 'Pacific mentality', a 'Pacific psyche', of laid-back friendliness. Yet there are contradictions here between Islanders who, we are told, go to great lengths to re-create their culture for the tourists but 'are not under any pressure to perform'; between tourists who will be rewarded for showing genuine interest but do not have to become involved, and who are advised to take some coke to kava ceremonies to wash away the taste; tourists whose 'conversation' may be limited to sign language which will nonetheless enable them to encounter 'real, traditional' culture. Or perhaps will know only what this racist discourse presents, will act only according to the race relations endorsed here.

'Students can see. . . . ' I have claimed this as a strength of such an intertextual, interdisciplinary curriculum, but I now need to problematise the formulation and its assumptions. As chapter one argued, the metaphor of 'seeing' is insufficient to describe the work of critical literacy. Moreover, I saw, and may have assumed too readily that I 'gave' this sight to my students in ways they could then use to see other texts and contexts.

Also problematic is the impoverished image of teaching this conjures up. It overlooks the pleasures of a good story, the detective intrigue of detecting inconsistencies in events and opinions, the ironic connections that arc between texts. It hides the shared choreography of the classroom in its shifting conversations. It does not 'see' the role plays, the performative and visual arts presentations. That my students participated in these pleasures I have their testimony in their writing and talking, their presentations and evaluations (for samples see Morgan 1992b).

But here too are further challenges. For a start, I was the one who had such expert knowledge of that range of texts, I was the one who was able to pull out a surprise text like a magician flourishing a rabbit from a hat. I occasionally drew attention to the way that I was implicated too in the meaning making through constructing this unit and directing the students' attention. Despite drawing attention to my authority, I was no less in control of texts and activities around them, and we expected that the students were simply to follow my lead. Yet my interest and interests were not necessarily shared by my class. There were few if any opportunities for students to experience the impact of actual language practices in contexts that were of direct concern to them. Hence their understanding was likely to be diminished if it was not learned and practised in contexts where it mattered and had consequences for them personally beyond the walls of the classroom. The next unit attempts to make some such connections.

So rather than repeating myself on curriculum planning and implementation, by way of critique I focus here on more general issues raised by some of my uses of the materials and students' reading of them. When critical literacy teachers bring into the classroom media and popular or everyday texts – magazines, advertisements, brochures, and the like – the temptation is to choose those they find objectionable on the grounds of racism, sexism and so on. That makes critique so much easier; it allows the teacher to burst heroically into the classroom with guns blazing from the hip. The pleasures of indignation and self-evident condemnation may not however be shared with our students, for whom (contradictorily, perhaps) the texts hold other pleasures. And their preferred texts they may prefer not to analyse in this fashion. While adolescents may be ambivalent about the texts of their popular culture, if we allow them no scope to explore these responses of pleasure and imaginative projection as well as scepticism, we are likely to miss the point and the opportunity provided by such texts.

The visually stunning texts that construct island holiday resorts, surf beaches, outback nostalgia or city chic offer so much pleasure. Here again we need to ask how adolescents are right, to respond with pleasure of the senses, mind and imagination, to feel desire for the lifestyle, products and selves on offer – even if they feel obliged to deny such feelings in critical classrooms where the only admissible pleasure is in reasoned debate and dismissal of irrational seductions. Students may not see these texts (which of course include clothing and other such accoutrements of youth culture) as we do – as toxic waste dumping. They are right in that the texts invite the involvement of senses and emotions, which adolescents will often give insofar as this gives them in return a sense of identity (as group members who may be against the – other – group). And we are wrong if we begin our work of critical literacy by trying to dismantle such pleasures. First (and my unit on tourism stands accused thus) we attempt to use the tools of reason on what cannot be undermined in this way, insofar as pleasure does not work by rational, conscious means. As Cherryholmes notes (1988: 35), 'Often power is most effective and efficient when it operates as desire, because desire often makes the effects of power invisible.' Second, if we try to part students from what currently 'hails' them and offers a sense of self as choice-making, stylish individuals and group members – then we ask them to hollow themselves out. We would leave them unable to answer that pressing question of adolescence: who am I? Instead – and it is a theme to which I shall return in the final section of this chapter – we need to work *with* those pleasures and desires, as well as on them, to redirect them and create an even more pleasing subjectivity.[1]

Hence our work with texts will consist not so much of debunking the truth-claims of advertisements and other such materials as of coming to understand how we are offered a reading position that creates and focuses desire. Since desire mobilises action or agency, it is all the more important to work *with* desire and not just against it. Many English teachers are not comfortable talking of desire: it seems too undisciplined, too risky, unless it is the disembodied-seeming pleasures of the aesthetic. But looked at differently, desire promises pleasure. And while desire therefore signals lack,

it also points to a capacity for choice. Representations in media and popular texts of what is desirable are productive: they shape both the desires
and their fulfilment in people. But they cannot determine one's responses
or actions. For any reader has a particular history, inhabits more than one
discourse and has therefore more than one way of being and knowing.
Given these multiple subjectivities, any readers may be ambivalent, their
response open to transformation, if a different desire beckons.

SPEAKING OF 'THE LOVE THAT DARE NOT SPEAK ITS NAME'

What would a pedagogy look like that embraces desire and does not just
distance it? To imagine, let alone implement it is not easy, particularly
where there are questions which reach to the heart of identity. Surely the
question that is most contested, even unspeakable still in many English
classrooms (Rockhill 1993), is sexuality – including both heterosexuality
and homosexuality. I use the term 'sexuality' instead of 'sexual orientation'
or 'sexual preference', since 'both can be objected to, the former because it
suggests a genetic programming, the second because it suggests a shallow
and changeable taste' (Misson 1995: 26).

Because we hardly know what a curriculum unit looks like that engages
with discrimination against the sexual other – which may embrace also the
sexual self – I must shift from description to speculation.[2] (For suggestions see however Pallotta-Chiarolli (1995) and in an American context see
Hammett (1992) for an attempt, thwarted before implementation.) I shall
conjure up a senior secondary classroom which extrapolates from the unit
on literacy and work and described in chapter three. Such a curriculum is
presently improbable, certainly impossible in many school contexts. But
critical literacy teachers must continue to imagine otherwise; for this
focuses and mobilises our desire for a less discriminatory society within
and beyond the classroom walls.

In this world of possibility, having just completed that auto/biographical
unit, I now plan to extend the scope of the students' investigation and
bring them, step by step, to consider representations of sexuality. We begin,
seemingly at some distance from that point, by picking up issues raised by
our informants and echoes in current debates about what students should
study in English – the works of the cultural canon, popular and media
texts, texts by writers of minority cultures or marginalised groups. We
negotiate the most appropriate forums for presentation and discussion of
their views. They decide on two: a debate before other members of their
year-group, and a written set of recommendations to the English
Department and to the state English Teachers' Association.

At the beginning of the unit, then, we draw on transcripts from our previous study and on other materials which present a range of views on the
'proper' focus of an English curriculum. We conduct surveys among

parents, teachers, peers. In discussion together we draw up a concept map of the positions. In order to explore those views more precisely, I focus on one example – an interview transcript – and model a useful strategy for analysis (developed by a colleague, Lindsay Williams). This is not an abstract exercise remote from the students' lives, for the interviewed speaker runs a 'temp' agency and students are asked to assume they want to register with that agency as workers. There would be very good reason for them to understand what she thinks about and values in literacy, how she wants them to behave as literate workers and citizens, and so on. I stand in for the figure of the owner and the students coach me in this role, explaining (with prompting) what I am going to look for in their resumes, what I am likely to ask about their schoolwork and the like. After this exercise in imagination, we will fill in a retrieval chart before small groups do the same with other speakers across the range of viewpoints.

> What do I think about . . . ?
> What do I believe about . . . ?
> What do I take for granted about . . . ?
> What is particularly important to me?
> What do I specially value?
> How do I behave towards others?
> What are my purposes and goals in this situation?

The point of this procedure is to help students to understand more about the ways social and cultural contexts shape people's ideologies, and how these ideologies in turn shape the way people think and speak and write and *are*. If students can grasp something of this, they may be able to understand that such debates are not just about right or wrong in some abstract sense but are, rather, *embodied* debates which are felt, acted out, lived by. (My hope is that by practising standing in another person's shoes for a while, students may come to be less single-minded about their own ideologies.)

There might seem to be several limitations in this procedure. Given its focus on individuals with names and idiosyncrasies, students may come to think that those views and attitudes are also simply personal. And this sampling of the tissue of a person for microscopic analysis might suggest that an individual has just one 'voice' and a single self, when instead we each have a number of identities we live out as we move from one cultural and social context to another. Certainly English teachers need to work with that understanding, to investigate how language is involved in these selves. This is no easy matter: for the most part those multiple identities are invisible to us and others (or at least inadmissible). But one must begin somewhere: these imagined students are just beginning that work by standing elsewhere in imagination and thinking and speaking otherwise than they might in their own skins. A little later, when we come to discuss a further issue, groups of students will be asked to speak as that person. Despite the risks of stereotyping, in this way the students may be able to embody, impersonate, that lived ideology, invoking it and so advocating it for a time. That is one way of moving on from the idea of a single identity and a fixed point of view.

That may not always be comfortable. Indeed, with so contentious a topic as sexuality even discussion may be extremely difficult, for a number of reasons. Many of these have to do with anxieties about self-definition. These can lead adolescents to police one another's gendered behaviour sternly and reinforce stereotypic patterns by ridicule or attack on deviants (Mac an Ghaill 1994). Particularly for boys, to ask them to countenance homosexuality as legitimate may be personally very threatening. To ask them to take up an alternative, non-hegemonic masculinity can seem to ask them to adopt an inferior way of being. And any more 'abnormal' person may have a skin too loathsome to inhabit, even if we ask them only to consider for a time how that person thinks and feels.

It is never easy for any of us to identify with the other and locate it in ourself rather than keep it at bay as a binary opposite. As noted earlier this chapter, recognition of sameness in difference (and difference in our sameness) will not be accomplished by confrontationist challenges to a self that is known and preferred, by self and society. For

> Without finding strategies for boys and young men to work toward the destabilisation of masculinity in a way that they have some control over, and *that taps into their existing patterns of desire*, their most likely responses may well be resistance.
>
> (Davies 1995: 1; italics added)

What that strategy entails is suggested by Misson (1994: 4–5):

> It can only be done by entering into other discourses that are more pleasing than the undesired, undesirable one, and thus constructing a new self. It is not simply a matter of showing the evil or the error, but of providing an attractive new way of being that will be as satisfying to the ego and seem as 'true' as the former one. There must be at least the possibility, the potential for a new positive construction; one can't simply eradicate these self-constituting beliefs and leave nothing.

As Misson notes in reporting on his research into homophobia in English classrooms, many students are perfectly in command of anti-homophobic, anti-heterosexist discourses which they can draw on as the occasion requires. The work for English teachers then lies not so much, as we have assumed, in teaching students those discourses but in 'making them want to use them more often than we suppose they do, and invest more in them' (1996: 6). This work of learning to perform masculinity differently may be no easy task in English classrooms if the subject is already identified as 'wimpish' and feminine in its fostering of 'sensitivity' (Gilbert 1994; Martino 1994).

Certainly the business of reattaching desire will not be accomplished in one lesson – or even one unit or one year of schooling. We might begin by identifying some aspects of desire for and pleasure in a certain identity. A paradoxical means to that end might be to attend to discomfort – the absence of pleasurable fulfilment. For when we are at home in our environment we tend to be unconscious of our ideologies, just as a fish is not aware of the water that buoys it up and gives it life unless it gets into water that is opaque or suffocating. So too I might ask my imagined students to be alert to those symptoms of discomfort when we are swimming around in different environments of ideas and beliefs and values. And then we can try to identify the match or mismatch between self and context, between environments that suit a dominant group but are uncomfortable for marginal groups. To consider others' discomforts may set our own in perspective.

This work involves two complementary aspects. One is analysis: scrutinising the ways language and image are used to give us a position for reading and desiring, for taking up a position as sexual beings. The other is imagination: understanding something of how the ideologies of our society are lived out in individuals in a specific time and place. We need to help our students understand the debates in this way: not as an even-handed assessment by neutral judges who have no interest in the matter, but as people's moves towards positions which affect their lives and others'. Easier to say than to do in the classroom, when students and teachers, parents and systems are uneasy about broaching issues such as sexuality which are felt to be too intimate for public scrutiny or too subject to moral regulation to be opened for debate. Indeed, the point is precisely not to probe into individual students' behaviour outside the classroom, but to ask how such views and beliefs about sexuality and so on get constructed and regulated.

Let me speculate further on how this might be done. Suppose my students and I are pursuing those discussions about which texts students should read and study in English, and in particular whether the views and voices of marginalised groups should be represented. A testing example comes to hand, an anthology called *Ready or Not: Stories of Young Adult Sexuality* (Macleod 1996).[3] All the stories are about adolescents, and their friends and parents, feeling their way into their sexuality as gay or lesbian – or maybe straight. Debates are raging about whether the book should be censored from school libraries and English Department bookrooms. Rather than condemning or condoning it sight unseen, the class decide that they will work in small groups to read at least one or two of the stories. Before they set to work, I take a sample story and trace with them the ways the text gives them a reading position on the people and events of the story.

Together we decide on some questions to help the students evaluate the stories and their responses. Here are some of those questions: does the ending of the story present a strong moral and tell you how to think and feel? Do readers get any sense of the complex pros and cons, the pleasures and the pains, in characters acknowledging they're different from the hetero majority? How is homosexuality understood by the characters and represented to the reader: as a sin or perversion, a biological fact, a disease, a positive way of life, or what? And so on.

As the students read and discuss these questions in their small groups, they are encouraged to take part in a developing dialogue via an electronic discussion group – at this stage limited to members of the class. This mode allows them simply to listen in or to contribute to more recent or earlier topics. (Later we will be able to trace the discursive threads via the transcripts.)

Now the story so far may suggest an easy consensus. Far from it. After some homophobic comments in face to face and electronic discussion groups dissension erupts one lesson. Some students are looking at a story by Jonathan Harlen, called 'Nicole Breaks It Off', that tells of a young woman who has become pregnant and wants her best friend Desley to be the child's other parent. The tale tells with some comic flair of a society mother and a father who thinks that money is all that matters. It is the mother who takes the phone call in which Nicole tells the news:

> 'So you're telling me – what are you telling me? You're in love with a *woman*? You want a *woman* to be the father of your child? Is that what you're telling me?'
>
> 'She's Jewish, Mum. Her name is Godsick. Maybe you know the Godsicks in Bondi. Her grandfather was a rabbi.'
>
> . . . .
>
> 'This is – why are you telling me this? This is meant to be a consolation? That her grandfather was a rabbi?'

While the humorous treatment of a minority group can target them for ridicule, when sympathetic it can break down hostility or defuse tension. The film *Priscilla, Queen of the Desert* is one example. Less zany, but equally effective is Gleitzman's *Two Weeks with the Queen* (1990).

Imagine now a story about this storytelling. Despite its comedy, at least one student is not amused.

'Yukk,' says a boy in the back row.

> That's revolting, a kid having a girl for a father. They shouldn't be allowed to get away with it. Normal families bring up normal kids who marry in the normal way. These lezzos are just going to make that poor kid turn out bent like them. Lesbians and gays like these just shouldn't be allowed to – to contaminate others with their own sickness. And this

story doesn't make it any better just by pretending it's a joke. I don't want to read any more of this stuff, and I don't think anyone should.

I hear myself reply, to the ripple of excitement, the interjections agreeing or disagreeing,

You know enough about my views by now to know I don't agree with the sexism in those beliefs that some people hold, that homosexual people are unnatural and sick and disgusting. We'll come back to those views shortly and try to understand why people think and talk that way, and why this leads them to think some books should be censored. And why other people think this is discrimination against those who have a right to express their sexuality in ways that don't harm others or themselves.

Not to pursue the issue with that student immediately, not to disallow those views, might seem too weak a response – despite my making clear I do not myself condone them. Indeed, I might be feeling some unease; that could well fuel my deflection here. Unease for others too, who might be listening with particular interest on matters very close to them. That is one reason why I might want to reframe the debate in terms other than those announced by my back-row student. But there would be another problem if that student were to be silenced by his advance knowledge of my views or the censoriousness of my response. Then my classroom would have failed as an arena for debate and confirms his view that I have nothing to say he wants to hear. In this case, I put the matter on hold for later, since his opinion (not only his – a wider discourse about homosexuality is speaking there) is already being set alongside a range of others that question it. This is far from capitulating to the objections of the privileged majority when their advantages are being challenged. Indeed, at times, this may entail a 'necessary insensitivity' (Eagleton 1985: 6) of not letting the democratic principle of free expression – the squeals of protest – prevent us from hearing what costs some groups have to bear when others are free to pursue their own advantage.

A classroom which is a forum for debate might seem ideal; it might also however suggest that all viewpoints are equal and that any can be freely chosen; indeed, that debate is the only game in town. Consider then this further scenario from our imagined classroom. While examining those stories and the debates about the banning of books on gay and lesbian sexuality from secondary schools, the students are formulating a statement reflecting their own view of some aspect of the issue. And I am doing the same. When these are completed, the students will use those previous questions on assumptions and values and so on to deconstruct their own statement for its ideology. This time, however, they will interrogate that statement for their own eyes alone. (This is particularly important on a topic where some students may have very good reason for being reticent about submitting themselves to public scrutiny. This process allows for both safety and challenge.) To show the way I first model the process by scrutinising my own statement – modelling also my willingness to subject my views to examination by myself and others. – Because I will not ask my students to take risks in doing what I am not prepared to do. Then, when the students have followed the same process they share only their more general insights about the ways our beliefs inform our lives, then proceed to discuss the social and political implications of holding this position or that.

This process allows some larger questions to be broached, of the kind critical literacy teachers often ask. In substance (they would need rephrasing for students) the questions are these:

Where is this view coming from (ideologically, socially, institutionally, historically, personally)?
Whose interests are served by this view? Whose are negated?
What are the political, social and personal consequences of holding this view?
Should these interests be served?

This last question goes beyond the social and political consequences to raise ethical concerns. The matter of ethics in English is a huge topic, and one addressed in various, if incomplete, ways throughout this book. Here I touch on just one way of encouraging an ethics of care for self and others and supplementing the analytical work of critical literacy. This concerns the performative dimension of English.

'HE DO THE POLICE IN DIFFERENT VOICES'
(of Jo in *Bleak House*)

As noted in chapter one, some critical theorists and sociologists of education (e.g. Bourdieu and Passeron 1977) have argued that education is a form of reproduction of present society. According to this view English teachers, including those who teach from a critical literacy position, are inevitably involved in producing students who will read and write and act in certain ways that become the norm in our classrooms and beyond. Bourdieu and Passeron, for instance, argue that successful students are those who are learning to impersonate an educated person, and in this way the tastes and style of the educated, ruling class are reproduced. But impersonation and performance may not amount merely to reproduction. For example, Miriam Ortega, the noted Chilean activist for political prisoners and women in poverty, described in a talk (given in Brisbane in 1996) how women's groups in Chile use theatre as a form of interactive teaching and learning. They identify an issue of concern to them, enact situations and events involved in that issue, investigate sources of the problem and the means by which it is perpetuated. Next they evaluate possible social and political action they can take, and then act out those strategies. This benefits not only their audiences but also themselves: as they rehearse and role-played the possibilities for change, such performance may enable them afterwards to enact such strategies in their everyday lives.

This kind of approach has value for secondary English classrooms. It goes beyond an exclusive reliance on 'teaching the conflicts' (Graff 1992) and the tactics of analysis in the previous units. For while we want our students to be able to argue logically and persuasively and to see what is illogical and falsely persuasive in others' arguments, and to engage with the range of texts that variously debate the values by which we live, this is not the whole of our textual work. For one thing, it is not useful to set up texts and views simply in opposition to one another, as if they are the antagonists and we the jurors weighing up the evidence and judging one 'right'. There are no innocent texts. For another, teaching the conflicts may enable our students to assess those conflicts only from a standpoint to which they are already committed. And as mentioned earlier, it may not get at those matters of desire.

To supplement this, we need to find answers to those questions raised earlier in the chapter, about working with and on our students' (and our own) desire and subjectivity. We need, I believe, to embrace a *performative* kind of English. This goes beyond, though it also includes, approaches that English teachers are comfortable with: as theatre, oral presentation, staged debate. In my speculative story the students are en-roled: they borrow others' voices and views and compare them with their own cus-tomary ways of thinking and acting. (And in any classroom teachers perform their roles, while students play to those in complementary roles of various kinds – which sometimes involve playing up or acting out.)

Not all performances that occur in classrooms or elsewhere are overt playacting. We sometimes adopt social roles, putting on a mask and cos-tume, while knowing that our face behind the mask is different from what we mostly show others. Our sense of such duplicity may enable us to know other possible ways of thinking and speaking and being than those that are closest to home. Through playing those roles we 'do' ourselves dif-ferently in different contexts. Indeed, the performance can change us if we are able to incorporate what we have learned through acting in those roles. And sometimes our face grows to fit the mask: we enact a self that changes our self as we act.

This may be even more likely to happen when we are not so much play-ing a social role as performing our selves. In this regard Lemke (1995: 93) makes a useful distinction when he defines communities as 'systems of doings, of social and cultural activities or practices, rather than as systems of doers, of human individuals *per se.*' In the words of Judith Butler (1991: 18), 'how and where I play at being . . . is the way in which that being gets established, instituted, circulated, and confirmed. This is not a performance from which I take radical distance, for this is deep-seated play, psychically entrenched play.' Nor is it determined, for a (gendered) self is not given; rather, it must be achieved – realised and shaped in particular contexts through regulation and repetition by self and others. Butler defines the performative as 'a reiteration of norms which precede, constrain, and exceed the performer and in that sense cannot be taken as the fabrication of the performer's "will" or "choice". . . . The reduction of performativity to performance would be a mistake' (1993: 24). Since Butler (1991: 23–4) offers a view of gender as performative, and Simon (1995) argues in similar terms about ethnicity, this view of selves as performative may be particularly useful for critical literacy teachers in helping students understand how subjectivity is constructed in 'systems of doings'.

Among those 'norms which precede, constrain, and exceed the performer' are language and gesture, the stories we enact and the meanings we give them. We make these ways our 'own' and they become 'normal' when we and others repeat them, in ways we are not always conscious of. That is why we need to find ways to help students begin to understand not only how we play the roles we choose but also how we perform our social selves into being – and the part which language and texts play in these. In developing that understanding, deliberate role-playing is important in questioning the notion of a single, essential, core self. (This is the story told by humanism, that we teachers can 'help students realise their true potential', or 'give voice to their own inner identity'; cf. Lemke 1995: 90–2.) So too developing an understanding of the social construction of the selves we perform helps us and our students get away from the idea that we can be anything we choose to be. (This of course is the story told by those popular psychology books on self-realisation.)

Now any performance, any performativity, occurs in time and space. These have bearing on the practice of critical literacy teachers. First: as beings in time and space we are inevitably embodied. Bodies and not just minds feel pleasure and pain, and these are very important ways of controlling people. The different physical conditions in which different people live are material – they matter. If critical literacy teachers overlook the ways in which ideologies and discourses get embodied and the physical effects these can have on people, we limit also our students' understanding of the role of language in our world. For bodies are not 'merely' material; they carry meaning not only by the way we carry ourselves and the gestures we make, but also by the words we use of them and the discourses that tell people how to conduct themselves physically. All of this is the business of critical literacy.

Second: since we perform our selves repeatedly, it is likely that we will do so with a fair degree of continuity. But since we embody our selves in different contexts and times, there is always a possibility of change in the selves we perform and hence are. The scope for change will always be constrained by the forms and norms of our society, but the potential for change remains since we each embody those forms and norms individually. And since our selves are shaped – and we shape ourselves – within our culture, both we and our culture may change. This too is the business of critical literacy, insofar as we may in language imagine otherwise. Such change is more likely to happen when we catch ourselves in the act – that is, if we are not completely immersed in what we are doing, but have a sense that the self or role we are performing is a performance. If there is a kind of distance from that role, we may be able to critique it – not by being our 'true', 'essential' self, but by standing in some other place, some other self, to perform that work of critique.

This work can take various forms. As the curriculum units sketched in this chapter have suggested, we can help our students deliberately and consciously play other, assumed roles and imaginatively inhabit other selves. We can help them give voice to others' words. They can take up a position which is not their own, habitual place. And so they *may* become relative to other selves, outside or inside. George Otte (1995) calls this deliberate playing of other roles 'in-voicing', arguing that

> the point of in-voicing other voices is not to make for risk-free, semi-engaged games of pretend; on the contrary, it's to make apparent the risks of a practice we all constantly enact, speaking [what's] already spoken, whether by teachers or . . . talk-show celebrities. Whatever is said is . . . mostly borrowed.
>
> (Otte 1995: 153)

If teachers and students are willing and able to do this kind of 'in-voicing' they may to some degree incorporate, embody others: take their gender, ethnicity, sexuality and other forms of difference 'personally' (Jay 1994). But one should not be too sanguine about the ease with which students may take on such others. A 'Method' approach via absorption of the acting self into the acted self is likely to be rejected in cases where imaginative sympathy is not already engaged. Then a Brechtian enactment is more likely to be acceptable in its interrupted stagy display of character and events. Despite these limits, I would like to hope that by this means students may become engaged with others, caught up a little in their emotions and thoughts and actions. It may also help them understand a little better the self they have invested in emotionally, the self they prefer to perform.

But 'in-voicing' can also lead to subversion or resistance and critique, when one voice is set alongside and against another. These two aspects, of engagement and of critique, are complementary, and both are necessary to performing and 'being', and to the 'doings' of critical literacy. As chapter one argued, there is no end to the debates and the contests among ideologies and the performative selves they produce. I provided no tidy resolution to this third unit, being unable to imagine a happy ending in consensus. That is precisely the story to be told. There is no possibility that as teachers we can lead students to some place of enlightenment beyond the struggle. Our job is rather to help our students to become more motivated to continue that engagement. All the more need, then, to explore the performative possibilities of critical literacy.

A PEDAGOGY OF ECSTASY?

Given the ineluctable difficulties of critical literacy teaching raised in this chapter, to talk of *ecstasy* seems absurd. But I have in mind its derivation from a Greek word that means standing outside oneself. Standing elsewhere than in one's own skin is necessary to the curricula discussed here; it is rather different from seeking to move students immediately to a position of alienation – that sense of being elsewhere than one prefers to be. Indeed, critical literacy teaching entails various, complementary moves of the kind just mentioned. One is performative: the risky business of standing outside oneself in (partial, provisional, temporary) identification with another. This may also involve a ludic element of pleasure in playacting as well as the ironic play of perspectives or the subversive playing around with forms and meanings in rewriting events and texts. As I argued in chapter one, the enactive, dramatic, even the theatrical – these help to mobilise students' pleasure through interest in imaginative play. So too, Usher and Edwards contend, 'the denial of the ludic is a denial of desire. It is a reaffirmation of a universal reason and a formal-computational rationality as the primary focus of discourse and practice' (1994: 224). As they explain further:

> Without engaging with the ludic we are left with the forms of social analysis which become totalising despite their intent and remain oppositional but ineffective because *as forms* they lack the emotional investment of a *desire* for change.
>
> (Usher and Edwards 1994: 16; italics in original)

The ludic or affective, and the analytical or rational, should not be thought of in oppositional terms: the latter is imbricated with the former and may also be the outcome of desire – in this case, a desire to understand further what we have played with imaginatively. Desire is the engine of change. Without in the least suggesting that it is an easy matter to 'change the subject' – the self we and our students are at present (the resistances are so many and so deep), surely this performative, playful and imaginative work is a practice of 'ecstasy'. Surely such forms of rehearsal of possibility might help to mobilise us (teachers and students) to become a more pleasing self that is also a 'better' person, in ethical terms.

Another means to self-invention is writing. Two curricular units which focus on this are the subject of the following chapter.

Notes

1 I owe this insight to Ray Misson.
2 The approach described here was developed in the company of a group at the International Federation for the Teaching of English Conference in New York, July 1995. I would like to thank other members of that group: Lela DeToye, Hilary Janks, Ray Misson, Marnie O'Neill, Gordon Pradl, Pauline Scanlon and Kathryn Schwertman.
3 Other anthologies are by Pausacker (1996) and Bauer (1994).

Chapter 3

School writing and textual selves

Our new teacher [in Grade 6] . . . wrote down lots of rules and the high-light was that we all wrote in pencil, and were all dying to begin writing in pen. So Mr Dankielo made a deal with us. Every morning for one hour we were given spelling cards. Then each one we got completed he would check the spelling and the way we wrote. If it was good enough spelling and was readable enough, we were presented with a pen licence. . . . Our teacher told us that if our writing failed, he would take away our licence and give it back again when he thought our writing picked up again. It kept all of us determined to keep our licence.

(Kathryn)

When I was in preschool I wrote with my left hand but as we were in an 'old' country school this wasn't allowed. I used to get my hand hit if I picked up the pencil with my left hand. This caused problems later when in Grade 4. The teachers were trying to figure out why my writing was so messy. I had heaps of special activities to do instead of the normal work. The school tried to change my hands over again so I did actually write with my left hand but it was too late. Due to this I had many trips to the school nurse to see if it was a problem with my eyes as well. . . .

The problems in writing have caused my work to be rejected when being selected for competitions even if it was of a good content, all because it was too messy.

(Catherine)

These two 'horror' stories were related by students in the same class. Other classmates told similar tales of sometimes coercive discipline, competition and regulation in primary schooling. One might think these are tales of the bad old days before student-centred learning and progressive education brought a more humane approach to English, but the events told here took place no earlier than 1988. They are a useful reminder of a marked uneven-ness of practice in the teaching of writing and the persistence of the 'old school' in new times.

As these events and others recounted suggest, in some primary schools the writing that counts is penmanship. In Kathryn's story the regulation of writers takes a most literal turn with the issuing of licences: those judged sufficiently in control (or controlled) are now permitted to drive a pen. Another point of order has been driven home by this means too: the over-riding importance of putting the right letters in the right order. In the second episode, Catherine's writing posture requires bodily correction. Lefthandedness is a sinister deviance deserving punishment; it may also be a symptom of a further pathology in need of diagnosis and cure. But despite interventions the girl's 'messy' writing persists as a stigma. Even as she writes this autobiographical fragment (its theme the development of a frus-trated subjectivity), her body writes the autograph of a schooled subject.

SPEAKING OF WRITING

Both episodes bear witness to the persistence among teachers and stu-dents – and parents – of that folk discourse about the value of a literate 'hand'. (That metonomy is revealing: our anatomy holds the key that gives entrée to polite, lettered society.) Like many primary teachers, secondary English teachers would be keen to dissociate themselves from such coer-cive disciplining. Certainly in the higher grades the focus shifts somewhat, from the letter and word to the whole written text, from the physical to the rhetorical position. But primary school practices, in their variety, surely persist as a palimpsest, even though overwritten by later forms of writing instruction. Writing in schools, as in the wider society, is obviously not always and everywhere the same; as chapter one suggested, it is produced within various sociocultural contexts with their ideologies and discourses. Each of these in turn produces a set of teaching 'technologies' designed to produce a certain, valued, kind of literate capacity in students.

It is the production of writing and writers in critical literacy secondary classrooms which is the subject of this chapter. Two curriculum units taught in senior English are explored, each in a rather different way fol-lowing up some of the issues raised here already. One describes my taking a teaching stand on the ground claimed by 'progressive' teachers as their heartland: personal, autobiographical, writing. (Here is *par excellence* per-sonal 'growth' through English.) This unit however examines the (student) writer as not so much an expressive author as a textual self, constituted by others' discourses and her own in the acts of memory and inscription. The second unit also takes biography as its subject: the students collect stories from community members and trace there the discourses of literacy at home, at school and in the worlds of adult life and work. Both units are experiments in developing the work of a poststructuralist critical literacy via a focus on writing.

Writing is an aspect of English curriculum in which critical literacy has generally been less evident than in reading. One reason is perhaps the various discourses and practices of teaching which produce students' compositions. As noted in chapter one, the discourse which has been most identified with the development of students' writing is the child-centred growth model and its transatlantic cousin, the Gravesian 'writing-process' movement. Since the mid-1980s much has been written about the limitations of this writing pedagogy, especially by critical and poststructuralist educators (e.g. Gilbert 1989). They have taken issue particularly with its emphases: on the 'individuality' of an expressive – not socially constituted – self; and on the implicit or invisible nature of the teaching, which (according to arguments mentioned in chapter one) may serve to reproduce the hegemony of the dominant, cultured, middle class. Since the process writing movement has been judged incompatible with a socially critical stance it is therefore mostly unavailable to critical literacy teachers as an ensemble of practices and beliefs, even though they may use some of the technologies of drafting and conferencing, revising and publishing.

Another more recent discourse, the genre movement, is also writing centred. However, unlike the process movement, this approach does not care to foster in students an enthusiasm for the practice of writing (whether 'creative' or 'functional'), nor does it value young writers as the fount of subject matter. Instead it concerns itself with instructing them in the reproduction of generic conventions. As we saw in chapter one, the genre school has also been subject to some criticism but has defended itself by drawing on the rhetoric of social justice, which has enabled it to become allied to critical literacy in parts of Australia.

In this chapter we return to those unfashionable humanistic concerns with writing or speaking subjects and the texts they generate, but in a different way: the point now is to help students explore how personal texts are also about the textualising of the personal. Before we come to the particulars of those tales, it may be helpful to extend the remarks made in chapter one about what the various discourses of English have to say about writing: about what it is taken to be, and the techniques that generate it, hence the technologies of writing instruction and the 'technologised' writing self that ensues. As noted in chapter one, none of these discourses is likely to be realised in a pure form – and my simplified account also does discursive work in retelling the story from a critical literacy angle. Granted these limitations, it may still help us to understand the attempted syntheses and ensuing tensions and contradictions in my and others' practice as teachers of writing.

A 'back to basics' discourse understands writing to be a matter of following the rules (not regarded as mere social conventions), whether these concern the structuring of a five-paragraph essay or the necessity to never split an infinitive. Such 'etiquette' can be learned from books; hence writing instruction involves instruction in fragmented subskills and repetition for 'mastery'. Each subskill is a self-contained system and can be taught and tested separately from others. Successful writing ultimately means competence in all of its components: spelling, vocabulary, the grammar and syntax of sentence construction, paragraph development and cross-paragraph maintenance of a topic. The learning theory and teaching practice of this approach to writing aim to form writers who mind their p's and q's and ensure their slips never show in public. Form, understood as good form and form-following, is all, and function is left to tag along.

A cultural heritage discourse creates a chasm between 'real' authors and student writers. Great authors have genius which school pen-pushers appreciate in written responses. Composing their essays of literary criticism involves a kind of reiteration: the purpose of the exercise is to reflect back to the original an accurate copy by showing in explanatory prose what is 'there'. Of course this act of running commentary unwittingly supplements the original and gives a rational cast of explanation after the event to an experience that is supposedly aesthetic. Many student writers fail to bridge that chasm with their essays, despite their teachers' efforts to demonstrate – usually in metatextual commentary in teacher-led discussion – what a cultured response is and how one substantiates a line of interpretation with reference to the text. In this kind of exegesis lies the only scope for students to exhibit originality, and this is of a limited and dependent kind. Learning, then, is to take place by immersion, osmosis, mimicry and therefore students' assimilation to the culture of cultivated writing. No need to repeat in detail here the arguments of social critics of this form of literacy, that it reproduces in the next generation a self-appointed elite who 'naturally' have what it takes. Its proponents would argue for the worth of the writer so developed: a judicious and mature reader who can elucidate the moral vision of the best products of our culture in urbane, authoritative prose fit for those who are fitted to understand.

The process movement celebrates writing as an exploration of self and world through the power of the imagination to order experience symbolically. Such writing originates within the individual and is expressive before it is communicative. Yet though its source is personal, the processes of shaping are social: feedback is sought from readers and their responses are taken into the revising, so that when the finished product is made public in publication it will indeed communicate the writer's 'own' ideas. The mysterious electrifying charge of inspiration may be kick-started by various kinds of stimulus applied by the teacher. (Some readers may recall with embarrassment darkened classrooms lit by candles and filled with eerie music.) More characteristically, the writing classroom takes the form of a workshop, in which students choose the materials, tools and end product and work together in the crafting. It is founded on a theory of learning by self-directed activity and discovery, by active involvement and initiative in all aspects of the process, by feedback and self- and peer-evaluation. The teacher's role in this is indirect, a mostly invisible 'facilitation' of that learning. The self that emerges is a creative individual with a personal voice and a child's freshness of vision still. By playacting what 'real' writers do in the writing process, they too in turn may become real authors.

Again one discourse cuts across another: to critical literacy advocates the cult of the personal voice denies the part played by culture in constituting the personal. That culture includes the classroom, whose teachers are covertly more manipulative than they admit. Indeed, to the extent that the sociocultural and the pedagogical remain unacknowledged, it is argued that a writing process English favours middle-class students whose forms of life may already be congruent with its ideology and practice and may thus be subtly maintained.

Those who teach the written genres argue that the business of writing involves understanding that people's social and communicative purposes take certain characteristic and relatively conventionalised forms within a culture. Within those broad cultural contexts the particulars of any social situation will necessitate certain choices to do with register (field, tenor and mode, in Halliday's terms) to ensure that the communication is appropriate and effective. Genre teachers do not believe that students can be left to develop their own understanding of these interdependent factors by simply encountering and informally experimenting with a range of genres. They see their role as one of master to apprentices: of explicitly analysing the textual features of an instance of a generic form and relating these to its function; of modelling before and with their students the construction of a sample text and so 'scaffolding' the students' learning; and of setting up a context within a curriculum unit for the students' subsequent independent construction of their text in the same genre. This pedagogical practice follows a sequential logic and is founded on a belief in the sufficiency of rational explication. (Critics argue that it is founded on an insufficient understanding of learning as explicit teacher-centred instruction.) The writing self that is to emerge from these technologies will be competent in the public and powerful genres of the culture and will therefore be personally – and, it is claimed, sociopolitically – empowered. This writer makes the right choices for rhetorical effectiveness – or may simply know what form of dress, rather than address, is demanded by a particular occasion. For once again the critics dispute the sufficiency and efficacy of this kind of teaching which instructs novices in obedience to the forms which are presented as static and self-contained.

The denouement of the story as told so far is evidently the arrival of the *deus ex machina*, shrouded in a cloud of enlightenment. But each of these not-so-vanquished pretenders, these Englishes, has a challenge for critical literacy. What is your theory of learning and how does writing fit in to this? Is there any place in your English for focused practice on a point of grammar, and if so, how would you frame it? Are you guilty of inverted snobbery in refusing to acknowledge the legitimacy of the essay and the scope it provides for expatiating on an idea? What are the cognitive, imaginative, aesthetic, processes of composition? How do you incorporate these in your teaching programme and how do you relate them to your sociopolitical understanding of literacy? Is there any place for literary creativity and play in your programme? Show me how you would simultaneously teach the genre and teach against it. Some of these questions may be answered in the pages of this book through its exemplars of curriculum units and teaching practice. Others require further attention by critical literacy teachers.

Certainly, as we have seen, critical literacy has had much to say about the sociocultural contexts that condition the acts and products of writing, and about the selective and interested nature of such representations of the world in texts. Some such analysts have gone so far as to suggest that in writing the writer is not substantially the agent; rather, discourses write through us and write us. As James Gee says (1991: 5), 'individuals do not speak and act, but . . . historically and socially defined discourses speak to each other through individuals.'

Given some ambivalence about agency, critical literacy theorists and teachers have generally had little to say about the appropriate technologies of writing instruction. The major exception in Australia is probably the work of Corcoran (1994) and Morgan (1992a, 1994f), who have drawn on aspects of a process pedagogy and advocated a playful approach to the reading and writing of experimental texts. The 'technologised' writing self that ensues is to be a 'resistant' reader and writer. As we have seen, 'crit lit' teachers are often inclined to be suspicious of pleasure and play as ultimately self-indulgent. But such an exploratory and ludic practice is valuable still and needs to be reincorporated into a critical literacy curriculum.

A critical literacy curriculum could well examine the phenomenon of writing itself as a sociocultural practice on the model of work on reading already done by Wallace (1992) and others as described in chapter two. The writing-based curricula that follow here however focus on just one aspect of that larger phenomenon of literacy: the constituting of the writing subject through schooled and societal discourses and practices.

SELF AS TEXT

Autobiography is generally thought to be the most personal kind of writing. What follows goes some way towards challenging that assumption by focusing on the interweaving of the personal and the sociocultural. It describes my planning and teaching of a unit in autobiographical writing; my writing here is also necessarily 'personal' and must therefore also be contextualised and interrogated.

At that time, in the early 1990s, I was teaching secondary English at an independent school for girls. The students were very comfortably middle-class, and the ethos of the school was academic without being ruthlessly competitive; it aimed by non-coercive persuasion to turn out graduates who were cultivated, polite, and ready to take their place in society, further education and careers. In the comfortably progressive and cultural heritage atmosphere of the English staff room I must have appeared intellectually rather radical as a self-declared poststructuralist. The unit I devised was very far from being radical, however. I chose most of the texts, the nature of the assignments, and I structured the teaching encounters. Nothing less was expected by parents and students or permitted in this conservative school. Any 'experimental' qualities in the unit derived from my under-standing of the role of language in constituting self and knowledge. (For a fuller account, including samples of students' writing, see Morgan 1993a.) It is offered here not as an exemplary instance of critical literacy but as a basis on which such work may be built.

Planning: an act of theory

According to poststructuralists autobiography is a self-reflexive, self-enacting discourse (Hooton 1990). This view shaped my selection of materials and teaching strategies in order that my students might in turn grasp something of those theories without direct instruction in their abstractions. What follows spells out the premises of the half-semester unit I devised for Year 11 students (aged from fifteen to sixteen).

For writers and readers the most interesting parts of autobiographies are often the formative years and formative forces of childhood and adolescence. They can therefore be particularly useful in helping students to reflect on their shaping by cultural influences, family patterns and their own particular but historically located experiences. If they are to observe these forces impinging on their developing self, it is necessary for students to 'decentre'. That is, even in writing which seems a transparently personal act of 'self-expression', they need to distinguish their past (experiencing) self from their present (narrating) self and the (written) self of the text. We are made different in this act:

> the observer who is a measurer of his [sic] past self changes the object in the very process of observation and recreation. And . . . the transformation of the past self changes the nature of the observer, who is never the same at the end of the work as at the moment of writing the first page.
> (Colmer and Colmer 1987: 2)

Such attempts to explain the kind of person we have been and therefore are often take the form of narrative. We trace – or rather, construct – a chain of causes and consequences, and present ourselves acting and reacting in particular ways in situations to which we give a particular character. These acts of narrating our lives can be consciously and deliberately crafted; they have already been perhaps unconsciously (re)constructed by a selective memory and the discourses that tell us the meaning of such stories. Most classroom use of autobiography centres exclusively and unproblematically on the emotional and cognitive development of 'oneself' as told in that story of an unfolding life. My intention was rather to present a life as a text traversed by discourses that constitute our reality and endow it with meaning.

This view of the storying of a life entails a further point. Poststructuralist critics have challenged the notion that the proper subject of autobiography is a single, existential self who becomes ever more individuated as he (it is characteristically a he) moves along a clear straight path towards an end consistent with his beginning. They argue that human beings are not autonomous and unified, but are a process: always in the making, always contradictory and always open to change. We are not the same person in all contexts and interactions, but who we present ourselves to be depends in part on the language that we speak and that gives us our meanings.

This gives rise to a second argument: that the classic pattern of the genre is less a reality than a construct, one that has constituted this 'reading' of a life as a journey in one direction. Feminist critics regard this pattern of life-storying as characteristically male and question the norm of form and achievement so created (see the discussion in Hooton 1990). (However, more experimental male autobiographies, such as Morris Lurie's *Whole Life*, 1987, explore how a man's life can also be presented as a kaleidoscope of disunified fragments, playfully shaped into a non-linear pattern.) They observe how by contrast to this 'norm' women writers have not often been able or do not choose to define themselves by distinction from their families and contexts in the way that male writers have tended to. Instead, women have recognised that their lives are interwoven in relationships which lead to a different version of selfhood as fragmentary, multiple, disunified, inextricably tied to the experience of place and 'encumbered', in dealing with domestic, familial, apparently trivial concerns. Such lives may not 'get anywhere', since they are not goal-oriented in any singular way; rather, they are circular in dealing with continuities and generations. Certainly I have noticed that the young women in my classes have defined their subject as being about family relationships even when they were ostensibly writing about some aspect of personal, individual development. A critical literacy needs to question with students – more than I did at the time – how 'normal', or normative, such accounts are, concerning the embeddedness of the female self and the singularity of the self-made man. In part this work can be done by examining such accounts for their historical and cultural discourses about a life-pattern.

Through their reading and writing of autobiography young writers can learn much about the cultural ways we bestow a meaning on the raw materials of life. We do not merely discover it in them as we select details, choose emphases and present ourselves in particular lights, according to our audience, purposes and the form of writing. The forms available to autobiographers are extraordinarily heterogeneous: diaries, letters, character sketches, poems, chronological and other narratives, descriptions, analytical exposition, reflection, among others. Most student writers can be accommodated in this range and may be encouraged to experiment with forms encountered in their reading. Indeed, such writing can help students demystify the texts they read. As they write about topics and in forms like those they have encountered in their reading, and as they deliberately shape their writing, they may become more conscious that those authors have developed their texts by similar processes and for comparable purposes. It is a first step towards an understanding of the textual making of a self.

Reading and writing selves: an integrated approach

> Mind is never free of pre-commitment. . . . There are . . . hypotheses, versions, expected scenarios. Our pre-commitment about the nature of a life is that it is a story, some narrative, however incoherently put together. Perhaps we can say one other thing: any story one may tell about anything is better understood by considering other possible ways in which it can be told. That must surely be as true of the life stories we tell as of any others. . . . If we can learn how people put their narrative together when they tell stories from life, considering as well how they *might* have proceeded, we might then have contributed something new to that great idea [that the only life worth living is the well-examined one].
>
> (Bruner 1988: 582)

No selective account can do justice to the complexity of texts or the moment-by-moment production of meaning in classroom interactions around them. At some remove now from those events, my impulse is to sweep under the carpet of oblivion the frustrations and failures, the untidiness – or (to maintain the housewifely metaphor) to tuck out of sight all the loose threads that would unravel the seamless garment of a successful teacher. When my tale is told I step back to critique it; meanwhile, readers must query my account as I give it.

To begin with, I separate here for convenience the reading and writing which went on simultaneously. So to the reading. And at the outset came a change of intention. Our shared text, *The Scent of Eucalyptus* (Hanrahan 1973) did not arrive until three weeks into the unit, so – happily, it turned out – we had to begin with some shorter texts: poems and stories (others were introduced during the reading of our central text) which served to introduce questions about autobiographical writing such as the processes of memory, the wisdom of hindsight and the like. The class under my direction discussed their tentative views on a number of such questions. We would return to these at the end of the unit, to confirm, extend or modify those first opinions.

The Scent of Eucalyptus was an obvious choice for students in Adelaide, South Australia, since it dealt with the pre-school and school years of an artist and novelist who grew up there during the 1940s and 1950s. (Hanrahan came quite literally from the other side of the track from my students – as a fatherless child in a very working-class suburb – and that too informed my choice of text.) One interesting quality of its writing is the unwavering clarity of Hanrahan's gaze on minute and intimate details of everyday objects and events. (The same attention is evident in her etchings.)

The students were asked to keep reading logs, for various purposes: to provide the basis for ongoing class discussion; to record memories prompted by their reading and therefore to serve as a memo of topics or approaches for their writing; and to be a source of ideas and insights for later reflective and analytical writing. What emerged most clearly from those logs and from discussion was the students' difficulty in 'getting into' this text. Even the more experienced readers found it especially perplexing to track a path through the first few chapters, which move in very fluid fashion between one time or place or person and another. From the novels they had read previously they were accustomed to a clear narrative line. They needed help to see how this text is organised according to topics or places which are dealt with in sequence as the growing child moves ever further afield into the neighbourhood from house and family. The students' perplexity was often compounded by a marked distaste for the frank, intimate physical details Hanrahan dwells on so minutely. Again, nothing in their reading had prepared them for this kind of level-eyed close-focused exploration, since details of bodily functions or 'unrespectable' behaviour are usually passed over in silence according to the etiquette of polite society and also the decorum of conventional narrative. Perhaps the students found it offensive and embarrassing because such writing disrupts the boundary between what may be noticed and expressed in our polite, adult, public discourses and what children are fascinated by. This text makes the reader complicit with the child, who is not a naive, sentimentalised child. These adolescent readers, who were still learning to attend to the world as adults do, may in many cases have repressed the memory of observing details like those in Hanrahan; and perhaps they needed to maintain that refusal. A few students however were less repulsed, a few were more open and receptive; and one or two admitted to a similar curiosity in themselves as children. There is scope here for exploring further what I only touched on with the students, the prevalent cultural and social construction of a 'sanitised' childhood.

My hope that the setting of the book would give my students an entry point was vain: not only its time but also its socioeconomic milieu were to most of them as remote as Alaska. I did what I could to explain those aspects of working-class lives which were foreign to them and to encourage a spirit of sympathetic understanding. But I failed to help a number of them to find points of contact or a generosity of interest to bridge the gap. It is not surprising that many could not find pleasure in what was strange and unfamiliar. For while they had encountered texts which present other periods, races and social classes, such novels have been unproblematically realistic narratives. They wanted what confirmed rather than challenged, what reassured rather than confronted. They could not believe that textual territory on the other side of the tracks could speak to their own lives. (As I shall suggest later, there may be ways of encouraging the 'sociological imagination' many of these students lacked.) Nonetheless, when I was able to use some episode or detail to trigger common memories of childhood experience, the girls shared reminiscences in a lively manner. I used these and our shared text to prompt reflection on such questions as how reliable memory is and how 'true' our life stories are; how we develop a sense of self; and how that self is represented in story through the selection of details and the significance they are given.

Among other supplementary texts were samples of autobiographical writing I had collected from my students at a former school. These too served to help the girls explore various aspects of the topic: the choices of lexis and grammar which reconstruct a child self in words, for instance; or the ways one can move between seemingly direct sensuous apprehensions of a child's world and the writer's subsequent perceptions of their meaning; or the staging of a narrative through the motif of a series of places which delineate the dimensions of a family relationship. I am still convinced of the uses of this kind of scrutiny of more technical matters of crafting, for I believe that such scrupulous attention is part of what it takes to be critically evaluative – that is, valuing the aesthetic and rhetorical effectiveness of texts. We need that capacity for appreciation to motivate us to undertake the next step, of inquiring into the sociopolitical effects of such texts. Besides, if this kind of scrutiny can help young writers to achieve greater control of textual features, in a context of experimentation such as this they may begin to transgress the bounds of mere literary conventionality that confines (and produces) so many adolescents as schooled writers.

After sharing and comparing a number of autobiographical pieces, short and long, by published adults and their own student contemporaries, which included reflections on the purposes of life-writing, I reintroduced those questions about the nature of autobiography which we had explored at the outset and which could now be reflected on more sharply. For example, we compared Hanrahan's proliferation of precise detail with the frank confession of Elizabeth Bowen, another Adelaide writer, that she had reconstructed pre-war Adelaide in memory and could not vouch for its truth. And we contrasted the former's social insecurities with the latter's more assured sense of being a legitimate member of the civilised world. (Again, I now sense a missed opportunity here, but I wonder too how much a teacher can expand on every chance to 'do' critical literacy.) My memory tells me that a good number of the students could at that stage, through their reading and my interventions, see with greater sharpness what they had only half recognised before, in their earlier reading. They could also appreciate the justice of such points – about writers' various intentions in representing themselves, or the selectiveness of memory, or the way that the act of writing can change our sense of self, for instance – through their own writing.

I had taken the girls through a set of preliminary writing exercises – constructing a 'lifeline' and a photo essay, and describing an object that was the repository of memories and meanings. These 'warm-ups' prompted students to consider the shaping of memory through selection and emphasis in both recall and writing. In another exercise the girls selected two incidents separated in time and explored the (causal) connection they made. My purpose was to enable the girls to see, from their writing, how we often give sense to the events of our lives by linking them and so creating the 'plot' of our life-stories. Such exercises provided starting points for the students' more developed autobiographical writing, which was to take the form of a folio of a number of short pieces in various forms and on various topics, for various purposes, all chosen by themselves, mostly from a set of suggestions arising out of their reading. Much classroom time was devoted to the crafting of those pieces. In setting up these 'discontinuous' autobiographies I intended to help the students construct their text according to a different organising principle than a simple linear chronology. So too the range of forms, like those they had encountered in their reading, was designed to encourage the students to move away from a naive, direct transcription of personal experience. In this way they might come to understand that how you say it constitutes what you say. Another subsidiary reason for the choice of topics and forms was to enable students to avoid having to set out for a teacher's scrutiny matters that might be too private or painful.

So far this writing agenda might seem – although overly interventionist – not much different from a 'process' classroom. What sets it apart is two things: the direction of the concurrent reading commentary with its focus on the textual construction of a life as story; and the written reflections I asked the students to append to each piece of their writing. In these they were to comment on such matters as we had raised in class discussion. They wrote for instance about the selectiveness of memory, the challenges of experimentation as a writing self, and how in their writing about others they were also writing about themselves. By their reflecting on the different ways in which they had represented themselves and their purposes in so doing, and by recognising the forms and styles which shape the episodes of a life, I wanted the girls to see more clearly how 'discourses speak us', and how we may be multiple, even contradictory selves in narration. I knew that some would resist being encouraged to feel uncertain about 'who I really am'; I hoped it might also free them from the determinism of believing simply 'I am who I am.'

Through discussion around the various texts the students showed they were beginning to understand something about the textuality of selves. But in their reflective comments at the end of the unit they fell back on the discourses of humanism and of developmental psychology which tell them a very different tale about selfhood. According to this story, we develop in a logical way (cause leading to consequence); are the source of our own freely chosen actions; are unique individuals; are consistent personalities (or should be); and thus we can know who we are, as rational human beings; and that in such acts of memory and writing we come to know (not construct) our 'real' selves:

> As a result of my autobiographical writing this year I am able to reflect that this form of writing has helped me sort out myself as an individual. . . . I found that writing worked best for me when I was using my writing to find something out about myself. In this way I used my writing as a means of sorting myself out. Rather like Clive James, I used my writing to help myself understand my development over the years.
>
> (Catherine)

One girl's final reflection chastens me further. I understand better now how hard it is for students to decentre from the self they have so deeply invested in. Some may, with good reason, be wary of digging up emotionally intense or disconcerting episodes they have long buried. They may not want (changing the metaphor) to open up the text of their life in writing and then reading about it, for that can present themselves as characters to themselves as readers with uncomfortable clarity:

> I have come to the conclusion that I don't like remembering. When this topic ends I will be able to lock up my memories and throw away the key, so to speak. I will block out my past quite happily. What I often recall makes me feel sad, guilty or embarrassed – negative feelings. There are so many unanswered questions in the past, so many blanks, like a puzzle with half the pieces missing. The people of my past make me feel sad. The children I grew up with are all gone and I find myself wondering about them, wondering what they look like. Often remembering incidents, or things I've done, I somehow feel I've betrayed myself, I feel so guilty and embarrassed and I really just want to forget what happened. The past is soiling me.
>
> Another reason I don't like remembering is that I'm beginning to understand what kind of person I am, and was, and that scares me.

Why? Because I don't want to know. Exploring the past and me only brings pain. I believe that some things are best left buried.

As a child I've always felt that I was different. There is one aspect which makes me feel very alone. My father. When I was two my parents split up and my mother took me to Australia. I never saw my father again. . . . I desperately want to know what part of him I have in me. I wish I could feel a closeness to someone, other people have father, brothers and sisters. I have none. My mother and I are not really very close. So there it is, one of the huge gaps in my life, and one I'd rather forget.

Getting back to the previous point of understanding myself, I've tried to analyse myself. I think too much. Sometimes I feel I'm just a character in a book, I question who am I and what am I doing on earth.

(Gitte)

Gitte speaks of autobiographical writing as unlocking memories, revealing gaps and hollows, dirtying the mind that touches the detritus of the past, and exhuming what should remain interred. These are powerful metaphors which speak of the painful effect her writing has had for her. But even in her desire to close off those memories she is disclosing herself to herself – and to me, her teacher. This too could be cause for concern, if autobiographical writing becomes one more avenue for pedagogical, pastoral surveillance, as Hunter (1988) puts it. Yet Gitte's final sentence also speaks of her search for meaning as a textual self. In that I take hope.

The writer critiques herself

Inevitably my aims were very imperfectly realised, that the students should have developed a fully fledged understanding of textuality in our lives. Insofar as it deviated from the norm of personal writing I still believe it has potential for developing useful understandings. However, in most other respects it was a conservative curriculum which was likely to undermine any new ways of thinking. It could even be argued that to encourage so sustained a self-absorption is to promote a kind of solipsism. This need not be true of self-knowledge; the question to be asked is, how have we come to know what we do, and what are the consequences of such stories we and others tell about this self? I concede that the students' writing was politically disengaged, whatever incidental reference was made to matters of class and gender in our reading. The shaping force of these factors might be recognised in others' autobiographies; in their own the students adhered to the modernist view that the self is the cause and origin of its actions. So too they read their lives as having been made simply out of their 'experiences' rather than shaped by their culture's ideologies, institutions and practices.

How might these girls' views have been opened up more than they were? To all appearances these middle-class girls (Gitte was a marked exception) had the luxury of being able to maintain a rather stable sense of self. It seemed that very little in their mostly secure social and economic lives prompted them to think of themselves as fragmented, fraught with contradictions and radically provisional. And despite their passing discomfort with Hanrahan's vulgarity, these students were further confirmed in their competence in a middle-class literacy by the exclusively literary texts I selected. This is an especially urgent question for girls, since their very success in 'literary literacy' in their secondary school careers may be irrelevant and even detrimental to their career prospects beyond school (Poynton 1985). There are challenges enough here for a critical literacy teacher, but there is one further, larger challenge. Freire and others mentioned in chapter two have modelled approaches to pedagogy for the dispossessed. But if there is to be significant social and political change, do we not also need to think through what might be a most effective critical literacy pedagogy appropriate for privileged students like these?

BIOGRAPHY: LITERACY IN AND BEYOND SCHOOL

It was partly my dissatisfaction with this autobiographical unit which led to my second experiment. This curriculum unit attempts to bring together self, story and literacy in a new configuration, one which takes up the functions of literacy within and beyond formal education. I had become concerned that the best efforts of critical literacy teachers in presenting knowledge of texts and culture could be undermined by the ways in which such knowledge is generally taught within school contexts. The problem is twofold, at least. One is the presentation of knowledge across the school curricula – as received from authorities, and not also constructed by knowers; as certain rather than provisional; as public and universal rather than partial and contested; as unrelated to students' own lives (except in the matter of credentials); and as neutral rather than always bound up with power. The second problem is the school-bound nature of the kinds of literacy predominantly studied and practised. The previous unit demonstrates my belief that the formal study of culturally valued texts and the practice of writing for personal purposes can be legitimate and useful. Nonetheless for most students these kinds of literacy, these kinds of knowledge, do not translate readily to out-of-school situations – unless those students are preparing to enter an academic or professional literary subculture. Teachers who argue for instruction in genres claim exemption from this criticism, given their emphasis on those genres which are 'powerful' because they are valued in our society. Perhaps; nevertheless the instruction itself, within the frame of schooling, may still inhibit the transfer and transformation of that knowledge. Students are likely to drop that schooled literacy the moment they pull off their school uniforms. Given these problems, the question I set myself was, What kind of critical literacy curriculum will not be 'idle', not unrelated to students' present and future lives? My hunch was that some understanding of discourses could help them make this connection between schooled literacy and out-of-school literacy.

As previous chapters have argued, to explain language in terms of discourses is central to critical literacy theories. The students I encounter at tertiary and secondary levels can be persuaded (in terms appropriate to their knowledge) that words cannot be pinned down to a single, stable meaning, that ideologies shape texts and readings. But as my students in South Australia showed me, it is far harder when they are asked to consider the role of ideologies and discourses in forming them as persons, or rather subjects. Knowing themselves as individuals, they are less likely to take on the idea of discourses as shaping them. However, my belief in the value of an understanding of discourses was not diminished by my failure to develop a curriculum to help develop this.

In 1992 a letter arrived on my desk, and with it an opportunity to develop a critical literacy curriculum which might enable students to make a connection between schooled literacy and out-of-school literacy and so develop some understanding of discourses. (After teaching in South Australia I had moved to Queensland and taken up a position in a university.) I was very pleased to receive an invitation from Lindsay Williams, the Head of English Department at Park Ridge High, a new school in a mostly lower socioeconomic area on the sprawling outskirts of Brisbane. Here Lindsay has been developing a critical literacy curriculum that pushes further 'the central focus of the Queensland Syllabus, on the varieties of language as used for social purposes. I was invited to be a friendly critic of his curriculum, to inservice the English staff in ways of implementing critical literacy theories, and to advise them as they developed and taught their units. In the course of this work an opportunity arose to work with Lindsay on a unit of work for Year 11 students. In Semester 2, they take a unit called 'The Language of Work', which incorporates a period of work experience in a chosen field. Next, as an option they may undertake 'The Language of Biography'. I wondered if the latter could build on the former, and so enable students to make the connection between schooled literacy and out-of-school literacy by means of a focus on discourses and practices of literacy in each sphere. After much discussion we developed and Lindsay taught the unit. (I participated in as many lessons as work commitments allowed.)

A collective biography project

First, our reasons for using biography. Narrative is common to classrooms and community; both alike use the language of everyday life. And when we link others' experiences and stories with our own we may come to understand more about ours and theirs. Students may well become 'interested' – personally motivated as well as intrigued – insofar as they can make connections and contrasts in those stories with aspects of their own experience. Most of us want to understand our own past lives, our present behaviour and our scope for shaping our future, and so any theorising is more likely to emerge in relation to our own lives. But, as I found earlier, students are so close to their own experience, known and felt as personally and uniquely theirs, that when they focus exclusively on their own life-story they find it difficult to see the shaping roles of society's structures, practices and discourses. But to read and write biographies might, I believed, permit some distancing to occur. Then, out of the particulars of a range of narrated lives students may come to trace some of the cultural threads, the discursive threads, out of which unique-seeming lives are woven. They may be able to see those patterns more clearly when some biographies tell of events from an earlier generation. Much of the past is already so remote from present adolescents that the contrasts with their own lives will be the more salient. This can make their own experiences strange by contrast. But where there are continuities, in discourses or literacy practices, these too can be traced. In such ways what is usually invisible or obvious or personal may become more accessible to a different view. Such biographical or oral history work can also be useful for another reason, to deal with the problem of bounded knowledge mentioned above. When students carry out oral history research into literacy practices in school and community, they are no longer simply the consumers of others' knowledge which has already been transformed into schooled knowledge; rather they will in a sense be producers of information.

There is yet another reason for undertaking biographical work in a critical literacy classroom. An example may make the point. In the 1920s a girl called Pearl was growing up in New Zealand, in a fundamentalist religious home. Many years later she told this episode.

> My mother wouldn't ever let me get my hair cut, because she believed in the Bible text that said, 'A woman's hair is her crowning glory.' My hair was very thick and heavy, and I used to get terrible headaches from the weight of it. When I was in my teens I was always vowing and declaring I'd get it cut off, but my parents wouldn't hear a word of it. One day I went into town. . . . Then I sent a telegram home, and they knew what it meant when they read, 'The deed is done.'

Here is a telling literacy event! Pearl not only had mastered the genre of the telegram, but also had judged well the force of her few words, using them to announce the power she had exercised as an agent, openly defying the religious discourse that bound beauty to religious subservience. When she came out of the hairdresser's salon with her hair bobbed and shingled, she had identified herself with another discourse, of 'flapperdom', which spoke about a particular form of behaviour and looks and attitude that gave a young woman 'It' – sex appeal – and a new form of beauty. No wonder her parents were alarmed. They knew what flapperdom involved: loose talk, loose morals, loose purse-strings. Of course Pearl's 'deed' did not mean that she had escaped from religious discipline into a realm of pure freedom; and she was still contained by the discourse of the flapper. Nonetheless, she evidently felt it gave her more space for acting, as perhaps it did, relatively.

Now Pearl's story is so remote from my experiences that my interest is captured. (For further examples from her autobiography and a discussion of their discourses see Morgan 1994a.) What I feel while reading is not a simple empathy, because I cannot 'be' her, cannot dwell in the body and the discourses that she inhabited. Yet I do draw on experiences of my own that are similar enough to allow me to transform them in imagination and in this way come to sympathise with her (sympathy meaning literally 'feeling alongside'). Admittedly this might lead to my projecting and even superimposing myself inappropriately and so rereading her story as identical with mine. But I think that risk can be reduced the more conscious I am of it, and the more I come to know about the ways in which social, cultural, ideological and discursive forces work together in particular ways at particular times. This may enable me to stand alongside my informant, in thought as well as feeling, to compare her story with mine. Such positioning can lead to an imagining that is not so much personal as interpersonal: formed in the spaces and links between two individuals' stories. And if I try to trace the discourses at work in my informant's story I may come to understand more about the discourses that have shaped me, for they may well become more salient by comparison. Thus, as I return my gaze to my own experiences I may know them from a perspective that is not simply egocentric. Such is still my hope for students of English, that we can find ways to help them develop that kind of 'sympathetic understanding'. It will not necessarily arise in every mind, of course, as my earlier students remind me (as do my imagined students in chapter two), though it is more likely to occur where there is already an interest in the other person. (This proved to be the case with the Park Ridge students.) I also believe it is a necessary corrective to the form of critical literacy which is becoming orthodox in some Australian classrooms. This sometimes goes by the term 'resistant reading' and is rather narrowly understood as rejecting the text or reproaching the teller for some ignorance or political incorrectness. I believe it is possible and necessary to develop a more sympathetic and partial form of resistant reading: one which can see things from the point of view of another whose views diverge from ours even while we still see things differently.

In an eight-week unit one must concentrate on a particular field of discourse. As mentioned already, it was decided to focus on the discourses about and practices of literacy in school and in people's working lives. Here were the unit objectives Lindsay gave the students:

During the course of this unit you will

1 examine the role of social and cultural practices (especially literacy practices) in shaping our identities and consider the implications of these possible influences
2 consider the links (or lack of links) between literacy practices and work
3 consider a range of issues associated with biography, e.g.

- truth, fact and reliability vs 'lies', fiction and unreliability
- the constructed and reconstructed nature of biography
- biography as 'authorisation', 'justification' and 'rehabilitation'

4 interview a person in the local community and write a mini-biography of that person
5 analyse the ideologies that seem to come through in the biography.

In the previous term the students had been observing workers and recording workplace literacy practices. At the outset of this unit Lindsay drew on those investigations to construct a shared definition of literacy and its uses and values. Lindsay, and I as occasional co-teacher, shared with the students anecdotes from our own lives and others', including Pearl's, about being schooled in literacy. (Among the episodes offered in turn by students were those quoted at the beginning of this chapter.) We discussed how this affected their sense of themselves as members of a community, then and later. And we mentioned the various kinds of literacy that people bring to work with them, and how new times require new literacies.

This initial work was extended by means of some short auto/biographical texts which Lindsay brought in – magazine articles about Steven Spielberg, for instance, to introduce questions about the uncertain nature of a life that cannot be seen as a linear progress of linked episodes; or the reflections of a young woman on her growing up surrounded by the gendered discourses that gave her an identity and a role, which she first rejected and later, for a time, succumbed to. The students also selected a biography from the school library for independent reading.

The next task was to identify a biographee – a known adult, perhaps a relative, who could have interesting tales to tell or an unusual life to share. Their choice was discussed with Lindsay, who needed to ensure that there would be a good cross-section of community members of an older generation. Then, when the students had to learn how to conduct interviews and write up their biography, a local biographer and oral historian gave a series of practical, procedural lessons. And so the students set to, working with their informant to map his or her uses of literacy, in school and workplace, and to identify one or more significant episodes. They prompted that person to elaborate on the details of those episodes in audiotaped interviews, then selectively transcribed and revised their narrative, going back to their informant as necessary for additional details or corroboration.

My earlier experience had made me concerned that even a set of bio-graphical stories would still be read as the lives of individuals seen in individual terms, and that this would not necessarily enable listeners and readers and writers to get a purchase on wider social structures, discourses and practices. It was therefore our intention that the students would be crafting one autobiographical episode of their own, related in some way to the community members' biographies. They would therefore have to discuss the emerging patterns of similarity or difference, and as a class they would organise an anthology of student and adult stories about literacy and work. I saw this collection as a collective biography, wanting to emphasise the links with a feminist form of research, in which women share episodes from their lives pertaining to a chosen topic (Haug 1987, Crawford 1992). It is collective in the sense that the stories are told, retold and analysed in a group process. In form and function collective memory work is rather like the consciousness raising groups of the 1960s and 1970s, which was based on the understanding that when a number of women shared their experiences they would be able to see how 'the personal is political', and how events and responses that seem individual or particular are instances of more general tendencies which do not simply originate within each individual or within a fixed biologically determined pattern of behaviour.

In a shortened term it proved impossible to construct a properly collective biography, but I still think it would be valuable, as a class-produced resource for subsequent analysis. Nonetheless, we attempted to initiate the process with those Year 11 students. Lindsay made their task easier by breaking down ideologies into a cluster of related views and behaviours: what a person appears to value and believe about a certain matter, what institution is given allegiance, what the purpose of the particular practice they engage in seems to be, and what roles are set up for participants in such a practice. (In chapter five students can be heard conducting just such analysis, unsupervised, of a 'maverick manager'.) He demonstrated through shared analysis how one may detect the traces of ideologies in texts, and so began that work of tracing some more general patterns across texts. The students then conducted their analyses of their own informant's biography individually, considering the ways that literacy practices, and the ideologies and discourses that construct them, have been at work shaping a person and a life. And then they compared their analyses with those of another student and wrote about any similarities or differences they detected. Not all of them could manage this in any comprehensive way – that is to ask a great deal of Year 11 students. But one must start somewhere, and any first inklings here may be extended in Year 12 and beyond.

Here are parts of two such analyses. Both testify to the scope of the students' overview of the life patterns they have been tracing. And both begin to acknowledge the interplay of the social, historical and educational in the complex plot of a life.

Maurie finished school with 8 A's (suposadly) and scored a job as a clerk at Stewarts and Lloyds (tubemakers), which he continued his career with for 40 years. An assumption I can make with a link with early life and his choice to stay with his company is that he had a strong loyalty to his family based on his upbringing which it can be said that he was loyal to his company like he was loyal to his family.

I can also derive from my information gathered that he was inversely linked with his childhood and career choice i.e. he loved and participated in a lot of sport during his teenage years, but he chose a career with nothing to do with sport.

Although, this mighten be the case because when he left school, he probably tried to get any job he could, so when he got a job as a clerk, he enjoyed it so he stuck with it and didnt see any point in changing his career path.

Comparison

The simularities I could derive from the biographies is that a lot of the people interveiwed that were grandparents of students, were effected by the war, left school early and got a job, they also had alot of brothers or sisters.

There wasn't a strong link between things they did at school and the career paths the took. Most people just got any job they could and whether they enjoyed it or not decided whether they stuck with the job.

(Tim)

Links between literacy learning and work

Literacy events have not played a huge part in Hilary's life. She attended primary and high school where she learnt the basics like any other normal scholar. Naturally it has been used in her everyday life but nothing amazing from those years has affected her path in life.

The main aspect has been her amazing musical talents. Right back to when she was 3 years old to the present, 45 years on, her life has 'revolved' around her being able to play the piano. Her teenage/early adult years were taken up by her participation in America with the Christian Music Team. Her work was secretarial and organisational but none of that would have come around if she had not met Gordon Moyes through playing for him. Her university courses were a result of her working with music in a Nursing Home and local schools. Possibly this is when literacy events came into play and those have had a very positive impact on her life.

(Tracey)

'If language is the site where meaningful experience is constituted, then language also determines how we perceive possibilities of change' (Weedon 1987: 86). And if discourses are contingent, historical, and if subjectivities take on their form within discourses, then subjectivities are determined only to the extent that certain discourses prevail. If students can explore through their writing the discourses through which they and others become selves, this may provide possibilities for changing the subject in and of literacy.

The next chapter also changes the subject: there, four teachers at the same school as Lindsay discuss the remaking of their teaching selves as they take up a discourse new to them, of critical literacy. They too have shared my experience and Lindsay's: that its practice is shot through with contingencies and contradictions, self-sabotage and resistances. . . . But also that teachers and classrooms can be sites of change, however uneven.

Chapter 4

Between authority and freedom
Teachers negotiating the discourses of English

> In my first term at Park Ridge, kids started questioning me about why I wasn't doing the same sorts of things the other teachers were doing and started telling me that what I was doing wasn't *real* English.
>
> (Lindsay Williams)

As we saw in chapter one, a version of critical literacy in Australia is no longer a subversive and revolutionary alternative to mainstream English education; rather, an 'orthodox' model is endorsed in policy documents and government-funded professional development packages. Despite this, very few studies engage with its actual practice in its peculiarly Australian forms, and in much writing about critical literacy the voices of teachers are curiously absent. It is especially useful at this early stage in the institutionalising of critical literacy in Australia for education theorists, researchers, teacher-educators and teachers to listen to discussions about relations between older and newer discourses about English as these are being negotiated. For at the foundation of a discipline, as Foucault has argued (1970, 1972, 1979), a crucial process occurs, of determining which forms of knowledge and practice are to be valued and upheld or devalued and discarded. Therefore if we are to understand the phenomenon we need to know more about the relationships among the theories and exhortations of 'crit lit' academics, the theorising teachers do about their teaching, and their practice of critical literacy in school settings. For example, how do teachers deal with any incompatibilities they find between their critical literacy and those more traditional approaches to English teaching which are part of their inherited professional repertoire? What versions of critical literacy theories in and for practice might therefore evolve in a particular 'ecological niche'?

In this chapter we will be listening to four teachers in the same school discussing the critical literacy curriculum and pedagogy they are developing there. Such discussion does not belong in the realm of 'mere' theory: these teachers' reflective talk is itself a discursive practice and a component of a pedagogy which is inevitably the performance of theory, despite sometimes being trivialised as the mechanistic implementation of a set of techniques (Salvatori 1994). In the first sections of this chapter we will be tracing the various discourses of English through the teachers' discussions. We will follow the teachers as they negotiate their way among those 'Englishes' which they may see as contrasting or competing with or complementing their critical literacy. (As noted in earlier chapters, critical literacy is of course not a totally distinct 'successor regime' occasioned by the cataclysm of a paradigm shift.) This leads us in the final part of the chapter to consider a set of recurrent issues in their talk, concerning matters of authority and freedom in the construction of theory and practice, readers and readings, and teachers and students.

FRAMING THE TEACHERS

The Queensland education system is the least constrained of those of all the Australian states in having school-based curriculum and assessment in Years 1 to 12 within very open syllabus guidelines. It is underpinned by a broadly sociolinguistic model of language, with an emphasis on the ways its features vary according to cultural and social contexts and the purposes of its users. Subject English is in turn encompassed by a broader policy of social justice, *The Departmental Standard for Inclusive Curriculum* (Department of Education 1994c). This is congruent with federal government initiatives to provide equity for various groups systematically disadvantaged in Australia.

These frameworks have made it easier for Lindsay Williams, whom we met in chapter three, as the Head of English at Park Ridge State High School south of Brisbane, to develop a coherent critical literacy curriculum from Years 8 to 12. Uneven though it must be as implemented by more than twenty teachers, in its scope this curriculum is probably unique in Queensland and indeed in Australia. Of those twenty, four voices will be heard here: of Lindsay and of Spiro Jovic, Vicki Bothwell and Ivy Monteiro, teachers of senior and junior secondary English who have been at the school since the introduction of that curriculum. All four have a first-level tertiary degree and a postgraduate teaching qualification. Vicki and Spiro have studied critical sociology and taught it in high school and through this have access to a radical cultural studies approach to English. The cultural diversity of the four was not my reason for concentrating on them – though certainly fascinating stories could be told about the culture, history and education of these teachers in an attempt to explain why they were prepared to take on a critical literacy and how they arrived at their particular beliefs. (Lindsay is from a mainstream Anglo background. Spiro Jovic's family are Serbian, and although he concedes that he has been 'assimilated', he still defines his perspectives on the world as non-Anglo-Celtic. Vicki Bothwell is of Chinese descent; she came to Australia from Singapore via Hawaii and New Zealand. Ivy Monteiro is of Indian ethnicity; she grew up in Kenya but took her degree in England.) My reason for selection was much more pragmatic: while other teachers came and went, I had interacted with these four during more than two years of contact with the English Department at Park Ridge High. The focus of this chapter is not so much on the individuals themselves as on the discourses about literacy that these teachers produce and that also produce them as teachers – on 'how persons acquire literacy practices within the context of a particular field, domain or discipline' and on 'the tensions and disparities between the ways in which field knowledge is learned, employed, and valued in different contexts' (Beach 1992: 105–6).

In keeping with my arguments in previous chapters, I am using 'discourse' here to refer to the language which social groups characteristically use to explain events, define themselves and others and make sense of their world. To think of discourses of English conversing and arguing with one another helps me to interpret the dilemmas and tensions I hear in the teachers' talk as they negotiate a position and construct an identity as critical literacy teachers out of the bits and pieces of other Englishes and other educational practices available to them.

Their 'critical friend'

Knowing of my work as a teacher trying to 'translate' recent literary theory into classroom practice, Lindsay had asked me to conduct a series of inservice workshops with his fellow English teachers in 1994 and 1995 on the theory and practice of critical literacy teaching. I was also invited to be a resource and critical friend as they planned and implemented their curriculum. During that time I held discussions with the teachers in a variety of situations: semi-structured individual or paired interviews at regular intervals, to explore with the teachers their understanding and practice of critical literacy; interviews with individuals concerning their curriculum units; and pair-then-share sessions in which the teachers engaged with opinions they or their colleagues had previously offered on aspects of the reading and teaching of texts. The voices heard in the rest of this chapter are drawn from transcripts of those discussions.

The teachers' work is not just framed by the various discourses of English and pedagogy and all the 'educratic' directives that organise their professional lives. In my work with them as adviser, academic, teacher, researcher and writer I am also 'framing' them by my knowledge, even at times exposing them to interrogation in ways that may be condescending or oppressive, despite my intentions. For those roles entail multiple forms of authority based on my expertise. The teachers have wanted this expertise – but also, quite properly, have wanted to challenge its sufficiency at times. (Questions about authority in the relations between master/teacher and apprentice/student are taken up later in this chapter.) For example, when we came together in conformity with the genre of the interview, our conversation mutually constituted us as researcher and researched, and this constrained what could be said and how and what information was thereby generated. And of course their responses to my prompting could never encapsulate the rich complexity of their experiences and understanding of them. Spiro and Vicki each expressed their concern that their off-the-cuff comments, made in the few minutes of interview snatched in the midst of a rushed school day, when taped and transcribed could be subjected to analytical scrutiny which the words were not intended to bear. Indeed, they had trusted me, when they exposed their uncertainties and vulnerabilities, and any evaluative commentary I made could seem a kind of betrayal of those confidences – and indeed, of their confidence in what they were doing.

The narratives told in research interviews are already a selective interpretation of past events and thoughts. They become in turn the raw material of academic research writing and thus undergo a second order of selection and interpretation. Such writing is a form of textual display of 'knowledge', authorised by the expertise and status of the writer as demonstrated by his or her conformity with the genre and the technologies of research procedures. Given these transformations, like other researchers who work within an interpretative tradition I cannot subscribe to a naive belief in a single development from the 'data' of interview transcripts to analysis, interpretation and so at last to generalities – theory.

Nevertheless I am aware that this chapter may still appear to give ultimate authority to my interpretations of what Lindsay and Vicki, Spiro and Ivy said, for even as I have tried to present their meanings I have inevitably appropriated and re/presented them in a partial and interested way. However, the teachers had the opportunity to override and 'overwrite' those meanings: after my initial analysis and drafting they were asked to interrogate it and to supplement or supplant my interpretations with points of their own. (This is not to say that the teachers' 'last word' is necessarily more authentic and final either, since our meanings, always constructed within a context, are always subject to reconstruction in other contexts. Indeed, the teachers are no longer the same as when I first interviewed them or drafted this chapter: their negotiations among the discourses are still evolving.) Their comments, sometimes rightly critical, concerned not so much any particular point of interpretation, but rather the judgements I appeared to be making on their theorising. These were based on a poststructuralist, postmodern discourse of language and meaning which they did not have access to. 'My' critical literacy appeared to be different from theirs, based on premises other than those they had been encouraged to implement in their teaching. They might ask of me and my text that classic question of critical literacy: who profits from this? That is, whose knowledge is privileged? Who is helped to learn from this? Who gains in power and status? These are questions which have been taken up elsewhere, with those teachers, so I make only two more general points here. First, critical literacy begins at home, and our own practice – whether as teachers or researchers – should be the first object of our scrutiny. Second, since, as we saw in chapter one, critical literacy is no monolith but has a number of different and sometimes discrepant forms derived from discourses that have contributed to it, so we need to continue to debate the nature and agenda of those forms. I hope that, rather than appearing to advocate one 'correct' version based on my supposedly superior and superimposed understanding, this chapter will be seen as contributing to that debate as these and other critical literacy teachers contribute to the endless (re)construction of that field.

CONTRASTING, COMPETING, COMPLEMENTING DISCOURSES OF ENGLISH

Accepting some of the basic premises of chaos theory like uncertainty and all the rest has helped me not be dogmatic about what I believe. . . . Beliefs gradually evolve. There probably isn't 'The' critical literacy – one way of doing it.

(Lindsay)

An impure discourse

Lindsay's students in his first term at Park Ridge were aware that there may be disagreement about what counts as English; like their teachers they too were taking part in a conversation among (and about) competing discourses. As we shall see in the sections that follow, Ivy and Lindsay, Spiro and Vicki have variously defined critical literacy in relation to other discourses: as a totally contrasting paradigm; as a perhaps competing component of English in its various aspects; or as completing or complementing other forms of English teaching. Lindsay does not insist as Head of Department on uniformity; as he told the teachers at an inservice session, 'It isn't necessarily bad that we don't all have totally the same understanding of what it [critical literacy] is.' But quite understandably when the other teachers were in the first stages of implementing the critical literacy curriculum, they wanted an explicit, common definition to guide their planning and teaching. (They did not feel then that they had made the concepts securely their own.) Spiro for example wished for

a nice coherent written statement of values about what we're on about, where we're coming from. . . . I think I know in my own mind what the limitations of this [critical literacy] are and where we're meant to be headed, but we haven't been told that and it's usually just criticise,

criticise. But there needs to be a conceptual or philosophical framework that's embedded in.

As I understand them, the teachers wanted a framing definition and rationale to work with, not necessarily to be confined by; for it is much easier to test out and redefine an explicit statement in the light of practice and reflection than it is to measure up to an amorphous aspiration. Of course the opposite is also possible: an authorised rationale-cum-definition may come to seem unchallengeable in its power to dictate practice.

Seeing through metaphors

When we enter a new field of knowledge and are groping in uncertainty towards the elusive glimmer of clarity, we often have recourse to metaphors – as this sentence does. Such metaphors may stand in for or supplement other attempts at definition; their poetic suggestiveness can enable us to apprehend as we try to comprehend. So it has been for the Park Ridge teachers. And as Vicki commented on reading a draft of this section, when they were undertaking that very difficult work of reinventing the subject they might tend to use already formulated ways of speaking and thinking where no new language is yet available to them. In her experience this was a necessary stage on the way to such transformations.

Their metaphors have most often to do with opening eyes, removing blinkers or creating sight where there was blindness. Vicki for instance said she had explained the rationale for critical literacy in this way to students who were resisting her analysis of gender positioning: 'If we just open your opinions, your eyes to some of these things – whether you accept it or not now is another thing – you can sort of broaden your horizon a little.' This is certainly in keeping with the project of enlightenment on which a 'classic' critical literacy has been founded, as we saw in chapter one; it also informs the units in chapters two and three. And in keeping with that project, this metaphor suggests that the teacher's role is one of intervention, even in the face of student resistance. But Vicki still wants the ultimate decision to rest with the students as to whether they will take on this offered view 'now' (her hope is that they will eventually).

Other metaphors the teachers used are similarly visual and spatial: critical literacy offers breadth instead of narrowness, making spaces by removing the restrictions of walls or narrow paths. For instance, when I asked Lindsay if he saw critical literacy as 'leading students out of the dark into the light,' he was at first inclined to reject this metaphor, and preferred a related image:

> I wouldn't have thought about it in those terms . . . maybe not dark. But the sort of roles we all are put into are very narrow and confined. It's a case of, maybe, removing blinkers or removing walls. . . . I think we tend

to move in very narrow paths and we don't see all the other things going on around us.

(On another occasion Lindsay gave an aural emphasis to the same metaphor of spatial breadth when he defined critical literacy as in part 'opening up spaces for other voices to be heard' which may have been silenced in the dominant texts of a culture.) There is certainly a difference between being in the dark and being blinkered, the former suggesting a gloom in which one simply happens to be immersed and might find one's way out of, the latter a deliberate act of (partial) blindfolding on the part of someone or something else which prevents one from seeing what surrounds us in the light. Later in the same conversation Lindsay returned to that metaphor of blindness giving way to sight:

> My argument to the kids is that we're often blind to things that are happening in the texts that surround us. You need to become aware, to the stage where you can't read things in the same way as you once read them. And I'm really happy when kids start saying that to me because what it means is that they're able to see things which they weren't able to see before.

Using another spatial and visual metaphor, of depths as opposed to surfaces, Spiro at an early stage defined critical literacy as 'looking deeply into things to establish meanings. . . . You look deeply at a text, you find the assumptions. Who's writing? The way they're writing: what's their purpose, what's triggered them to write?' In this account, the real meaning of a text lies there under the surfaces of language; it can be seen if we pierce through to those depths by understanding the writer's motives. This is congruent with that conception of impediments to seeing what is 'truly' there. Later however Spiro had moved to a view of texts which emphasised more how they are made and remade (by readers) in their cultural and historical contexts.

I perceive some shift in these metaphors, between removing barriers to the clear sight of what is 'truly' there and providing a new way of seeing or rather reading the world and its texts in order to produce another 'reality'. This may seem a minor difference, but I believe each entails a significantly different view of the relations between texts and knowledge and teachers' work. It also raises questions about the authority of the text *vis-à-vis* the reader.

Evident in these metaphors of blindness and sight, depths and surfaces, is the teachers' concern for their students' clearer understanding: things are not always as they seem. According to Vicki, the aim of a critical literacy curriculum is to produce 'discriminating readers' who are aware of the 'ability of language users to manipulate and influence one's thoughts and actions'. This raises an issue for me, and for the teachers (we shall hear more of this later). For even if we accept that our readings, like our students', are partial, nevertheless we are bound to be interested in promoting our own. We may think ours is superior in its power to bring up the invisible ink of those hidden, encoded meanings; or we may think that the act of setting one reading alongside a different one may itself do the work of shifting perspectives, thus showing that any reading is partial and none is final. If we believe the former, we may still have a scruple about how overt we should be in leading students to substitute for their untaught readings the interpretations we endorse. That scruple was perhaps at work in Vicki's parenthesis quoted above: 'whether you accept it or not now is another thing'. Of course, our culture and its discourses coach us in all our reading practices. And if we accept that no readings are neutral and disinterested, no thoughts are 'pure' – ours alone and freely chosen – then we may have the less compunction in confronting one reading of the world with another we find less noxious.

In such scruples I hear a dilemma for English teachers who may be positioned in somewhat contradictory ways by two discourses: the critical project of deliberate enlightenment and a progressivist facilitation of student growth. The democratic and liberal impulses of the latter encourage readers' right to 'free' choice, while the former asks how far students may be allowed to stay with their ideologies, hence meanings, when teachers in their wisdom find these wanting. (And as we saw in chapter one, insofar as teachers aim to have their students reproduce their preferred readings, those teachers have 'failed' if the students apparently persist in wearing their blinkers, for this indicates that they have not developed a critical consciousness.)

That desire to enlighten students while still permitting them to make a 'free' choice can lead to other metaphors in the teachers' talk. Vicki's passionate concern was evident when she said,

> I see my aim as throwing these challenging ideas at them [students], because they've never been confronted with these sorts of ideas; and whether they accept it or not, . . . hopefully, when they leave school some of it will stick. And at least they have been thrown another way of looking at the world. . . . And if they still totally reject it, fair enough: at least we've thrown the alternatives at them.

Offering challenges becomes in Lindsay's expression of a similar concern offering an opportunity for (capital – and cultural) investment:

> I'm not trying to change their [students'] opinions overnight. So they can decide if they'll buy into what I'm trying to say. . . . I don't believe we're necessarily going to change their [students'] minds, but they're at least now aware that what they believe might not be totally in kilter with what everyone believes. . . . It's a case of denaturalising what they believe.

The version of critical literacy produced through all these metaphors is consonant with the traditions of critical theory and cultural studies which Vicki, Spiro and Lindsay encountered in their tertiary studies, and with the critical sociology which Vicki and Spiro have taught. Indeed, the practice of looking deeply into texts for their 'real', hidden, meanings is common enough in these and other discourses of English teaching, while the idea of developing less blinkered readings goes back at least to Leavis – although the understanding to be developed in critical literacy by such practices is claimed to be very different.

The discourse of social justice

These teachers' agenda, of confronting one reading of the world with another less harmful in its social and political effects, fits with the ideals and policies of social justice on which the Park Ridge curriculum is explicitly based. Consequently some assessment tasks developed early in its implementation required students to conform to the imperatives of social justice. For example, students were set to construct a children's picture-book which deliberately subverts stereotypes of gender, age and the like. Lindsay judged the success of this project by the fact that it

> got them [the students] to question their own ideologies . . . to the point where now a lot of kids make a joke out of being politically correct, and they weren't doing that at the beginning of the year. What they've done is suddenly see how they're not politically correct and . . . they are obviously starting to realise that the things they believe might be out of sync with what other people might believe.

(See chapter six for the way Lindsay has since reframed this task and for the wider range of assignments based on the teachers' changing understanding of critical literacy.)

Spiro was less sanguine than Lindsay about the unmitigated benefits of a politically correct social justice agenda:

> Kids have used the word politically correct: 'I've got my story and it's politically correct, sir,' and I don't think I'd used that [term] in class until then. That's one of the concerns that I would have with what we're doing. I know that with a social/critical literacy we take a political view of language . . . but I also think that we're pushing – it's not just English, we're also pushing a baggage of political values as well and that's the part that worries me the most.

He commented that the issues which concern him and his Yugoslav friends may not be the same as those given priority by the educational bureaucracy and added, 'Our [school] political correctness is an officially defined political correctness.' Ironically perhaps Spiro's affiliation with a marginalised cultural group has enabled him to produce a resistant reading of the Park Ridge social justice policy and curriculum.

These teachers give clear expression to a dilemma which is shared by other educators in their writing on critical literacy. How far is it the business of English not only to undertake ideology critique but also to require students to conform to a certain behaviour – and be assessed for that? It can be argued that English teachers have always been involved in normalising students – defining what they desire as a norm and encouraging students to conform to that; but perhaps they have not always done so explicitly or argued the grounds of their stance. Nonetheless, Spiro's concern must be heeded, that in their very desire for social justice critical literacy teachers may be participating in the work of social control, of 'governmentality'. In a more extreme form, it takes up the dilemma of Lindsay and Vicki in the previous section, of coercion or persuasion, teacher authority or student choice.

So where does the teacher's role centre, and where does it stop? Lindsay defined his role, within a social justice framework, as helping students 'identify the consequence of accepting this position that these texts are offering, and not just the immediate consequences but maybe some of the [social and political] consequences further down the track.' He added,

> There is a place where the role of the English teacher has to stop, and we're not necessarily able to take action [with our students] in the outside world – not in Queensland schools, anyway. . . . Nice Anglo-Saxon middle class parents aren't going to be too happy if their teachers are inciting their students to revolution and riot and overturning or dropping out of society. . . . At some point the role of the teacher has to stop and the role of outside community organisations and families have to take over.

I believe we can also hear in all these comments debates about the nature and work of social justice itself. Despite his general endorsement, Lindsay does not accept all aspects of its agenda uncritically. His social justice means attempting to accommodate both a cultural relativity and an ethical commitment to principles and practices of equity. He argued that students need to understand that while different and perhaps incompatible ideologies and practices are 'normal' to those who hold them,

> it's not the same as saying anything goes. It keeps coming back to the idea of ethics. We need to say to kids, there are some options that are there but maybe they're not particularly good options to take up or good things to regard as normal or worthwhile doing.

And he cited as 'an interesting dilemma' his students' doubt whether they might criticise Aboriginal polygamy and patriarchy as described by Daisy Utemorrah in her children's picture-book, *Do Not Go Around the Edges*

(1990), when they understood that these had been culturally acceptable practices at the time.

Such cultural pluralism can lead to scepticism: if all beliefs are relative, then perhaps none can be preferred to any other. What might prevent a slide into nihilism? We have heard Spiro before on the limitations of a curriculum based on endless critique (it is a point shared by many critics of the postmodern):

> I'm worried that we're heading towards a moral negativism. . . . I think I know in my own mind what the limitations of this [critical literacy critique] are and where we're meant to be headed, but we haven't been told that and it's usually just criticise, criticise. But there needs to be a conceptual or philosophical framework that's embedded in. . . . I think normally when you start criticising, asking questions, you should know what the aim or the purpose is.

Ivy too was concerned that there should be an ethical framework to contain critique, wondering 'why you should question power, not only when you should question it'. Both questioned the insufficiency of raising a critical consciousness without the grounds for and means of social change. Lindsay agreed:

> It does concern me that we throw something out and say, 'Well, we can't believe these values' – but what do we replace them with? You talk about being nihilistic and . . . that is a danger, and I try to work out what are the values we're going to bring through this English. I mean education, let's face it, is about teaching values.

(I later suggested to Lindsay that English could also be about enabling students to understand the discursive and textual means by which various systems of value are represented. Given his views on language and meaning which we have heard already, he agreed with this point.) Although he did not spell out these values at the time, it was evidently an ethics of social justice he had in mind. Such an ethics is the more likely to be taken up by the teachers if it offers a corrective to that negativity of critique. When Lindsay talks of 'teaching values' and when Vicki 'gets on her soapbox' and 'comes down like a sledgehammer' on the conservative views of students, this seems to entail a teaching practice that differs from the progressivist ideal of implicit advocacy, of modelling of a set of values and behaviour, or of setting up the conditions under which those values may be fostered. As we have heard (and will do more later) the teaching of values has caused these teachers some misgivings about their authority as it relates to students' autonomy of choice, since the latter is also an ethical desideratum. Here again perhaps we can hear these teachers negotiating their position among various discourses of moral education through English.

Cultural or critical aesthetics

A number of discourses about the cultural canon can be heard in the talk of the teachers. While Vicki, Spiro and Lindsay roundly rejected the discourse of the Leavisite Great Tradition, in various ways they were still engaged with questions of literary value and the educative function of such works of 'the' heritage. From the texture of their comments one could infer some ambivalence, the warp of teacherly concern crossing the woof of personal enjoyment. To my view they certainly represent in microcosm debates among the discourses. In the tapestry of critical literacy some have been threaded beneath the surface; their resurfacing here reminds us that they need to examined again for their part in the fabric.

One of those boldest threads in critical literacy has been its dismissal of the perennial aesthetic worth and universal truth of the best literature or even of its claims to distil the essential qualities of a culture. (This view is given most forceful expression by Eagleton 1983.) Such critique of 'high' culture is a discourse well represented among the Park Ridge teachers. Lindsay for instance has talked about his commitment to critical literacy as a 'paradigm shift' which has entailed 'giving up' a cultural heritage model of English. (But as we are already seeing, it is not so completely abandoned.) Vicki and Spiro also mistrust the claims of the heritage discourse to represent the 'best' of 'the' culture, arguing that the promotion of certain authors, texts and subcultures excludes others from legitimate study. In a throw-away comment Spiro for example shrugged, 'I come from a non-Anglo-Celtic background, so – big deal, it doesn't mean that much to me.' He later elaborated that knowledge of his own, often richly oral, tradition gave him an alternative perspective – though certainly there were also works from the Anglo tradition such as Shakespeare's which he loved. However, he would not insist on students' studying such texts which were not always suitable for them, though he also regretted the Park Ridge underemphasis on poetry. And he felt that the traditional terms of literary criticism, as part of the 'nuts and bolts' of English, had been lost in the school's 'heavy emphasis on the socially critical and looking at ideologies'. He would be prepared to coach students in traditional literary criticism if that would help them achieve their goals of academic success, since there are 'two parts to education', both of which fell to his responsibility: not only broader social goals but also preparation for future study and work.

In these comments I hear a number of discourses and their debates. One has to do with the identification of valued literary works: 'a' tradition or a number? – and according to whose system of valuing? Another has to do with the capacities (for appreciative reading) or competencies (in literary criticism) to be fostered in students by induction into a literary tradition. This entails another: about the teacher's mandated responsibilities to ready students for employment in relation to the teacher's ethically and politically educative role. Yet another, which we now turn to, concerns the relations among enjoyment, value and critique.

Much of the curriculum and the teaching at Park Ridge is based on a critique of a high culture and a monoculture. But this critique can in turn never go unchallenged. Ivy, for instance, maintained that there was value in teaching the literary 'greats', as she put it – Shakespeare, Dickens and others: to ensure that students 'don't miss out on so much of the culture'; to provide acquaintance with the classics 'that have given rise to today's literature'; and to give them experience of 'another time' and an imagined world. However Ivy, like Spiro and Lindsay, concurred with Vicki's advice that canonical literary works of the past should be studied 'in the context of their time, but this time with the blinkers removed.' The value of literature became a parental as well as teacherly concern for Ivy and for Vicki: both expressed concern about their sons' reading of non-literary texts and magazines which Vicki derided as 'pulpy'. For themselves, all four teachers have freely declared their enjoyment of canonical texts and conceded that such reading brought them aesthetic pleasure and historical-literary understanding.

Nonetheless, a discourse of aesthetics seems to sit in a rather problematic relation to critical literacy; this is evidently perceived by some students as well as their teachers. The romantic view that 'we murder to dissect' is echoed by a student who, according to Vicki's report, asked, 'Can't you say, "I love this book, I really enjoy this story? – and not have to justify and feel guilty about it? . . . You can't have a positive experience [in reading] if you keep pulling things apart."' The teachers have defined a critical literacy reading practice as involving 'healthy scepticism' (Lindsay) or 'strategic doubt' (Spiro); such distanced discrimination could I think seem incompatible with absorption in the pleasures of the text and compliance with the views it proffers. (Yet many readers alternate between unselfconscious engagement in the act and more conscious, critical evaluation afterwards.) Certainly the teachers expressed diverse views about the relations between literary aesthetic and socially critical reading practices. We have heard here hints of these: as contrasted and incompatible discourses; as perhaps competing components of a program of study; or as complementary – critical literacy completing traditional literary study. For the most part however, the teachers rejected the argument that an aesthetic response to literature promotes a refined sensibility, hence a moral maturity. Moral and ethical responsibility ('active and informed citizenship', as the Queensland English Syllabus puts it) are more likely, in their view, to be fostered by a resistant rather than compliant reading of the texts of a dominant culture.

These discourses of aesthetics and critique are open to further debate among the teachers. Lindsay announced the agenda when, at the end of an inservice discussion, he mused,

Can we invent a term like 'critical aesthetics'? Or 'critically aware aesthetics'? . . . In my version of critical literacy I would also have to
question the notions of things like aesthetics and appreciation. Those
notions would become quite different in my version. . . . There has to be
some room for that [critically aware aesthetics] because you have to ask
yourself: What's the role of uncritical aesthetics? Are you simply going
to accept everything and say it's beautiful, therefore we can't analyse it
or comment on it or criticise it?

In this speculation I believe Lindsay brings together two aspects of the critical: first, the acts of valuing which are, second, the basis for evaluating.
These and further comments make it clear that he did not believe one
should be naively accepting of the pleasure which encourages us to value
what we read. He argued that pleasure can open readers to manipulation
and to acceptance of the meaning proffered by a text; hence it is all the
more important to examine literary texts such as poems through a critical
literacy perspective, 'because you're more likely to be moved and go along
with the poem because you like it'. In a hint still to be developed, Lindsay
suggested a way of negotiating a position that evades such binaries
between pleasure and critique when he acknowledged that his habit of
scepticism still permitted him to enjoy texts. For if pleasure is impermis-
sible, 'we have to question the whole notion of reading for enjoyment' –
though this may be a reader's legitimate purpose.

I believe these discussions usefully raise issues for critical literacy teachers. To read (and view) *for* enjoyment, as the (sole?) intention and outcome
of the act may be rather different from reading and viewing with enjoyment as a concomitant and perhaps a byproduct of a more consciously
judicious practice. The latter can perhaps more easily be accommodated by
critical literacy teachers as being more compatible with the practice of
scepticism they advocate. But there are debates still needing rehearsal
among critical literacy theorists and teachers, so that their implications
can be enacted in curriculum and pedagogy. One has to do with the relationship between a literary sensitivity to the workings of language and a
critical consciousness of those workings. If there is a dilemma here, is it to
be resolved by applying a disciplined scepticism which will presumably
lead to a different, enhanced pleasure, of critical enlightenment? Another
debate, discussed in chapters one and two, has to do with teachers' stance
towards students' investments, of emotion and desire, in the texts which
help form their subjectivities. How can teachers work with students' iden-
tifications in pleasure and not just against these when they interrogate the
texts of young people's culture? Again this raises questions of readers'
freedom, in textual pleasure, and the constraints on them, through manipulation via such pleasure. It raises questions of students' freedoms
(illegitimate if not scrutinised?) and teachers' authority to subject students
and their readings to such scrutiny.

Grammar and genres: the discourse of a 'functional' literacy

This discourse of English education also surfaces in the teachers' discussion, and here a 'pragmatic' commonsense often speaks to or across the 'theoretical' commonsense of their critical literacy. Does a critical literacy complete or rather compete with the teaching of writing? Lindsay believes the former: a critical literacy curriculum can help students develop their capabilities in writing. He cited his own experience of becoming a better writer when he became aware of 'the wider issues' and '*why* language is used in particular ways', and he argued that there should be a similarly 'strong flow-over effect' of rhetorical understanding from students' reading to their writing. The other teachers inclined to think the latter, giving voice to their concern that a critical literacy emphasis (presumably seen as instruction in reading) might be 'at the expense of writing', as Vicki put it. Ivy advocated for her students the conservative training she had had in learning correct expression through writing exercises and a cycle of 'reinforcement, correction, reinforcement, correction'. Vicki worried that some students 'can't even string ideas and sentences together, and when we start worrying about the critical literacy aspect, it's minuscule in comparison to some of the problems they have in terms of their writing.' She quoted such students, who had raised their doubts about the usefulness of critical literacy, as saying, 'How's this going to help me write better?' It was her belief that this concern may be a source of students' resistance to the critical curricular emphasis, since 'writing is so important, especially when a lot of them are going on to some form of tertiary study'.

It was Spiro who most often expressed his dissatisfaction with the neglect of the 'nuts and bolts' of a functional literacy. Underlying this was his concern that such neglect may perpetuate the disadvantage of a working-class community:

> If this is a working class area wouldn't it be good if some of these kids picked up and did go to uni [university] and qualified as doctors, lawyers and things like that? . . . In some ways I think we're foreclosing their options. . . . My own parents were post-war migrants etc and most of us at my high school became blue-collar workers, apprentices and things like that. So I wonder whether we [teachers] really are being critical or in some way are reinforcing dominant ideas about not going to uni and so on. We just focus so heavily on alternative structures [of social and political organisation], in some ways I think this may not be the message to be giving a working class community. That's a dilemma I'm tossing around.

Instead of appearing simply to encourage disaffection from mainstream ideologies, in Spiro's view the curriculum should set higher standards for students' written products and offer more opportunities for structured practice in traditional school genres – imaginative, descriptive, and especially analytical expository writing. He was concerned that the Park Ridge students might not perform well on the publicly examined Core Skills Test in Year 12 (a component of their publicly moderated English portfolios by which their 'exit achievement' grade is determined), which he called a 'litmus test of critical literacy'. In that case there might be a 'backlash' from the school's administrators as well as legitimate disappointment from students and their parents.

One aspect of a 'functional' literacy which traditionally gets much attention is grammar. In Queensland 'grammar' is now generally understood by English teachers to mean the Hallidayan, systemic functional grammar (Halliday 1985) endorsed by their Syllabus. Its exponents argue that, unlike other merely categorical and prescriptive grammars, this helps readers and writers understand how the language systematically works to produce meanings. It is therefore often advocated as compatible with critical literacy (but see Pennycook (1994) for incompatibilities between a sociolinguistic emphasis and a more ideological view of discourses). As we shall see in chapter five, Lindsay is attempting to use grammatical analysis to help students see what they could not previously, that (as he put it) 'discourses operate at a very subtle level' – 'because [our use of] grammar is another thing that becomes naturalised and we regard it as [being as] natural as talking in particular ways, without thinking through the implications of what using that particular grammar is doing.' (For an example of such grammatical analysis see Lankshear and Williams 1996.)

Nevertheless, despite his continuing commitment to such linguistic analysis, Lindsay's estimation of its sufficiency has changed. In 1993 Lindsay had told the teachers at a workshop he was conducting, 'Looking at the language features in this text we can see how the author has used them, probably unconsciously, to encode her ideology about social relationships.' A year later, while he still believed that such analysis 'can help to confirm your intuitive response to a text, or it can actually reveal things about the text that you might not have noticed otherwise', he critiqued his earlier phrase, 'we can see . . .':

> . . . as if as soon as you do that [analysis] you can automatically see, as if that deconstruction automatically reveals the ideology. . . . Once you've done the analysis, yes, it might reveal what the actual construction of the sentence is, or whatever. But you still have to place an interpretation on that, and that interpretation is going to come from your own ideology. So it's not as simple as what that last comment makes it.

There is a shift here from a systemic, structural and rational notion of meaning as located 'in' the text and ideology as 'encoded', to a more interactive, provisional model of meaning-making as chosen but also constrained by both conscious ethical deliberations and generally unconscious discursive conditioning. Nonetheless, when I was reading the transcript of this discussion I thought I heard here some ambiguity concerning the 'mechanisms' of language. It seemed that the reader could determine with certainty the grammatical elements, and this activity was separate from and might be prior to reading as interpretation. On such a view grammar could seem a neutral tool for analysis instead of itself being a discourse and a reading practice which already produces meaning. And this kind of reading might seem somehow superior in its capacity to neutralise by such analysis the workings of power through language. Lindsay and I later discussed my queries, and he conceded the plausibility of this latter view of grammatical analysis as discourse. However, he still thinks it can be strategically useful in classroom critical literacy work.

In general the Park Ridge teachers, like most of their peers in Queensland, have focused on one aspect of functional grammar: genres. These are defined in the Syllabus as 'any purposeful activity that is characteristic of a cultural group or community. It has a characteristic staged generic structure'. Particular cultural contexts and social circumstances lead to the production of texts which instantiate a particular genre (Department of Education, Queensland 1994a). The teachers' focus on genres is almost inevitable, given Syllabus directions that students must read, view and write a range of 'literary (narrative and non-narrative) and non-literary (transactional, procedural, report and expository)' genres. So too the task and criteria sheets teachers draw up for student assignments must be explicit about the generic demands of the writing or speaking to be produced. (This matter is taken up further in chapter six.) Given these directives, Australian teachers of English have in general tended to represent genres as static, recurrent, even formulaic structures and teach their students to reproduce these. (Freedman and Medway (1994) give a North American perspective on genres as more dynamic and interactive; for discussion of the Australian version see Richardson 1994.)

For a critical literacy teacher there can be risks in disciplining writers into habits of conformity within the confines of genres. It can also encourage the view that the possibilities for subversive rewriting lie only in content and not also in form and function in specific contexts. This however is not always the case with the Park Ridge English curriculum. The first unit of Year 11 sets the students to read and write a range of unconventional narratives; the rationale for this is partly to enable students to understand more about the constructedness of texts and their openness to reconstruction. Further units at this and other levels require students to transform texts or parts of texts from one genre into another. Still other writing tasks direct students deliberately to write texts which are subversive in content or approach or which counter dominant ideologies.

According to my reading of the teachers' talk, the discourses of writing instruction have been negotiated in various ways *vis-à-vis* critical literacy, as competitive or complementary. Affecting these negotiations is whether writing is seen as 'writing likewise': a functional replication of correctness in genres and grammar (a competence that leads to study and work), or in terms of 'writing otherwise' texts and their realities. Here is again a dilemma for these teachers, as for any critical literacy teachers, of balancing their mandated responsibility as writing instructors (a role inherited from a long-dominant discourse of English) with their ethical concern for a more broadly defined 'empowerment' of writers.

Individual readers or positioned readings

The 'personal growth' and 'reader-response' discourses of English, discussed in chapter one, have emphasised the active role of students as readers and writers in bringing their own understandings and concerns into their English classes. We have seen how it values students' autonomy and gives teachers an identity as cherishing those individuals, 'facilitating' their learning through indirect and often 'invisible' pedagogies. In what we have heard the teachers say in this chapter I believe are traces of this discourse too. Of the four, Ivy has been the most committed to its kind of humanism – and this fits with her continuing commitment to the 'great' literature of a humanistic tradition. At times this contrasts with a more interventionist critical literacy; for while she approves of the way the English teachers are 'moulding' students, the latter must still be helped, she said, to fulfil their potential as individuals.

According to Vicki, Ivy and Spiro, the meanings that students make of texts have their origin in both personal experience and cultural context. Nonetheless they require students to substantiate their interpretations by reference to the text. (I hear in this an older discourse-practice of close reading, which locates the authorised meaning in the text rather than in a reader's personal response.) Lindsay put the emphasis on the cultural rather than the personal when he queried the notion of an individual, idiosyncratic meaning:

> People don't have personal responses but they have responses that are shaped by the way they've been brought up, the values they hold, their beliefs. . . . Responses are shared. . . . If you've got thirty kids in the class, you're not going to have thirty different opinions. You'll have clusters of opinions.

All the teachers appear to conceive of these readers as unified selves, whether they are unique individuals with a personal response or members of a group. However, they do recognise that one can change one's reading or writing position and so take up a different subject position. This tension between an emphasis on personally constructive readers and culturally positioned readers should not be seen as a 'problem' to be resolved but rather as a 'problematic', a matter always in question.

A connected tension appears in some of the teachers' talk between an emphasis on readers who bring meaning to the text and on the text as itself providing its own one correct meaning. Ivy voices this dilemma: 'Your opinion depends on your culture, your background, your experiences . . . but there are some kids who can totally misinterpret the simplest things.' The teachers are not prepared to give all authority to the text as the repository of a single, determinate, correct meaning nor to students in their untutored readings. Rather, for Vicki, Ivy and Spiro it appears that a three-way negotiation needs to occur: the student's initial reading is to be refined through the teacher's interrogation of the student about the text; after this, the teacher hands back to the student the ultimate decision about interpretation. (We have heard Vicki already on students' freedom to take up or not the challenges she has 'thrown at them'.) At an early stage of his learning to be a critical literacy teacher Spiro gave expression to this view of English teaching in citing the kind of conversation he had with students in order 'to make sure that they have read the book and in toto. . . . I guess they miss things or gloss over some things.' His characteristic questions were designed to get students both to substantiate their readings and to recognise their relativity:

> How do you know the author means that? Give a word / phrase / sentence to prove your answer. . . . Why do you select this interpretation? Are there different views? Why? . . . How might other people interpret your stance? Would you like to comment on other statements made by class members? . . . Well, what about this bit here? OK, if you don't want to take it on board, good. If you do, fine.

He then commented, 'They're doing the thinking and they've got to fit it together, they must make the ultimate decisions. My role is more or less about getting a discussion going and saying, "What about this part? What about that part?"'

In such comments about acts of reading comprehension I believe the teachers are grappling with elusive questions of authority and authorisation of meaning. This could be heard as an inconsistency in their stance; I detect instead an unwillingness to take a position on one side of a too tidy binary between a view of the text as the authorised repository of a 'complete' meaning and a recognition of multiple possible unauthorised readings. Such ambivalence permits a particular kind of teaching that is characteristic of much critical literacy. When a text lays claim to its 'givenness' and the certainty of its meanings, it is the reader who must destabilise those by constructing alternative readings. And where change depends on the reader, this of course enables and justifies the teacher's work of interrogation of students, texts and their readings.

These conversations among discourses about textual meaning and readers' responses have brought us once again to questions of authority and freedom, choice and its constraints. We now turn to consider these more closely.

DILEMMAS OF AUTHORITY AND FREEDOM

In what we have heard the teachers say so far have been three broad kinds of framing. One had to do with state educational policy and syllabi. (The curricular boundaries between areas of learning is another often rigid framing.) The second concerned societal, school and parental expectations of teachers' responsibility to make students competent in socially valued forms of literacy. The third framing, our chief focus, was the discourses of English education: the terms they set up for thinking and speaking about critical literacy and the constraints these may entail on thinking and acting otherwise. Conversations among these discourses raised a number of questions about the legitimation of teachers' authority to intervene in their students' attitudes and opinions. When and how far is cultural critique (including of students' subcultures) legitimate? Is it justifiable if students are already subject to the constraints and controls of ideological manipulation of texts, so that critical literacy interrogation of these becomes a means to 'freedom' from them and 'empowerment' of students? When does such intervention overreach itself to become coercion into political correctness? And what of students' freedom of choice – to refuse the offer of such empowerment, or to give themselves to the pleasures that are in a text or represented by it? Is there some middle ground, of persuasion, between coercing students or abandoning them to the autonomy of maybe misguided choices? These kinds of questions surface again as we consider two further aspects of power and freedom the teachers articulate: concerning texts and readers, teachers and students. As we do so we should recall the point made in chapter one, that emancipation (or education) is only possible within a discourse and practice in which are also immanent possibilities of oppression.

Between readers and readings

'Is the aim of your critical literacy teaching to get students to re-examine their uncritical readings? Or to lead them to a more valid reading? To encourage multiple readings? Or something else, or some combination of these?' These were questions I asked the four teachers at the end of their first year of implementing the critical literacy curriculum (each of these aims had been stated previously by one or more teacher).

Each chose a different aim. Lindsay refused any of the options as too simple.

I give the kids a model of reading where we talk about the language the author used, and the ideology of the reader. . . . Your meaning comes by the interaction between those two things. So someone coming with quite different beliefs and values interacting with the same text could come up with something quite different. Meaning isn't just coming from language in the text. . . . Meaning has to be coming from other things as well, because there are huge gaps [in the language of the text].

Nevertheless, Lindsay conceded that less critical students should be encouraged to read more critically. As for leading students to a more valid reading, he was uncomfortable with the idea of 'closing down some readings'; however, he admitted, 'I would have problems with a kid who was voicing really racist comments in class or highly sexist comments.' He would in general prefer not to close down readings but challenge them, especially those which are at odds with the principles of social justice. This does not necessarily mean, I think, stopping the play of possible meanings but recognising that the play has been stopped with the privileging of one (perhaps unjust) meaning – which must be unsettled again.

Which kinds of readings, which ideologies are permissible and which are unspeakable is always a dilemma for any teacher who wants to set up a liberal classroom where a plurality of views may be heard but also one where not 'anything goes'. Vicki said her aim was to promote multiple readings as well as getting students to re-examine their uncritical readings. Nonetheless she was prepared to 'close down' readings by attempting to contest her students' interpretations and to substitute hers. For example, her feminism led her to vigorously challenge her students' compliant reading of the lyrics of the popular song 'Dirty Dog', despite their claims that its misogynist insults were dramatically authentic and therefore acceptable because they were vented in anger.

Ivy was inclined to be less overt in her direction of students' reading. She wished to accept a plurality of viewpoints but was also concerned about the possibility of misinterpretation. 'In this last unit on advertising I was more accepting than influencing them. Some of the kids went way off anything that was logical or relevant.' So in the end she articulated her aim as being 'to lead students to a more valid reading from their own experiences. They don't understand things unless they can relate it to what they've experienced themselves. . . . They have a preconception [after first reading] but very soon, after discussion, it's totally changed, very often. They see things there that they never did before.'

When asked about his aims for a critical literacy reading practice Spiro expressed his preference for promoting multiple readings, and he echoed his earlier questions to students: 'What is this saying and what are the assumptions underpinning it?' Such questions draw attention to the contextual conditions and constraints on a text's meaning. Of themselves such questions do not necessarily lead to a diversity of readings; however, when Spiro, like others, juxtaposes a number of texts whose ideologies are discordant, he encourages students to read across from one to another and therefore challenge those assumptions and question the sufficiency of any one meaning.

In these various responses it seems there may be some tendency to emphasise one aspect of multiplicity rather than another. What seems to be stressed in general by the Park Ridge teachers is the multiplicity of readers who each bring different ideologies and histories to the text. The other, relatively less emphasised, is the multiplicity of readings which are latent in a text, given the potential of language to generate many meanings. There are two reasons perhaps for the teachers' preference for the former. One is the democratic, culturally pluralistic discourse of their critical literacy. The other is their desire to substitute a more critically conscious, resistant reading for a more compliant one, rather than to hold in suspension a number of possible readings, each of which is relative to the other. But the teachers have also expressed their concern that in a critical literacy classroom a non-dominant, non-normative, alternative reading might ironically become the normative one. So we return to the familiar conundrum of freedom and control. One way of evading that either-or is suggested by Knoblauch and Brannon (1993: 62): 'Critical teaching begins . . . not with a power struggle over preferable readings but with the *reading* of those readings, contextualised by the life experience of those who produced them.' However, the sheer difficulty of opening up our classroom to other voices and interests and their contestation (recall the issues raised in chapter two) may lead any of us to return to the more familiar, institutionalised practice of transmissive teaching based on our authority and our privilege to adjudicate between meanings.

Before we turn to questions about master-teacher readers and their readings in relation to the apprentice work of students, I want to pause briefly over that issue of the constraints on readers and meanings *vis-à-vis* the freedoms of readers and the instability of texts. For this has bearing on the textual work of critical literacy. (In what follows I am drawing directly on the work of Misson 1994.) The fields of reader-response and poststructuralist literary theory are enormously complex and I make no attempt to do justice to them here, only to indicate some of the parameters within which those matters of freedom and constraint need to be negotiated in a critical literacy theory for classroom practice. What is in question is how a text constructs possibilities of meaning and how a reader is able to realise that text's potential for meaning (and how different readers produce different meanings). This means that in our thinking and teaching we need to problematise both textual and reading processes: to keep them both in play.

On a poststructuralist view, language and texts are indeterminate and unstable. For one thing, there are always more meanings that can be made of any words, any text. Some of this excess of potential meaning may be suppressed by the dominant meaning (the one a text encourages a reader

to make). But different contexts of reading may make any of these meanings more salient. For another, no text can say everything, but has gaps and
silences. Despite this indeterminacy, texts are also subject to constraints,
such as the structures of available genres and the discourses that condition
what can be said and how. Such genres and discourses implicitly carry
ideologies, so the constraints are also productive of meaning.

Yet it is for a reader to take up those textual invitations to make meaning:
the reader is the site where the potential of the text is realised, though
always in a partial way. The question remains of who or what sets the
bounds of possible readings? The term 'reader-response'

> can be misused to seemingly validate a view that one reading is as good
> as another as long as it is an honest response to the text. . . . This matter
> of limiting the range of possible meanings is obviously important for
> teachers, because without it we could not readily discuss a text and we
> could certainly never think that we or our students had come to a better
> understanding.
>
> (Misson 1994: 21–2)

Bounds can be imposed by teachers shutting down meanings; but texts
also seek to impose their views on readers by calling us to take up a particular reading position and therefore to be a certain kind of person (or
subject). This may feel more or less easy and 'natural', depending on the
congruence between a text's ideology and its readers' – for they are also
subject to the constraints of their culture. Thus when readers have to fill
gaps in a text they tend to have recourse to what is culturally typical,
because discourses and genres shape our ways of thinking and responding
in that they encode social purposes and make a text 'readable' by working
with cultural assumptions shared between the text and the reader.

> It is easy to talk airily about resistant reading as if it were a simple and
> single thing, whereas most of our reading is a mixture of resistance and
> compliance. . . . The set of ideological positions we inhabit when read
> ing a text is the result of complex negotiations between already existent
> subject positions and those that the text is trying to impose.
>
> (Misson 1994: 29)

In those endless negotiations among the freedoms and constraints of texts
and readers lies the critical work of critical literacy and also the possibilities
it seeks to realise for reading and writing otherwise.

Between teachers and students

That work takes place partly within the productive constraints of schools
and classrooms. I do not intend to tackle that topic fully here, but to return
to the testimony of my teacher-informants and take up two themes

touched on already in this chapter and others: the teachers' desire for authority based on certainty of knowledge, and students' resistance to this authority.

We have already heard Spiro's call for an explicit ethical framework for his critical literacy practice. Of all the teachers he has most consistently expressed his need for a handbook with rationale, terms and definitions, to guide him in his planning and teaching and to give students a consistent set of key terms and concepts. In that way he and they will have common ground, the students will be more likely to retain the concepts and therefore be able to use them in analysis. As noted before, such a compendium can have appropriate uses but also risks, if it defines the agenda for teaching and the reading processes and products that can be generated with its aid. It could thus legitimise the teacher's authority and help maintain the traditional power structures in the classroom, where the teacher holds the text and the certified (here, the theorised) reading over the less adequate student readers and their 'spontaneous' (inexplicitly or incorrectly theorised) readings. Nonetheless, it could also foster an explicit understanding among teachers and students, where the teacher's purpose is to share the (text-based) authority. (But its dogma needs also to be questioned.)

In traditional English classrooms the teacher's authority has been defined and justified by the authority of the text and the teacher-authorised readings which are shown to emanate from it (Baker and Freebody 1989). When privileged texts have lost their unquestioned authority, and when no reading can be conceived of as single and correct – then a new basis for the teacher's authority may need to be found, if this is felt necessary. The Park Ridge teachers have invested in a teaching practice of critique based on an officially sanctioned social justice. One consequence might be that the teacher's authority within this practice may become identified with a particular form of moral regulation.

Teachers in general expect to be certain, and confident. It is after all our traditional role and identity to be knowledgeable. To lack such authority in the adequacy of our knowledge can therefore be daunting. We might not be able then to represent ourselves to self and others as consistent in theory and practice. In various ways, especially in the early days of the implementation of their curriculum, the Park Ridge teachers have expressed such unease. As Vicki put it,

> Every time I take one step forward [in understanding the theories] I'm taking three steps backward. The more I think the less I know. And that's the frustrating part for me. And I just want to say 'I don't want to learn any more so I don't feel so inadequate.'

It must be noted however that Vicki, like the others in various degrees and by various means, have stayed with the struggle, and now report that they feel much more confident in their theoretical understanding and have been able to develop a repertoire of teaching approaches. These strategies are not so much tricks of the trade; rather, the teachers believe they are now teaching 'from the inside out' – from concepts to practice. However, they recognise that the converse can also apply. The practice, scaffolded initially by Lindsay's shared materials and suggestions or by workbooks such as those published by Chalkface Press, has been a principal means by which they have come to develop insight into the concepts of textual representation and the like.

Their students have also had to deal with the strangeness of such critical literacy concepts, according to the teachers' accounts. This has taken a variety of forms. As we have heard from Lindsay's testimony, some students have learned to read otherwise than they had done previously. Some have maintained their previous beliefs and interpretations and take the stance that 'I disagree but I won't say anything', according to Vicki. Others have more actively resisted a critical literacy agenda: 'Why should we worry how women are represented – whether it's a traditional or resistant reading?' they say, and 'What's this going to do for me when I leave school?' Still others, as Ivy reported, have been busy reading the teacher for the acceptable line to take. There is nothing surprising about this range of student responses, but they do pose a set of dilemmas for the teachers.

One of these has to do with the students' expectations that their teachers as authorities will provide certainty of interpretation. Vicki reported a conversation she had had with a student who asked, '"What is the correct way [of reading], then?" And I said, "There isn't one." And I found that then he sort of sat there and looked at me and said, "Well? So?" And I just felt I'd taught that lesson really badly and poorly.'

Vicki also felt a tension between her passionate desire to influence students for the better and her concern that they might merely mimic without taking on those understandings 'for themselves', as she put it.

> The students are . . . looking at you and following – [imitates a student's voice] 'Now hang on, I want to take that home, I know what she's like, I know what she's after. She wants it written that way.' And I thought, I don't want to be like that, I don't want it to come across as that.

Ivy concurred:

> The kids in Year 11 hang on your every word. They believe in you so totally because you're the teacher. They've got to listen to what you've said, because when they put it down in their assignment that's the way they've got a handle on what you want. That makes me very uncomfortable because I'm happy to accept whatever they say but they won't accept that.

Part of Ivy's discomfort lay in her not wanting to intervene overtly and superimpose her subjectivity on theirs. However, some students who have been reading her reading lessons and others' have evidently felt that while all interpretations are equal, some are more equal than others, which is why they have been so keen to find out the 'real' answer.

This tension between discourses of pedagogy as authoritative or facilitative, transmissive or negotiated, perhaps comes down to two models of teaching. Teachers who work within any of the discourses of English discussed in the rest of this chapter may demonstrate either or both in different situations. One of those is a model of authority. The Park Ridge teachers manifest this as they take on the role and identity of the enlightened, critical teacher who is an authoritative reader of texts and culture. The other is a model of freedom. As we have heard, the teachers speak from within this discourse when they express the scruples of a liberal humanist progressivist teacher concerning the student's freedom to choose whether or not to accept the authority of the teacher's textual exegesis. Vicki summed up this dilemma of pedagogies: 'I tend to stand on my soap box. . . . Even when I'm trying not to impose I'm sure I'm coming down like a sledgehammer on them.' Nonetheless, her own self-criticism indicates that Vicki is trying to find ways to exercise power that are neither oppressive nor covertly regulative. Of course, the daily, momentary interactions of the classrooms of these teachers will inevitably be more complex than her metaphor suggests, more full of partial resistances, complicities, compliances and negotiations on the part of teacher and students. But the telling of that story must wait until the next chapter.

THREADS OF CONVERSATION

Out of the threads they share with others in their state and elsewhere (syllabi, discourses of English, the commonsense of schools and the like) the teachers at Park Ridge are weaving a tapestry which resembles no other. It is after all a new school with a still developing curriculum, with the freedoms and the press of work this brings. We cannot therefore simply take their talk and teaching as a microcosm, a pattern that may be replicated on other looms. – Not least because they are, like Penelope, unpicking those threads, reexamining them, and reweaving them into yet evolving figures in the fabric. But even if the product is unique in its configurations, the processes – those conversations among discourses – may be shared with English teachers elsewhere.

To my understanding these are sometimes overlapping, sometimes competing. At times I have discussed these voices as conveying 'dilemmas' or 'tensions', but I do not wish to suggest thereby that any teacher can or should take up a pure consistent position within one discourse of English teaching. Nor should we think of those tensions in terms of simple oppositions or alternatives, such as between freedom and control, one of which needs to be chosen to the exclusion of the other. They are 'problematics', matters always in question and without an ultimate answer. As I think we have seen, Vicki and Ivy, Spiro and Lindsay (each, and as a group) have not taken up a fixed position within a single discourse but have negotiated within and among discourses: sometimes rejecting, at others making accommodations and modifications. Their various moves may lead to the partial transformation of older Englishes by the newer; they may also bring about the partial absorption of the emergent discourse of critical literacy by those residual but still persistent 'others'. It might be that the radical potential of critical literacy could thus be partly contained. But it is an exercise in 'the art of the possible', among teachers who are inventing themselves as they evolve a version of critical literacy for their ecological niche.

That version is certainly still evolving. One discourse has not yet become so dominant as to be naturalised; there are very few signs that a 'commonsense' version of critical literacy is coming to prevail at Park Ridge. And while the teachers have expressed unease at their uncertainty, this is certainly productive when they continue to engage in the development of theory and practice. They and others in their department who are similarly conversing are not transmitting a knowledge (a theory and pedagogy) transmitted to them, but by reflecting critically on their practice are producing knowledge, as they co-construct and reconstruct a discourse of critical literacy – while at the same time also being constituted by it.

Of course, while any discourse of English remains capable of transformation, if it gains institutional status it can to all appearances become sedimented into the rock of certainty. It would be regrettable if critical literacy in its Australian forms came to be seen as an orthodoxy for which all the answers have already been provided, instead of as a continually questionable, retheorisable practice. As these teachers at Park Ridge have shown, that work of unsettling falls also to classroom practitioners and not just to curriculum researchers, academics and advocates of critical literacy. It is especially important at times of change in a discipline for such researchers and advocates to try to understand teachers' negotiations among discourses in the light of their daily practice in school. It is the teachers after all who are attempting to translate their commitment to social justice into the specifics of classroom teaching, for this particular group of students, in this unit of work, on this day. For such transformative work they have not been given many models, yet in teaching (practice as a present participle) are the 'speech acts' of the conversing discourses of English.

In the next chapter we listen to the conversations among a critical literacy teacher and his students and watch him inventing a different practice within and alongside the customary business of classroom interactions.

Chapter 5

Classroom talk

Business as usual

Teacher: Okay, before we go to – well, obviously the microphone is on, because Dr Morgan wants us to record this again today.

Student A: Is she a doctor?

Teacher: Yes.

Student B: Is she psychoanalysing us?

Teacher: No – she's not that sort of doctor. A Doctor of Philosophy.

Student C: How will this help?

Teacher: Well, she's interested in the way – with the sort of work we're doing, she's interested in the way that classroom talk occurs, and particularly in the sort of way that I talk.

Student D: I know, she thinks we're special. [Students laugh]

Teacher: No, it's not a case of being special; it's a case of – in Wendy's work, it's a case of being *interested*. I don't know whether that's – I often don't know if that's good or bad, trust me.

OPEN FOR BUSINESS

Field Notes: 10.10.95 Year 12 English
Bell has rung for lesson commencement, but students are still at Student Representative Council, listening to speeches by candidates for next year's School Captain. Students begin to drift in. Some boys wear ties and brushed hair, though one or two have hair hanging loose below shoulders; several are wearing baseball caps, which they don't remove. One girl has a short shag of purple hair. An eclectic ensemble of school uniform items, approximating more or less to the standard. Socialising listlessly (very hot afternoon: fans on high) they dump school bags on floor or tables grouped in islands around empty central space. Teacher's desk to front, right of whiteboard and OHP. Posters of popular films,

charts relating to lessons and crit lit concepts on pinup boards around room. Windows give on to grassed oval ringed with gums and scornful crows. Teacher takes up stance centre front, in empty space, begins talking in carrying tones.

It is both instantly recognisable and very strange, that peculiar subculture of the secondary classroom. (I have used this term throughout the book as a metonym for the verbal and physical interactions, rituals, and the like which go on within its four walls – though of course these are also conditioned by what goes on without them.) This chapter focuses on one aspect of that classroom – the almost ceaseless stream of talk through which relationships are negotiated, identities displayed, knowledge transmitted or generated, amid a host of other official or unofficial functions. It is unfortunate that on the page those words become disembodied, for the speakers' habitual disciplines of dress, their schooled postures on and around the standard issue tables and chairs, their learned position and movement within the space of the room, as well as their articulation (murmur to a neighbour, laughter in a group, sharp loud command ringing round the walls) – all of these condition the communication. Readers will need to supplement with their knowledge and imagination the thinness of the transcripts reproduced here, already at several removes from the utterances as produced by bodies in time and place.

Consider the following exchanges. They would be very familiar in kind to anyone who has taken part in an English classroom; this is 'business as usual'. It would not be hard for example to identify the teacher by the nature of the questions and comments and to assign the students their roles in the interaction:

1: But can you think what would happen if – just say you could – you picked up, say, a little group of them and brought them to the twentieth century, and took them to a court case?

2: So what are you saying?

3: They'd all be in jail.

4: They'd all be in jail for life.

5: It would be now, for what they've done; then, they weren't even getting talked badly of because of it; now, if there was capital punishment, you'd probably be killed.

6: Romeo wasn't – he wasn't sentenced to die when he killed whatshisface –

7: No. He was close –

8: Yeah, but that's why – he would of if he hadn't killed the other fellow.

9: Yeah. If Tybalt hadn't of killed Mercutio, then he would have. But it was only because he was getting revenge for the dead one that it was accepted, and even then –

[Much student talk: 5 secs.]

10: Okay. Now, look, what we've got so far is one sort of hypothesis we're starting to form about the way women are being treated here. Now, what I'd probably stress to you is what we need to do now is to go and have a look at the rest of these bits from Act I and see whether in fact there's a pattern of women being treated as sexual beings, or whether in fact women get treated in a variety of ways.

Many readers would identify the teacher as asking the initial question, designed to get students speculating about how Shakespeare's play would 'translate' in their own society; student speaker (turn 2) seeks clarification while another student (3) replies. The teacher partly endorses this reply by repetition and partly corrects it by extension (4). In 5 a student continues the speculations; in 6 another responds to that by drawing on 'evidence' from the text, and the teacher in 7 embarks on an explanation of the reasons for Romeo's lenient sentence. At this point two more students (8 and 9) – enthused about the developing line of argument? – follow up the explanation. In 10, however, the teacher evidently feels the need to get the conversation back on track and breaks across with a general 'hypothesis' (presumably not so much a hunch as an end point – an idea which students are to 'discover for themselves') and an instruction about how to follow up this lead.

This makes the kind of sense we expect, because the pattern is so endemic. But in the actual exchanges that took place in a Year 10 classroom at Park Ridge State High School in outer Brisbane, the teacher, Lindsay Williams, spoke only exchanges 2 (the question for clarification) and 10; the rest were shared among four students, with much peripheral participation by others. It is a useful reminder that however predictable, even dominant, the usual pattern of classroom talk is, the roles can be modified. Perhaps it is also a reminder of how well students have learned to 'do' classroom talk, so that they too can conduct 'business as usual' and speculate or ask questions and make evaluative responses in a manner that resembles their teacher's. (Admittedly this was a rare exception to the usual pattern.) But it is also salutary to note the teacher's return to a role we, and he, take to be his by right. Indeed, no student in a 'normal' classroom, where the relations of power are too unequal, could have uttered that final point. For even most progressive or 'crit lit' teachers assume that as the accomplished knower their responsibility is quite properly to design and implement discussion and activities to enlighten the learners in their charge. As a rational process a curriculum can be determined in advance; but as all teachers know (ruefully, perhaps), not only can these intentions change in the moment by moment

decisions of a lesson, but also the processes of interaction can produce effects
different from those planned. This chapter examines both the intentions of a
critical literacy teacher in two secondary English curriculum units and how
they become articulated in classroom talk.

Catechism or communication?

Traditional teachers have long practised the rituals of catechism, to enable
students to display their knowledge by giving correct answers to questions,
and teachers of all persuasions still at times use the technology of interrogation and response for various ends. But since at least the pioneering work
of Barnes and his colleagues (Barnes *et al.* 1969, Barnes 1976), progressive
teachers who adhere to a constructivist view of learning have encouraged a
different kind of student talk for different purposes: shared exploratory talk
to develop thinking and understanding. Classroom talk of both kinds has
therefore also become a rich field for discourse and conversational analysts
(e.g. Sinclair and Coulthard 1975, Baker and Freebody 1989, Baker 1991),
interactional sociolinguists (e.g. J. Green and Harker 1988) and more generally for researchers and theorists of education (see Edwards and Westgate
(1994) for an overview). Some of those voices will be heard (metaphorically)
in this chapter, but the voices we will be most interested in listening to are
those of one teacher and his students in Years 10 and 12.

We shall find, as we have already in previous chapters, that the patterns
are less tidy than the critical literacy advocates sometimes suggest, across
a range of more complex and sometimes contradictory interactions. We
shall not find an unproblematised 'community' of learners beloved of progressivist teachers. (The critical pedagogue Zavarzadeh (1992) calls this a
'hegemonic pedagogy' and describes it as a Stanislavskian theatre of entertainment in which students are seduced to accept the 'reality' they are
offered.) Nor shall we find a pure radical pedagogy, if by that is meant an
unrelenting practice of confrontation (the 'Brechtian' theatre advocated by
Zavarzadeh). Indeed, as we have seen, in accounts of critical pedagogy
there are often tensions between an authoritative teacher's conscientisation
and the processes of progressive teaching or 'open dialogue' through
which the project is to be realised.

Yet in many accounts of critical literacy the view of language in classrooms is relatively unproblematised: explicitly or implicitly a dyadic
'apprenticeship' model of teaching is endorsed, in which teachers 'are to be
understood as actively intervening in and guiding their students' learning'
(Christie *et al.* 1991, I: 21). Such interventions may easily slide into an authoritarian style of transmissive teaching. And even where a more liberal,
constructivist view of learning prevails, that theory may itself be problematic
if it sets up learning as simply building bridges between the known and the
new and conceives of it as individual, internal cognitive processes or social

interactions narrowly conceived. Such models of learning and teaching – transmissive or progressive, constructivist or apprenticing – tend to de-emphasise the positions of students as subject to discourses and knowledge and the power these produce in as well as beyond the classroom.

Hence the focus of this chapter. By the analysis, or rather interpretation, of a sample of these discourses I hope we shall understand more of the process of learning how to negotiate communicatively, for this is one way in which learners become inducted into their culture. In this case it is the subculture of a schooled critical literacy and those techniques of 'reading' texts and social practices which are specific to its classrooms. After all, one of the most familiar guiding principles of critical literacy teaching is that language practices are social practices: that ideologies and social institutions condition the kind of language which may be used in certain contexts; and conversely that the ideational and interpersonal aspects of language as used in those various contexts have social effects – that they even shape the subjectivity of those who talk together. Yet while critical pedagogy theorists scrutinise the forms of language which represent ideologies and re/produce a culture, they have rarely turned their attention to the nature of the talk that goes on in classrooms – unless it be in the more general terms we have seen concerning the politics of teacher–student interaction and the desirability of open, equal 'dialogue'. But as we saw in chapter one, their postcritical critics have insisted that the reality is rather different: there are multiple forms of surveillance, regulation and oppression in the most enlightened teacher's practice, and myriad kinds of compliance, resistance, mimicry and the like in students' schooled interactions. All the more need, then, for a close study of those language practices if we are to move beyond assertion and counterassertion about the micropolitics of the classroom.

Technologies of analysis: producing talk as text

However, while there is a set of research technologies available for discourse analysis, such close-grained investigations into decontextualised face-to-face interactions and the mechanics of conversation have been found wanting: they have failed to critique the wider sociopolitical and ideological contexts which condition classroom literacy events and their interpretation. Certainly in recent years there has been a broadening in conversational linguists' understanding of the social constitution of language (see Edwards and Westgate (1994) for an overview). But other, more politically critical sociolinguists such as Kress (1985), Gee (1990) and Fairclough (1992a, 1992b) have gone further. They have attempted to analyse the connections between the 'micro' (the utterance or text), the 'meso' (the social context of discursive and social practices) and the 'macro' levels of cultural and ideological structures. However, because these sociolinguists have not sustained a close scrutiny of classroom discourse, they do not suggest what such a multilevel analysis would look like. I hope to maintain some awareness of some of those wider contextual features (not all of them knowable by participants, observers or analysts) both in my analyses and commentaries in this chapter and in the other chapters and their larger concerns. But my aims here are more modest than this kind of multilevel analysis. Through my more microscopic focus on language use I will gesture only towards these practices and institutions which constitute it and which it instantiates.

For if a classroom, like a school, is not merely a given context already 'there', but is instead created, maintained or modified through the flow of talk and action; and if speakers and listeners are also reciprocally constructed through that discourse, then we must see the work of critical literacy classrooms in a different light and give it a different value. That is, the point of such work is not merely directed to what occurs elsewhere in space and time, whether in the textual representations of a culture or in students' eventual critical consciousness and sociopolitical action in the wider world. It exists centrally in and for the practices being jointly negotiated and enacted within those four walls on a particular period and day. Such pedagogy is, in Lusted's (1986) often-quoted definition, 'the transformation of consciousness that takes place in the intersection of three agencies – the teacher, the learner and the knowledge they together produce'. Hence my focus here on the transforming processes by which teacher and learner (whose roles may be exchanged among the participants) produce that knowledge – knowledge which also produces them. It is likely that the largely tacit and consensual understandings about classroom interaction (the immediate social world) strongly condition what understandings can be developed there about the wider social world. It may even be that the messages conveyed by the pattern of interactions subvert or contradict the theoretical and political promises of critical literacy.

Any investigative methodology needs to be congruent with the broader theories that frame it – here, the constitutive role of language and discourse in shaping what can be seen, how it is understood and reported on. If meanings are always socially constructed and constrained, if texts are a partial representation of the 'reality' they constitute, and are uncertain, capable of multiple readings, then a positivist and scientivist model of research simply will not do. For example, the researcher's discourse community and ideology frame not only what can be seen but also what is to be looked for; any researcher comes laden with a toolkit of theories as well as methods for analysing, or rather interpreting, what is indeed already interpreted. And given that there is no one transcendent conceptual framework, no single metalanguage to describe, that is, interpret, the classroom language, those theories and methods are necessarily partial – interested as well as incomplete.

Then, when the 'data' are collected, uncertainties proliferate. As the exchanges at the opening of this chapter make very clear, the researcher's presence affects the field of observation. And particular data are selected for focus to the exclusion of others. For example, I have chosen to record some lessons as more likely to be of interest and to 'yield' useful 'evidence'; I have not for example included one-to-one teacher-to-student conferences over a draft of writing. Words audiotaped are already a thin and partial record that excludes whatever – and whoever – is not verbally explicit. What can I make of the knowledge and power of those silent students? Let alone the banter, interactive comments and other 'maintenance work' among the students in the overlapping flow of conversation, which a recorder or transcriber cannot do justice to? Or the good-humoured intonation of most of the talk? Such words as are 'captured' are further transformed by the transcriber and researcher making decisions about sentence structure and format in order to tidy the flow of utterance into legible prose. It is an artificial stabilisation of a process (always in the process of being mutually constructed, negotiated and interpreted by the participants) into a seemingly fixed product.

And what is to be made of those words on the page? – if we do not believe a single, certain meaning can be 'there' in the transcripts waiting to be 'revealed' by the 'expert' analyst's scalpels. A fundamental problem is that meaning is not simply in a text but constructed between text and reader; any text is therefore available for the production of a range of meanings. For instance, no verbal form can be assigned a unique function, since there are 'many diverse systems of meaning available to members of a speech community' (Barnes and Todd 1977: 15). The same caution applies even more to outsider-observers with their intention to hear what makes sense according to their predetermined emphases, their different discourses, ideologies and theory-laden analytical methods.

Such will to knowledge is also the will to 'truth' and power. These intentions govern also the (selective) representation of 'findings' in written reports, whose genre cannot permit so great a degree of uncertainty and complexity that it would threaten the very rationality and conclusiveness on which it is founded. I am mindful of this regime and of my desire to 'produce the goods'. However, not only my scruples but also Lindsay's corrective comments on a first draft of this chapter prick me from too complacent a certainty. But we can only tell a story as best we may, and a story is made out of what it omits. At least this is not presented as a metanarrative with general application. The most it can do is point to what may or may not be issues in other contexts. Provisionally, then, the account that follows aims at 'a more literary approach towards the complex, irregular relationships between linguistic forms and their illocutionary force' (Edwards and Westgate 1994: 137).

As methodology follows from theories, so in turn do analytical methods.

Two main methods are used to 'read' the register of the classroom interactions according to two complementary aspects. The first of these aspects is the 'how'. In Halliday's (1985) definition of register this 'how' has to do with the tenor of social relationships. My interest is especially in the construction through language of power relations between teacher and students. These relations may range across a spectrum between authority and solidarity, hierarchy and equality, social distance and intimacy. To analyse those relations, I focus on topics (the organising and control of knowledge) and interactions (the 'turns' made by interlocutors and responses to those). My interest is in understanding what a critical literacy 'reading' of texts and culture is made to be procedurally, in the course of the lesson, how this organises the institutional relations of authority among teacher, texts and students, and how this constitutes the interactants as subjects or agents. It is sometimes suggested, for example, that the still characteristic pattern of teacher questioning generally known as the IRE sequence (in which the teacher initiates a turn by asking a question, a response is proffered by a student and the teacher evaluates the adequacy of the answer) carries and displays assumptions about knowledge, power and learning (Young 1984).

The second aspect is the 'what'. This concerns the field or subject matter of register. What is knowledge taken to be, what knowledge is valued by teacher or students, and what is knowledge shown to be procedurally? A rationalist, structuralist view of knowledge still prevails in most secondary schooling, where it is represented as revealed, not created by sociohistorical discourses; as universal and transcendent of context, not contingent on situation and therefore multiple; as certain, not problematic and contested; and autonomous rather than constituted by and constituting knowers. The status of the classroom knowledge and whether it is deemed to be constructed by language or not is examined by means of the language interactions of teacher and student, for this has bearing also on their relations of power and authority.

Two methods are used in exploring these aspects. One, for examining turns and topics, is a more structural analysis of transcripts, in both broad survey and closer analysis of passages selected for their representativeness or their peculiarity. For the most part the analysis is not technical or finely detailed, since my interest is not in the teacher's technologies – that repertoire of professional skills which has absorbed the attention of many classroom discourse analysts. Rather, these structural analyses can be useful to suggest how meaning is being established, who controls, directs and develops it and sets the agenda – provided we do not attempt to identify a single function and effect, for there will always be ambiguities and colorations, details and textures of dialogue that evade such definition. The second method (I move between one and the other according to my purposes) is a more discursive, paratextual commentary – which is also inevitably an interpretation – particularly of how the teacher manages the staging and (co-)construction of knowledge.

TWO CURRICULUM UNITS: DESIGN AND STRATEGIES

A lesson in a critical literacy classroom is designed to give students access to a discourse; it is a (sub)culturally organised way of describing and explaining the nature of the social world. The processes of the classroom demonstrate how such knowledge can be produced collaboratively. Critical literacy teachers may argue that, by acculturating students into this way of reading, writing and speaking about the texts of a culture, they are providing a discourse which is alternative to the hegemonic and therefore offers students a position for a different reading and speaking. But to Lindsay Williams, curriculum design is in other respects very much like what traditional teachers do, for it entails making decisions on students' behalf:

> You have to have some idea of where you're going. . . . I don't think you can negotiate everything with kids. There have to be some givens – curriculum givens. . . . I've decided for a whole range of reasons that studying work and issues in the workplace is important for them. And I suppose I've made that decision for them. . . . I don't think they would have come to that decision themselves. From there, I think it's a case of showing them why it's important, and then through the selection of texts letting them see connections and the consequences of particular ideologies.

This is very different from the Freirean approach discussed in chapters one and two, but such advance planning is one of the accommodations that teachers in public schools make to the 'system' and its insistence on instrumental rationality. Indeed, Lindsay is happy to draw on many of the student-centred techniques and activities of a progressive pedagogy, since students who would not have the patience for sustained critical analysis find them enjoyable, and those strategies can be put to his own purposes when he goes a couple of steps further.

In a 'regular' classroom the teacher has authorised rights and obligations to 'take the decisions necessary to achieving orderly interaction' (Edwards and Westgate 1994: 45) and the discourse is therefore relatively formal. In Lindsay's room this does not mean that the talk is for the most part contained within a central communication system emanating from the teacher. Lindsay's lessons are structured around group-based activities. Any lesson is likely to have a number of phases, whose sequence depends on the stage of the larger activity and the planned end point, and transition from one phase to the next is marked by a new disposition of bodies in the room. These phases include whole class inputs and instructions by the teacher, often standing at the board, to students seated on chairs in a semicircle before him; whole class forum for (teacher guided) feedback from groups and discussion of emergent issues, when Lindsay sits with the students in a circle; group work, in which six students work together on a task seated around tables pushed together and the teacher circulates, listening and interjecting occasional comments; group performance or reporting, in which selected students from each group, arranged at the front of the room as a panel, share each group's different work orally with class members, with Lindsay intervening occasionally to elicit a point; and individual work of silent reading or writing at the tables. In the lessons I observed group work and whole class forum predominated.

The language of the 'classics': a critical literacy approach to academic literacy

This is an extension unit for Year 10 students who want 'a bit of a challenge'. It is designed to introduce them to the principles of critical literacy 'through devious means,' as Lindsay puts it, 'that is through study of some classic English literature: *Romeo and Juliet*, Romantic poetry and Dickens' *A Christmas Carol*'. Lindsay is aware that many in the wider community value these texts and complain that school students do not study them.

> The brighter kids also have the view that Shakespeare is far more worth while than a lot of the other stuff [more popular texts], so I wanted to introduce them to that literature but at the same time get them to question the whole notion of classic literature and the canon. I certainly don't want them to go away thinking, 'This Shakespeare stuff is a lot of rubbish.' What I want them to do is say, 'Yeah, I enjoyed the Shakespeare but at the same time I have to realise that there are things about it that I need to be aware of.'

That awareness is to take the form of the students' first systematic introduction to critical literacy. To this end Lindsay was working from four principles, as spelled out in chapter two: that texts and their meanings are produced within the cultural contexts that condition them; that texts therefore offer a partial (incomplete and interested) version of 'reality'; that they are nonetheless capable of multiple readings, since readers draw on diverse ideologies in their own contexts; and that the work of texts (their production and use) is political. Lindsay aimed to explore these principles by means of a range of group-based activities, including some intensive study of the text and grammatical analysis.

The language of work: a 'get your hands dirty' sort of critical literacy

In the last term of their school days, many of the Year 12 students who are not headed for tertiary study have chosen this unit, which is designed to effect a transition to the workplace. 'It has a really practical part,' says Lindsay, 'which is reviewing how you apply for jobs, and job interview techniques, and filling out job application forms. The other part is a look at some of the issues of work in the 1990s: Key Competencies, total quality management and enterprise bargaining.' (In this second aspect Lindsay was drawing deliberately on work by Gee and Lankshear 1995.) By contrast to the direct and explicit approach to critical literacy Lindsay takes with his Year 10 students in the same term, with these more practical and less academically motivated students he feels it is necessary to 'take a back door approach'. He will attempt to meet their needs for practical, 'relevant' content, but attempt also to convince the students that they need a critical understanding of workplace issues.

> They think it [the unit] is functional; that's how I'm selling it. What I'm trying to convince them, through what we're doing, is that the principles of critical literacy are as important, if not more so, to them going out into very practical fields as they are for someone going into university. Look, if you're going on to university, you can sort of observe things at a distance. For them it's going to be very much 'hands on, get your hands dirty' sort of critical literacy.

Unit activities will not take the form of hard analysis but be short, often changing, and fun – 'slowly building up the concepts and understandings through a range of team-oriented activities.' Given the short time available for the unit, it is not possible to take the students out into workplaces (they have undertaken Work Experience in Years 10 and 11), but Lindsay does not feel a classroom-based study is at too great a remove from the workplace: for one thing, school is his worksite, and for another, many of the students already have jobs. Nonetheless, he concedes that in this or any other unit 'we're always removed from those situations in a fairly artificial environment'. His focus here on students' ability to work in teams (one of the Key Competencies) is designed to compensate for that remoteness. So too their learning to evaluate the (limited?) workability of teamwork, the underlying concepts and the managerial, economic claims that are made for it is designed to move them towards a critical understanding of what they are experiencing already.

Both these units, then, are doing very important work in taking critical literacy into two different sites: the 'heartland' of the apparently timeless canon and the 'headland' of the fast shifting world of work. Such work is exemplary: this is surely as good as it gets in Australian classrooms; it is also only as good as the norms of classroom work allow. Both the possibilities and the constraints need to be acknowledged together, if our understanding of critical literacy is to become more subtle and answerable.

CLASSROOM PROCEDURES: THE STAGING OF LEARNING

Students to centre stage

By their senior secondary years most students – unless they prefer the out-of-school discourses of resistant subversion – are very accomplished participants in the genres of classroom talk; they know how to get the register just right. In well-regulated classrooms it has all become second nature, so smooth a practice as to be almost invisible to teacher and students. However, this backgrounded understanding relates dynamically with the foregrounded knowledge that is being constructed in the particulars of topics and demonstration, argumentation and the like. To begin, then, it is necessary to make a little strange that commonsense business, to see how the authority, power and knowledge of teacher and students are achieved – for they are not simply brought into the classroom. The 'classic' patterns of traditional classroom talk are based on the teacher's (naturalised) superior status, knowledge and communicative 'right-of-way', as well as on the physical organisation of classroom space (McHoul 1978, Mehan 1979). But an overview of Lindsay's staging of classroom literacy events indicates that a different pattern prevails for a large proportion of the time. So it is with student-centred talk in groups that the analysis begins.

One example is a Year 10 lesson exploring gender roles in *Romeo and Juliet*, after the students have read the play in class and watched the film by Zeffirelli. Lindsay has initiated work on the ways women are described by themselves and others: as acting, acted upon, simply existing in some state, or as ordered to do something. (He is drawing on various aspects of what is called transitivity in a functional systemic – Hallidayan – grammar.) He has handed out excerpts – all the passages from Act I in which women appear or are talked about – and each group is assigned a different one to analyse for these functions. (In the next stage new groups will be convened, drawn from all the original groups. They will share their findings and discuss the implications before coming together in a whole class forum.) One group is working on Romeo's speech when he first glimpses Juliet (I.v.44 ff.) which begins, 'What lady's that which doth enrich the hand / Of yonder knight?' and contains the famous ode, 'O, she doth teach the torches to burn bright!' One student (A) is responsible for filling in their entries on a chart. Lindsay is circulating around the groups, available for enquiries. Here we see 'classic' textual analysis put to new ends; we also see how typical the patterns of interaction are. (We cannot see, or rather hear, from the transcript below, the overlaps among the students' exchanges and the sharing of comments among the group which support, question, suggest and confirm.)

 1 **Student A:** Sir, does 'enrich the hand' come under anything, or is that just a load of babble?

2 **Teacher:** Well, the lady is *enriching* the hand of yonder knight.

3 **Student A:** Yeah, so you reckon it's an action – enriches?

4 **Teacher:** Yes. It's a funny sort of action, though, isn't it?

5 **Student A:** Yes, because it's not something you can actually physically do.

6 **Teacher:** No, and although it's an action, you might want to qualify it. I mean, who's getting the goodness from this person?

7 **Student A:** The boy she's dancing with.

8 **Teacher:** Yes. I mean, that leaves open the question of what – you know, usually when something is enriched, when you enrich something, it usually deplenishes the thing that, you know, is doing the enriching.

9 **Student A:** So what – just write 'enriches'?

10 **Teacher:** Yes.

11 **Student A:** She teaches. She's a teacher. . . .

[unclear discussion with other students]

I know, but it's the verb that she's doing to – it's like enriches; it's not something – he's using it as a description, but it's not what she's doing. [With mild irony:] This is thrilling, isn't it? ['It seems she hangs upon the cheek of night.'] Oh come on, we can't have her hanging, as well. No, skip that one. 'As a rich jewel in an Ethiop's ear'. Okay, so is that what she's described as?

12 **Student B:** Yeah.

13 **Student A:** Okay, so she's a rich jewel. So she's beautiful ['Beauty too rich for use, for earth too dear'], she exists as beautiful. There's nothing [i.e. no Process] in that, is there? 'As yonder lady o'er her fellows shows' – I don't get it. What's that one mean, sir: 'As yonder lady o'er her fellows shows'?

14 **Teacher:** That lady is showing her fellows –

15 **Student A:** She's showing the others up.

16 **Student B:** [quoting gloss] 'In such a way does the lady over there, yonder, prove herself above her companions.'

17 **Student C:** Okay, so she's showing everyone that she's better than them.

18 **Student A:** She's in the spotlight. Right, okay.

19 **Teacher:** One of the things to think about is whether she's doing this deliberately or whether she's doing it by simply existing.

20 **Student A:** She's existing. Okay, so in existing she's showing – how are we going to put it? 'Shows fellows up.'

21 **Student B:** She's just proved herself over her companions.

The student initially asks questions of the teacher (1 and 3), for clarification of the category of grammatical Process. The teacher in response (4 and 6) begins to question the student to prompt further analysis and then extends the answer (7) with a statement (8) to articulate the point he has in mind. In responses 11 and 13 a student (with support from others) begins to make the connection and to glimpse the implications of the Processes: 'it's like enriches; . . . he's using it as a description, but it's not what she's doing.'

These exchanges are interesting examples of student 'meta-textual commentary'. This is more tentative in character than a teacher's preformulated exposition tends to be. The students' talk in 15–18 is also characteristic of such group work: each statement builds on the previous speaker's as they jointly construct their knowledge and confirm their understanding. As often happens, their questions are also to that end: to gain information, hypothesise or dis/confirm a hunch. (The typical teaching trio of IRE exchanges is completely missing from all the students' group talk I observed.) So when Lindsay prompts by offering the students something to think about (19) – again, to move them to consider the significance of a woman described as simply existing – the student replies confidently (20) and needs no evaluation of his reply from the teacher but instead gets it from group members.

In another instance, a group of Year 12 students are discussing part of a magazine article entitled 'Winning Ideas from Maverick Managers' (*Fortune* 10 July 1995). Lindsay has distributed a question sheet to guide each group's analysis of a different manager's ideology and prompt them to consider the possible consequences of that manager's approach. (Later they would be asked to take on the role of either a shareholder of one manager's company or a trade union official concerned about workers' welfare, and in that role identify and explain their responses to the article.) This group of students is examining the practices of a manager who encouraged all his employees to study the financial records of the company. (One boy is observing and recording the teamwork processes of the group for later discussion.) Lindsay is not present at this stage.

1 **Student A:** [Reading] 'Work out what the manager's ideology appears to be, by answering the questions below. What does the manager appear to value?'

2 **Student B:** Just like trust, I suppose; knowledge. . . .

3 **Student C:** Showing everyone everything.

4 **Student D:** Everyone's honesty, I suppose.

5 **Student A:** Honesty, yeah; everyone to be involved in the company's fate. I'd say it would have to be just to make them – to make sure all the employees understand and know everything about the company. That's what they're trying to do, isn't it, really?

6 **Student D:** What were they trying to do?

7 **Student A:** Yeah, they're just trying to manage it to get the value back –

8 **Student B:** – understanding –

9 **Student A:** . . . that all employees know everything about the company that there is to know, basically.

10 **Student B:** I mean, from the books you can tell just about everything about the company.

11 **Student C:** Perhaps if this big company shuts down the machines for a half hour, right? – for an hour, actually, [Reading] 'while its 800 employees break into small groups to study the latest financial statement'. . . . That's pretty zonked. I mean, you get an hour off work just to sit around and go, 'Oh yeah, we made 10 million dollars this week, fellas – you know, that means we got a fucking big pay rise.' I think it works, doesn't it? Keeps us working harder.

Lindsay's questions, listed on the worksheet, require a close reading to infer the manager's beliefs, values and practices and they lead to exploratory talk. Consider turns 2 and 4: the speakers are tentative, with their repeated 'I suppose', and despite the next speaker's move towards identification of a value (5: 'Honesty, yeah'), he is still working towards certainty ('I'd say it would have to be . . . '), and at the end seeks confirmation from team members. The (genuine) question raised in 6 leads to others' explanations; this information leads one student (11) to contemplate the peculiarity of workers downing tools to check the books, and so to imagine and dramatise an exaggerated scenario – in order to draw the inference about the managerial interests served by this apparent munificence.

These instances of speculation are promising, if they indicate a shared cognitive and affective engagement. However, when in the following lesson the groups report back on their manager, the representative of this team (Speaker A) tells it somewhat differently when Lindsay asks him what the manager's values and beliefs appeared to be:

Student A: Obviously financial training, employee understanding of the company, like more understanding it's just – I don't know, it's more trustworthy and everything; they just know what's going on. They're not just being overseen by one big manager telling them what to do. He also believes that best production is through trust, and everyone knowing what's going on. The purpose of work is to create more efficiency and more profit and therefore more bonuses, therefore everyone is happier, and the trees are greener, and the sun is sunnier. [Students laugh]

Such panglossian panache in that conclusion! The rest of his report however (only part of it reproduced here) is far less exploratory, as befits the genre of the report perhaps: this is knowledge already arrived at by the group and now rehearsed in summary fashion, for the benefit of others, by one student holding the floor. The temperature of the talk is therefore more lukewarm. It is also talk that is supervised by the teacher; Lindsay sometimes prompts with questions to maintain focus on aspects he regards as significant, to correct misinformation, or to obtain additional details for the sake of other students who have not read about the particular manager being reported on.

So far, though the ends are different from those of a mainstream classroom, the means (group work) would be familiar to any liberal or progressive teacher. On several other occasions however the pattern of exchanges alters somewhat. In the first of these, Year 10 students are in whole class forum, discussing whether women are represented in Act I as passive sexual beings. 'Are you suggesting that sex wasn't interesting for females then?' asks a student, adding, '. . . as in a passive sexual being.' Lindsay has been pursuing a line of argument about women being represented, in the play's opening comic interchanges between Capulet servingmen, as the objects of men's aggressive and misogynist physical attentions. Another student, taking up the first student's question, continues with a parallel line of thought concerning the Nurse's comment to Juliet about her not getting much sleep when she was wedded to Paris, and a third student adds a corroborative detail. Is the inference of this comment that women too could make bawdy jokes and show a marked interest in such matters – and in this way show response as sexual beings? It may be, because a fourth student takes up the topic introduced by her fellow:

1 **Student D:** Romeo touches Juliet's hand, and that's [inaudible].

2 **Teacher:** All right, touches Juliet's hand. Does Juliet get to do the reverse?

3 **Student D:** Oh, she puts her hand up against his palm – whatever.

4 **Teacher:** Can we just come back to the sexual beings point now. You've got the men joking about, you know, thrusting the women to the wall, you know, cutting off their maidenheads, robbing them of their virginity and that. And you've got the Nurse making sexual jokes too. What about Lady Capulet and Juliet? Do they make basic [vulgar] comments?

5 **Student A:** No. They're real discreet because they're rich –

6 **Student B:** And the Nurse is just a normal person – you know.

7 **Student C:** Do you reckon they're [Lady Capulet and Juliet] upper class? They don't make any of these references, but they know they're going to get it anyway, so they don't have to. [Students laugh] Do you know what I mean – they know that their husbands are going to do sort of do it all the time, so they don't have to –

8 **Student E (male):** They would have been having you girls on!

The student (1) may be suggesting that Juliet is a sexual being in herself and not merely passive in reciprocating an advance in equal measure. Lindsay does not take this up but wants to 'come back' to the topic as he has conceived of it and to lead on to a related topic, about the effects of class on women's freedom of sexual speech. Another student's final argument (7) makes a shrewd point that when you have wealth (of sexual intercourse) you do not need to flaunt it in vulgar fashion. In these exchanges, then, students introduce and pursue topics together, even if not all of these can be attended to by the teacher in the heat of the moment following his own train of thought. (Lindsay conceded later that in the hectic pace of a classroom he is bound to miss some of the half-formed or tentative insights of students.)

Later in the same lesson the class are looking at a passage (I.iv) in which Romeo complains, 'Under love's heavy burden do I sink', and Mercutio makes flippant remarks about a lover's weight on his beloved and advises him to 'be rough with love; / Prick love for pricking, and you beat love down.' The students catch the double entendre and laugh, then one comments:

1 **Student A:** It's quite funny when you actually understand it. If we went through the whole play like this . . .

2 **Teacher:** Well, I mean it is amusing. But what do you make of it?

3 **Student A:** If we all were to listen to this . . . [inaudible general student talk]

4 **Teacher:** That's right. But I mean, here's once again the sexual joking, at whose expense?

5 **Student B:** Hers.

6 **Teacher:** At the woman's expense, once again.

7 **Student B:** But they're not actually being *mean* to her.

8 **Student C:** Yeah, they don't mean to offend *her* or anything.

9 **Student D:** They offend the lower-class girls, when they say it, but they don't offend the upper-class girls.

[much discussion and agreement]

10 Teacher: [Bell has rung] All right. We'll finish there.

Here a student objects to what she takes to be the teacher's interpretation (6); this is echoed by another (7) and extended by a third (8) who makes a distinction between the men's treatment of women according to their class. – And then the higher authority of the timetable supervenes to voice its imperative. But the students have been heard first, expressing their reservations of the authority of the teacher's interpretation.

A more critical note is heard in another, lengthy, interrogation of Lindsay by a Year 12 student. Lindsay has been describing recent negotiations over an enterprise agreement between the Queensland Teachers Union and the Education Department. He confesses to the class that 'I really couldn't tell you, off the top of my head, what our agreement even has in it.' The student asks (or comments: the implication of catching the teacher out is there to be heard):

So, you're being critical before you even know about it?

Lindsay concedes that the teachers have let their union handle the minutiae of bargaining and have expressed their collective will in a mass vote. And he muses, 'What sort of pressure is there on you, when you're with 3,000 people, if you want to say no?' The student refuses to let Lindsay get away with that: 'Oh, none, because the voting – come on, it's your – it's just your opinion.' He then pursues Lindsay with a series of probing questions: 'You just voted?' 'You just voted it in?' 'And you still don't know what it's about?' And another student caps this with a clincher to conclude the interrogation:

Would you say if, now you've voted it in, in your situation you're powerless?

Extraordinary though this is, in that the students have usurped the teacher's role to grill and criticise him and draw an ironic inference about the surrender of power by democratic means, it still depends on Lindsay's initial confession. Nonetheless this looks like the work of critical literacy being taken up most competently by students. But Lindsay's explanation complicates the picture somewhat, for he identified his confession paradoxically as a 'control technique':

I often play the role, particularly with these kids, of – clown isn't the word – but the sort of dumb sidekick, if you like, where they're the ones who get to make the jokes and everything else, and at my expense, and where I can suddenly admit, 'Okay, well, I'm a failure again here; I don't know the answer here.' I suppose you do it for establishing rapport with kids.

He went on to explain his reasons further: to disabuse the students of any idea that he should be regarded as the font of knowledge (since the teacher's authority is deeply ingrained in students), and to demonstrate by example some of the weaknesses in the enterprise bargaining system. So how shall we understand this exchange now? – as the student gaining control of the floor for the time but only by the teacher's tacit permission, since the student is playing into his hands, enabling him to achieve his longer-range strategic goals.

One point to be made, surely, is that this is the same teacher who in the same lesson uses the 'classic' IRE sequence of questioning. That is, within the usual pattern the scope of interactions is more varied, the tactics of teacher and student more responsive to opportunity, and the relations of leader and follower more open to negotiation and co-construction (Dillon 1988), than researchers sometime suggest.

Teacher talk: upstaging students?

We now turn to examine some of those IRE exchanges – which are also varied in structure and intention. The traditional framework for whole class talk, according to researchers, has given teachers alone the right to direct speakership in a creative way (McHoul 1978): they begin and end the exchanges, allocate all those turns they do not claim for themselves and determine their length. Where this is the case, the consequences are far-reaching: the teacher's evaluation of those responses is 'central to validating the curriculum and defining competent membership of the class through demonstrating acceptable forms of participation and expression' (Edwards and Westgate 1994: 142). In this way students are obliged to respond within the teacher's 'epistemological frame of reference' (Young 1984). Thus although to a casual observer it might seem that the questioning teacher is eliciting knowledge from the students themselves and fostering cognitive development in each individual, to critics it looks instead as if students are being inducted into a pre-existent culture of valued knowledge and practices (Edwards and Mercer 1978). (This point is taken up further in the next section.) This may not be entirely bad, of course, and in any case knowledge is inevitably produced and used within a cultural context. The question to be asked here is whether the use of IRE is always to be abhorred as a covert direction to students to display their knowledge so that it may be tested, or whether and if so how it can be used in the production of new knowledge which can be appropriated by learners. Certainly the talk that fosters the latter is generally assumed to occur as 'genuine' dialogue, debate, collaborative problem solving and free-ranging speculation, but it may be that more traditional methods of interrogation may serve the same ends, in intention but also in effect.

Several kinds of teacher-directed questioning are apparent in Lindsay's talk. On only one occasion, across eight lessons recorded, did this take the form of 'guess what's in my head' – probably because the students did not catch on to the drift of argument being pursued through his interrogation. This is one form of the Socratic method: using questions to which the teacher already knows the answer and by a sequence of such questions and evaluations nudging the students towards a predetermined, fixed cognitive destination. This instance occurred in a Year 12 lesson in which Lindsay was introducing an article which they had not yet sighted. To alert them to the reading position that might be set up he drew their attention to the title, 'Enterprise Bargaining from Both Sides'. Here he interrogates them about the meaning of 'both':

1 **Teacher:** When it says both sides, what does that imply about the issue of enterprise bargaining?

2 **Student A:** That's just how it stands for the individual.

3 **Student B:** That they're sort of negotiating in this bargaining.

4 **Teacher:** All right. But this word – what does 'both' mean?

5 **Student C:** It's from their point of view that they're taking what the unions want, and taking what the employers want, and finding a middle point, and so. . . .

6 **Teacher:** Maybe my questions deceive you. What I want to know is, does 'both' mean *two* sides? Does it mean *two only* sides, or does it mean *two or more* sides?'

When students opt for the latter (because of the loose way in which the word is used in casual talk), Lindsay persists until he hears a more acceptable answer ('Two'), which he endorses:

Two. Two only? I mean, they're saying two views. They're making it pretty explicit when you go into the article.

(He has already explained that these are the union view and the employer view.) Having established this, he introduces a new line of questioning: 'Are they necessarily going to be the only two views in enterprise bargaining?' and continues prompting: 'Who belongs to the Australian Chamber of Commerce and Industry? Every industry, every business in Australia? What about the Australian Council of Trade Unions? . . . Is every employee in the union?' Having thus led the students by yes / no answers he arrives at the point he is set on making:

All right, so one of the things you might want to think about when you're having a look at these articles is the fact that, although it says both sides – right – and setting you up to believe that there are only two sides to the enterprise bargaining issue, are there indeed other viewpoints as well, that could have been raised?

This is a valuable point of critical literacy: that voices not institutionally sanctioned may be silenced. In order to make this point, it may be worth using such known-answer questioning. It is part of a teacher's repertoire of strategies which can be drawn on to serve a larger purpose of bringing students to conduct interrogations themselves of texts and their exclusions. Of course, pedagogical intentions are not necessarily matched by effects: it may be that students simply 'hear' such questioning as subordinating them to the teacher's knowledge long after the point of argument being made has been forgotten.

In other instances Lindsay uses strings of known-answer questions to elicit information and so generate inferences he intends shall be drawn from the text. Here the Year 10 class are examining Act I, scene i of *Romeo and Juliet*. It is not hard to see the direction of the questioning.

1 **Teacher:** Do the women perform any actions in this little bit about women here?

2 **Student A:** Yes.

3 **Teacher:** What are the women doing?

4 **Student A:** Rooting the guys.

5 **Teacher:** Is that the way it's described, though?

6 **Student A:** No. That's what they're implying.

7 **Teacher:** But is it the women doing it to the men?

8 **Student A:** No. The men are doing it to the women.

9 **Student B:** They're being used as toys.

10 **Teacher:** All right, so they're being acted upon, are they, are you saying?

11 **Student A:** Yep.

We should not read this probing as sinister in purpose or effect. Admittedly Lindsay is controlling the direction of thought via words, but his intention is to change thinking by introducing students to an alternative, feminist, reading. It is a problem only if we believe, simply, in individuals' rights to 'think for themselves' and 'make up their own minds'.

In whole class talk, as opposed to group work, Lindsay takes on the right and responsibility to guide discussion. His redirection of talk and thought from the line students are taking can at times be obvious: 'Can we just come back to the sexual beings point now?', 'Can I just draw our attention away from that?' On other occasions he can have no clearly predetermined direction, for his questions are genuine: he does not know the answer. Nonetheless, as the following example shows, he may use the opportunity to reach a conclusion that accords with his agenda. Groups of Year 10 students have just reported back to the class on flow charts they have constructed which invent and follow through various alternatives to the story line of the Shakespearian play. Lindsay has just commented in class forum, 'What you're starting to indicate there, is different directions which – if you were writing the story from your cultural perspective – you might take.' Evidently with a connection in mind he then asks why they laughed during the screening of romantic scenes:

1 **Student A:** It was so funny.

2 **Teacher:** Okay, why did you find it funny, though?

3 **Student B:** It was so stupid.

4 **Students:** Yeah.

5 **Teacher:** What was stupid about it? Why did you think it was stupid?

6 **Student C:** They were so serious and so old-fashioned.

7 **Student D:** Yeah. They were so lovey-dovey.

8 **Teacher:** All right, if you were Romeo and Juliet, then, how would you be talking to each other?

9 **Student E:** The difference in our talk –

10 **Student C:** Nobody shows their emotions like that much any more.

11 **Teacher:** So you don't think that sort of open display of emotions is something that –

12 **Student C:** Nowadays, if people, like, show that much emotion, they get all worried that the other person will think, well, hey, they need me that much, I can just treat them how I want; they'll always be there.

A shift occurs in 8, where Lindsay evidently feels a breath of wind that will fill the sails and enable him and his crew to make for his landfall with the freight of their learning. Shortly he describes that landfall to them:

Okay, I think that makes a lot of very nice points about just how different culture is, and the fact that I'm sure when Shakespeare wrote some of those scenes, he would not have intended for you to laugh at them. Right? And it says something – going back to one of the points that we made last week – that although a writer might write something, they can't guarantee how you're going to respond to it as a reader.

Afterwards Lindsay commented,

Although I wanted to talk about language issues and reading and writing issues, they were really talking more about content issues, and I really had to do a bit of probing and refocusing and reminding and summarising to get the lessons about language out of even these kids here.

'Getting lessons out of kids' is a revealing expression, but one that does not really do justice to what we have seen of the subtlety of the teacher's management of talk or the willing cooperation of the students in that guidance. In other cases Lindsay claims he learns from them instead: they teach him to see things in a different light. In one example, Lindsay built in to a lesson with his Year 12 students a critical comment one student had made the day before. When students entered the room this was attached to the board for all to read:

Shaun was fairly derisive when I asked if you were in a powerful or powerless position if you did not understand the articles on enterprise bargaining. He said it was nothing to do with power, that he was simply confused.

Is he right, do you think? Or can confusion place you in a position of powerlessness? How could confusion make you powerful? Does the issue of power really matter?

Lindsay is prepared to engage publicly with a student's scepticism and explore its implications, admitting to the class, 'I was thinking about this after Shaun laughed at this the other day – and it was actually enlightening, Shaun laughing and that, because I hadn't thought it was a funny question at the time.' In class discussion it transpires that Shaun had come to see that confusion could lead to powerlessness but had objected to the words 'power' and 'powerless' to describe his mental state. Lindsay then prompts the students to explore possible results of confusion about enterprise bargaining if they were in a workplace. With students' suggestions he constructs a 'futures wheel' on the board. (This is a set of concentric circles, with the situation for investigation listed in the middle. In each ring students list possible consequences, good and bad, and follow each of these through into the next outer ring.) Among other consequences, they suggest that ignorance might spur one to ask questions and gain information. At this point a student takes the initiative in questioning:

1 **Student A:** Would that be in a position of power? Can you actually say *'power'*?

2 **Teacher:** I don't know. Why are you saying that?

3 **Student B:** Wouldn't it happen that if you're an employee and you ask the union what's going on, everyone's going to ask different questions, you're going to get the same answers to that question, and

another person is going to come along and ask another different question, and then once that's happened, you've got what the basics of the thing is, you're going to go through and talk with your fellow employees, and then you're going to talk about this and say, 'Oh well, I asked this question and they gave me this feedback.' And then you've got two sides, and there you've got two answers for it – two questions answered.

4 **Teacher:** So you're saying that's good or bad?

5 **Student B:** I'm saying that's probably good, because then you're feeding your knowledge in, talking amongst the employees in your work.

6 **Teacher:** So, by teamwork . . . ?

7 **Student B:** Yeah. You get –

8 **Student C:** Yeah, but that course isn't easy street. You're going to have to understand what they're talking about, as well.

9 **Teacher:** Right.

10 **Student C:** So, if you don't get the question that that other person asks, then you also don't get the answer to it, yeah.

Here is an interesting variation to the usual pattern. A student introduces the topic (1) and seeks definition as an implicit move in investigating the question, 'Is inquiry to gain knowledge the same as "power"?' (This does of course derive from the question on the board, 'How could confusion make you powerful?') Another student follows this up (3) by speculating on the effects of getting a range of information when fellow workers pool their questions and answers, a point developed by a third student (8, 10). The teacher is here relegated to a minor role in the conversation. It may be that what facilitates this variation is Lindsay's willingness to take on a question that challenges his viewpoint, to put himself in the role of not-knower who wants to find out and who engages students in speculation about a hypothetical situation. The mode is certainly one of involvement and initiative – at least by some students. This culminates later in the same lesson, in a set of exchanges we have already looked at, when Shaun takes Lindsay to task for his irresponsibility in being ill informed about his own enterprise agreement.

In the context of mainstream schooling a teacher has both the authority and the obligation to organise for orderly (disciplined) and purposed inter-actions. Within this framework Lindsay's classroom interactions have shown a range from the more closed to the more open. We have seen obed-ient answers to closed, known-answer questions; 'guided discovery'; student-centred group discussion in which meanings are jointly constructed and negotiated; students' initiative in questioning and responsibility for argumentation; and their questioning the teacher's formulations and views. This is a practice, then, which is (within bounds) eclectic and flexible in its repertoire of interactions. It may sometimes be contradictory; it is certainly not monolithic in form or function. It is neither utterly innocent (the 'community' of unequals is sometimes built on collusion as well as on cooperation) nor entirely oppressive (there is scope for at least some students to challenge the status quo).

Students have their say

> Like in our groups, we have the power of our own views and that, and some might ask questions and want to know.

This Year 12 student has in one sentence reached the heart of the issues discussed above concerning the relative powerlessness and passivity of many students in whole class, teacher-directed interrogation. 'Mr Williams' and 'what he gave us to read' were identified as the main sources of knowledge, but the six Year 12 students I spoke to in a group interview at the end of the unit volunteered that 'teamwork' was the main mode of their learning. It was useful, they said, to help correct members' ignorance and mistakes within the group and to pool knowledge across groups when they had been taking a 'jigsaw approach'. They were also realistic about its limitations: it depends on good communication and cooperation, but the school situation is very different from the kind of teamwork 'when guys want to do it' – or have to do it. For as Kerry said, 'if you're not working, like pulling your weight in the team here, there's not like a really major big consequence, but if you have a business, you have to pull your weight, or things will happen.' By contrast, they said, in classroom groups members may lack clarity of purpose or focus of attention, and they may not have uniform enthusiasm and energy. The problem is one that teachers have tried to rectify by setting up 'lifelike' situations in classrooms, as Lindsay has done with teamwork here. And the students were appreciative: 'because we've actually done it in a practical manner, rather than just read, it's like we've actually been doing what applied in the workforce'. Nonetheless, while the value of group work is recognised by the students, when framed by school room and school curriculum it may risk being perceived as idle chatter.

One reason for this misunderstanding has to do with the power relations between teacher and students. While the interviewed students compared these to the hierarchy of boss and workers – the teacher has power over curriculum development and implementation and authority in the classroom, even though students outnumber him – they also identified significant differences. 'For a start, you're not getting paid,' said one (hence presumably there is neither the economic incentive nor the threat of financial loss). They specified 'knowledge' and 'our own grades' as what they were producing in the classroom, but fear of failure did not motivate everyone: other students 'just don't care any more' or 'they're focusing on other things'. Indeed, one student identified this as a source of student power: 'we can just sit there and say "No, we don't want to do anything," and then unless you want to pass in something you don't do it.' For the most part however they defined their power in relation to other peers and to knowledge. We have heard one student's comments, quoted at the beginning of this section. Another student added that such power is learned and appropriated from others who have more knowledge, and so 'you become more powerful'. Thus greater or prior knowledge gives you 'power over the group'. Power, then, is understood to be variously relational (and specific to a particular group: 'next year's Year 12s aren't going to have the power that we have; they have the power that they do, so it's always going to be different'). Interestingly, these students do not talk in individualistic, competitive terms: knowledge and the power it brings are not to be hoarded like capital, perhaps because for the most part these are not students who are committed to their 'own grades'.

The students identified ways in which talk was used to get things done: for exploring issues and problems through group work, thus for sharing information and so distributing power/knowledge. (We were discussing the ways talk worked in the classroom.) But when it came to another possible function – of controlling or regulating others' behaviour – one student identified this as a teacher's function: 'You need to have another talking person telling you to be quiet and get on with your activities'. He linked this with an internalised monitor who prompts him to govern himself: 'Some days you'd, like, think to yourself, "Oh, I'd better do some work today, otherwise Mr Williams is going to be mad at me." So you might sort of try and moderate your feelings a little bit more to do some work in the period.' Interestingly this student was Shaun, who was so ready to take on – that is, challenge – the teacher's superiority.

Talk works also on the imagination, to encourage the exploration of different possible consequences, the students said, alluding to the 'futures wheel' technique. But when it came to the more interpersonal aspects of talk, there were divergences along gender lines: to my question whether talk in class was used to share feelings, a boy demurred: 'That's not really a classroom thing, is it?' and denied that it went on to any extent there. A girl corrected him: students could and did speak of their attitudes and responses to topics. But both of them in thinking of 'the talk that counts' or 'talk that works' were perhaps ignoring the unofficial business of socialising. When reminded of this they agreed that socialising talk is not separable from group work: 'It needs to be both.' Another kind of ostensibly interpersonal talk, of conveying approval, they saw shrewdly in regulatory terms. It was therefore reserved for the teacher, because 'it would be hard for a peer to, like, do the praising thing to another peer' because 'that would be sarcastic'. Indeed, teachers could also use apparent praise or cautious acceptance in a way that the students read as covertly saying, for example, '"Brad, you're an idiot, where's your point?"' These students read their teacher well, and quite affectionately, in hearing the coded messages.

In the genuinely socialising, sharing talk of group work and class forums lies a most important function (and one which I had not suggested to the students): pleasure. Talk makes work 'more enjoyable'; otherwise 'in an English unit where you just sit down and write and copy notes off [the board], it's just going to be so boring.'

These evaluations by students of their classroom interactions have much to say to critical literacy theorists. These speak of students' pragmatic need to see the work of classrooms as authentic talk for real-life purposes within their equally pragmatic realisation of the teacher's authority to construct curriculum and govern lessons. Most important perhaps are the ways that pleasure (in sociable learning) and desire (for teachers' and peers' knowledge and the control it brings) work together with power. That capacity, both repressive and productive, regulatory and enabling, resides – unevenly – in teacher and students. The students have demonstrated important understanding in their talk about language, knowledge and power and the connections among them. In this too they demonstrate a point made earlier, that the (schooled) context of the talk, the speakers and listeners are reciprocally constructed. Thus the classroom – with its momentary mutual interactions in which intentions and meanings are produced – is therefore not only a significant site where critical literacy is being rehearsed for performance elsewhere but also itself a focus of such work. The question remains however of what learning is available to most students to be appropriated and (re)produced in other situations beyond school.

THE KNOWLEDGE THAT COUNTS

The interactions of these Year 10 and 12 students have been intended by Lindsay to develop various kinds of valued cognitive competence: interpersonal and procedural understanding (in 'working in teams'); propositional knowledge (the 'facts' about the Globe Theatre or enterprise bargaining); capability in logical and analytical processes (through close scrutiny of texts); and contemplation of possibilities (through imagination and speculation, narrative and anecdote). These are means to the chief goal: critical knowledge and understanding, for in Lindsay's classroom the emphasis has been on the cognitive rather than the affective. But as those fragments of classroom talk have demonstrated, such generation of knowledge is rather precarious, since the means of generating or transmitting knowledge is the mode of interaction, and this also conveys messages about the nature and value of that knowledge and its imbrication with authority (McNeil 1988).

As noted earlier, Lindsay refuses to accept the teacher's role as font of all knowledge with the authority to transmit to students the culture's knowledge and values. Such a role would be impossible to uphold: he believes that especially the senior students have a 'trained cynicism' of teachers. (Recall Shaun and his – friendly – judgements.) Despite that cynicism Lindsay also acknowledges that the students position him by their expectations of the role he should play as teacher: 'Students often want it to be "business as usual" and this conditioning comes not just from me but from their other teachers, parents, other students, the media.' Certainly those Year 12 students in an interview identified 'mainly Mr Williams' and 'what he gives us to read' as the source of their knowledge. (They also named other students with their divergent views, their teamwork and experience of worksites.) Indeed, they depended on Lindsay not to deceive them but to provide truthful information about matters of 'fact' in a unit on the realities of work. If he offered them 'fiction' (in one boy's words), it would be 'only wasting a unit' and 'you're best off doing a storytelling situation English unit or whatever'. What the curriculum offers as fact is evidently accorded a different authority from fiction, and students want to be able to trust that.

The status of the 'facts' themselves in non-fictional texts (articles about the workplace and the like) was almost never questioned by the students. Where they found it almost impossible to comprehend the articles (on enterprise bargaining, for instance) they tended to doubt their capacities ('just confused and bewildered') and blame their ignorance. As Lindsay commented, 'They come to texts expecting to have difficulties.' The students tended not to doubt the information itself, whose status as truth was therefore inarguable: they recognised that not having full, independent knowledge of the issue precluded them from judging the accuracy of a text's information. They also argued, interestingly, that accuracy of information in those articles was essential as a basis for the critique they were asked to carry out – or there would be no point in the exercise. As one Year 12 student reproved Lindsay: 'We're not talking about interests here [i.e. whose interests are served], we're talking about *knowing* it [about enterprise bargaining] first.' And recall Shaun's question of Lindsay: 'You're critical before you know about it?' Full knowledge is apparently the precondition of and basis for critique. It seems clear from their comments during interview that they saw the business of critique as having to do with values rather than simply truth or falsity ('we also had to ask whether it was right or wrong, whether it was a good or bad thing') and seemed confused when asked if there was a difference. Somewhat contradictorily the students simultaneously recognised that the texts themselves as constructed could be unreliable; Lindsay had 'told us to ask questions about what they're saying. They've worded it in a different way, so it might be biased'; or a graph might be inserted 'just to confuse people'.

Both these reasons for doubt about a text's palpable meaning could ironically enhance the authority of the teacher who provided that text, when he is able to 'see through it' and points this out to students. This might seem rather different from the argument that Baker and Freebody (1989) put forward in their examination of traditional primary classrooms. There the authority of the text and the teacher are co-constructed as the teacher points to features in the text which corroborate his or her reading of it. There are however some similarities. At times Lindsay also used such tactics, teaching that the persuasiveness of an argument depends on substantiation by reference to textual detail: 'Is that the way it's described, though?' 'What are the words that are used here?' 'What do the first two pages tell you?' However, his goal in such scrutiny is to bring students to – his – doubt about the sufficiency of the ideologies promoted by the text's characters, though not necessarily by the text as a whole. And in this way, though the text's authorised meaning is doubted, the text also provides the means of this 'resistant reading' which is founded on it.

In several lessons Lindsay guided the class through questioning to corroborate his point about different speaking and reading positions incorporated in or excluded from the text. On one such occasion he concluded, 'So this idea that that article is putting forward about two sides of the argument maybe isn't quite correct.' Such critical interrogation was directed by Lindsay's sense of what was significant. And while of course there was ample opportunity for students to identify what struck them as worthy of comment, such points would need to be validated by the teacher in the classroom exchanges. (Herein rests his almost invisible authority.) In these ways, then, students are the more dependent on the teacher – unless, as we heard them argue, their ignorance prompts them to seek out additional sources for comparison. Certainly fuller knowledge is set up in this classroom as a desideratum; and it is the teacher's responsibility to determine what knowledge is important.

'The knowledge that counts': the authority to define that is the teacher's, and yet it is not to be imposed on students. The knowledge is shared, but the knowledge deemed relevant is claimed by the teacher – for example, he and the students alike assume that he has the expertise to know what the appropriate questions are. In response to these riddles of critical literacy Lindsay approves of the principle of 'starting where the kids are', which he thinks has quite a lot in common with critical literacy approaches to subaltern knowledges. However, as we have seen, the relations between the knowledge, authority and freedom of learners and knowers in classroom interactions are rather more complicated and sometimes mutually contradictory.

You can't just have kids accept that what you're saying is relevant; you have to demonstrate that relevance to them; and also you have to listen to kids, and not just talk to them. . . . You really have to break away from the notion that your principles are ones the kids should also have; that your morals are ones the kids should also have. . . .

Even with our own values we have to look at them critically and think about what the consequences are of those values, and whose interests are being served by them, and that maybe the way we do things isn't the way to do it, and that maybe we've got something to learn from some of their outlooks on life. . . .

Rather than hitting the kids over the head, saying, 'You have to follow, you have to enter into this discourse', you enter into their discourse and learn about it, and help them learn about the discourse you're coming from and other discourses, as well. I suppose it's opening them up to other discourses and cultures.

And so they may be 'empowered' – if they accept the concepts and propositions about power which the teacher offers as knowledge. We have heard Shaun's 'derision' about the links between power and knowledge, or rather ignorance and powerlessness, and Lindsay's subsequent exploration of the issues. Lindsay later explained that students are 'very suspicious of words like power' and the ways teachers theorise about them, since these are alien to their discourses. 'You create a world according to the labels you give it. . . . And when you think about power, you see power relationships; but if you think about it as confusion, you think about it in a completely different sort of way.' As Lindsay sees it, this has consequences for critical literacy teaching, for 'as soon as you talk about power they start laughing and switch off, and just see it as Mr Williams rabbiting on again'. In interview later Shaun independently agreed: he thought that the suspicion of the managerial class, which they were encouraged to feel, was 'excessive': 'I think that sometimes we were a bit too critical'; 'I felt even more paranoid', as if 'the manager's out to get you', and 'even when he's trying to get on your level, he's only doing that because it's easier to manipulate you when you're on the same level'.

For the most part these students do not aim to be 'knowledge workers', in classroom or workforce, in the sense of having knowledge as a valuable commodity to 'sell' in order to produce a 'value-added product' (Gee and Lankshear 1995), let alone as 'intellectuals' and 'cultural workers' (Giroux 1988). (They are therefore less in danger of mimicking any esoteric academic discourse.) Rather they see themselves in more pragmatic terms. The knowledge they want and value is accurate, relevant information about the workplaces they hope to enter and the nature of work in the 1990s. They recommended to Lindsay that next year's unit should include more 'in-depth information of how it [any business or manufactory] actually works'. With this however went their recognition that they had learned about 'a lot of hidden agendas; it gets more complicated than you think. You have to watch out for a lot more things than just working every day nine to five.' 'We learned to be . . . really wary of what sort of situations were in the workplace' and 'who would benefit' from them. For the students this was also the utility of the unit: 'it gives you questions that you need to ask' in order to 'know your rights'.

Such pragmatism is an appropriate form for their critical literacy. Indeed, Lindsay had anticipated this and deliberately catered to it in his curriculum framing. Nevertheless, in some ways this focus of their interest 'subverted what I was trying to do'. One student, reflecting back on the unit, acknowledged both Lindsay's attempt to teach critical literacy and the difficulty of this endeavour: 'Mr Williams was trying to teach us – I don't know whether we got taught – not to accept one side of the story.'

Lindsay makes a similarly realistic admission to his Year 10 class when he has asked them to reflect on what they've learned through the various activities:

> I've obviously had some idea of what I've wanted you to learn out of the unit, okay? – but . . . what I, as the author of the unit, wanted you to learn isn't necessarily going to be what you *have* learnt. So if you're not sure about whether you've learnt the right things or not, I wouldn't be concerned about that one at all.

It is an interesting analogy, but in some sense the students are not just readers of his sole-authored text, external to it: they are subordinate constructors of it, who are for the most part apparently complicit with the story he is telling and they in turn tell him (and that tells them as characters). We saw above some of the ways in which the classroom interactions constructed this congruence of teaching intentions and learning outcomes. And so Lindsay is able to tell the students at the end of the lesson, 'You have picked up two things I would have hoped you'd have picked up'.

However directed these Year 10 students' learning, they have been supported to articulate in their own words some worthwhile points: about how the changing values of a society affect and constrain both how writers write and how readers read; and how there are links between power (or domination) and language and action. Lindsay concedes that 'understanding that the context shapes language isn't necessarily critical literacy, but it's a precursor to understanding some of the other issues in critical literacy'.

The knowledge that counts is also the knowledge that counts for marks on assignments. A sample of students' work from these classes is examined in the following chapter; the point to be made here is that the tasks in both cases require the students to explicitly acknowledge and evaluate a range of viewpoints about the texts and topics in the unit. In this as in other ways the nature of knowledge as presented by the teacher in these critical literacy classrooms is poststructuralist: it is shown to be produced by discourses, contingent on circumstances, multiple in meanings, problematic and contested, and shaping knowers. Lindsay intends that his students should come to this knowledge about knowledge. To the extent that he succeeds, they will hold a very different view from what is still propounded in a number of school disciplines (Cherryholmes 1988), where knowledge is taken to be revealed, universal, certain, and autonomous. However, as we have seen, such poststructuralist education may be incomplete and undermined by the very structures of classroom interaction. For instance, it is one thing to analyse a text for the ideologies of those represented in it; it is another to ignore the ways in which knowledge about those representations is produced by the discourses which prevail in the classroom. (This may mean being unconscious of them oneself as a teacher or choosing not to draw students' attention to them.) It is laudable to explore the cultural values that lead young readers nowadays to laugh at the 'lovey-dovey' bits in *Romeo and Juliet*; it is much harder not to fix on a preferred meaning and close down others from that multiplicity waiting in the wings. Sceptical adolescents may be very ready to accept that there is contestation over meanings; they may not be so immune to the authority of a teacher who seems to be ahead of the pack with his insider knowledge. And it is hardest of all, perhaps, to help students begin to understand how knowledge, hence ideologies and discourses, constitute those who know and those who are known within those systems of understanding.

And even if teachers could devise teaching strategies to explore these concepts – should they? A very experienced teacher like Lindsay, who is closely attentive to what his students can manage to take on board, believes there are some concepts which are appropriately introduced first, and that there are limitations to the tolerance of students for abstract analytic work beyond which it is pointless to press. And given the need, as he sees it, to get on with the business of those 'basics', for him to continually express his self-consciousness about his own role in the generation of knowledge could be a self-defeating self-indulgence.

From time to time however, Lindsay has shown ways to engage with the possible inconsistency between the view of knowledge being represented and the procedures of knowledge being presented in classroom interactions. (A further way, which he does not utilise much, is through role playing and other forms of imaginative, affective engagement as suggested in chapter two.) For example, in the previous year's unit of work, Lindsay had his then Year 11 students analyse their classroom talk for the relations of power and authority it produced – when this was germane to the topic of work. More frequently Lindsay offers his students a reflective moment of metaknowledge:

My intention for this unit has not been to teach you everything you need to know about management and enterprise bargaining and all the rest – okay? It's really to get you to think about some of the issues involved in enterprise bargaining, management and all the rest of it, and really try to hone up your critical skills – your ability to question things and think about them critically.

The activities we've been doing are really to let you think about *Romeo and Juliet* and whether the sorts of things people say about classic plays like *Romeo and Juliet* are true: that they have universal messages that everyone should be paying attention to, or whether there are things that are particularly relevant in these sorts of plays for us today.

At other times he pauses at the end of a phase of class discussion to synthesise the views and draw from them a general inference. In both cases it is of course his metaknowledge, not theirs, which is being articulated – although at the end of the units, as we have heard, he also offers students an invitation to reflect on their learning. Such opportunities could be extended, into moments (not more than that) of critical metacognition.

FACTORING IN THE CLASSROOM

It may be that the rewards of critical teaching must always be found in such small, tantalising moments of classroom encounter, not in measurable advances on the grand schemes that theoretically propel the enterprise.

(Knoblauch and Brannon 1993: 66)

Small, tantalising, their effects not measurable with any certainty – and yet the hints in such moments as we have heard in this chapter suggest it is worth persisting with the enterprise. And it is therefore worth scrutinising the factors that condition, even counter, the realisation of critical literacy in classroom encounters.

The most pervasive of these, and thus the one which becomes inaudible, is the characteristic discourse of teacher and students. It becomes not only normal but even normative, with its 'distinctive sets of interlocking rights and obligations' (Edwards and Westgate 1994). In secondary school teachers and students have developed a high degree of procedural competence in 'doing lessons'. The various teaching technologies of managing a line of 'shared' inquiry have long predominated as the customary means to customary ends. As Lindsay points out, they are characteristic also of the professional development workshops on critical literacy which he has attended, run by 'experts' such as Colin Lankshear, Hilary Janks and Catherine Wallace:

There was certainly little that was emancipatory about the techniques or, in many ways, the expert–novice relationship between presenter and participants. And of course, books on crit lit set up a very traditional relationship between reader (novice) and writer (expert). Even worse are many of the classroom oriented resources. Is it any wonder, then, that it's 'business as usual'?

Despite or because of their pervasiveness, there are two connected problems in those teaching technologies of managing 'shared' inquiry. First, if the means itself encourages in students intellectual accommodation to the institution of schooling and its commonsense and disciplinary knowledges and covertly discourages intellectual resistance under the guise of encouraging students to 'express their own point of view', then an emancipatory project is safely contained within hegemonic institutions and practices. Second, even when a teacher judges those customary means to be functional and uses them strategically towards other ends, students may hear in the pattern of classroom interactions only 'business as usual'. They may then import the epistemological framework of other subjects in which they are answerers of questions already known, not the askers.

Or it may be that the problem is quite the reverse: that the specific ways of talking and thinking (about 'power' for instance, or 'interests') that prevail in such a classroom are taken to be 'normal' and applicable for that situation only. Those ways of generating, communicating and displaying knowledge may serve as boundary markers, signalling and encouraging discontinuities between English and other school subjects, or between in-school and out-of-school talk. The question is how inseparable the discourse (classroom talk) is from the larger discourses (or ideologies) of critical theory and practice, and how much transfer is possible from one situation to another, each with its distinctive ways of talking, hence thinking and knowing, acting and being. It was suggested earlier that the process of learning how to negotiate communicatively is the process by which one gains entry into the culture – but how context-bound is that (sub)culture of critical literacy? We simply do not know what uptake is likely for most students so schooled. It may be that those whose primary discourse (Gee 1990: 150) – that first form of life acquired in intimate, family interactions – is closer to a critical literacy discourse will most easily take on this kind of 'cultural capital'. And so the intellectual and economic orders may once again ironically maintain their hierarchy and hegemony through the disciplines of schooling, even in critical literacy.

Critical pedagogy as an intellectual and social 'movement' defines its concepts and values, derives its aims and dreams of its ends. Teachers within that movement have to translate those broad outlines into the specifics of curriculum and classroom interactions. When these are studied in closeup, as we have done in this chapter, the clarity of the broad brush strokes dissolves into a mass of cross-hatching, some lines traversing others in no tidy-seeming pattern. Complexity is everywhere, nowhere identifiable as single, certain effects that manifest those dreamed-of ends of critical literacy. This is partly because the various institutions of school and society frame and contain such classrooms, and we cannot simply read off their influences from a transcript.

The text of this chapter also frames the classroom as a kind of still life when it produces knowledge about the generation of knowledge and therefore attempts to contain the possible meanings of those teacher–student interactions. All the more important then to come back to the point made in chapter one that there is something to be gained from giving up the pursuit of certainty and recognising that critical literacy is various forms of social practice, practised within and contingent on specific social contexts and relationships located in time and space. Its classroom discourse is therefore inevitably multiple, even inconsistent, sometimes sabotaged from within as well as from without. But those 'small, tantalising moments' may still be momentarily realised. I believe we have been privileged to hear some of them in this chapter.

Chapter 6

'A Daniel come to judgement'

ASSESSMENT: CAPITALISING ON ACHIEVEMENT

During my interview with those Year 12 students discussed in the previous chapter they compared their classroom to the workplace in various ways. So if they were workers, I asked, what were they producing here? One boy answered unhesitatingly, 'Like, our own grades, and stuff.' He went on to add that they were also producing knowledge; but here in his first response put so baldly is the economy of the mainstream secondary class-room, which in some ways operates like those of capitalism. To oversimplify somewhat: student-workers compete with one another to produce goods, usually in the form of written pieces; these are offered to the consumer (the reader-teacher), who assesses its worth by assigning a letter or number. In this symbolic exchange economy the grade carries a power equivalent to dollars: the capital so acquired can be put to work for the owner's economic and social advancement.

Such an analogy, expressed spontaneously by this student, has of course been the subject of critique by critical sociologists of education, as mentioned in chapter one. I do not intend to reproduce here those more general critiques of the reproductive nature of public schooling through assessment practices, especially standardised testing or public examinations. Nor will I discuss except in passing the policies and procedures of certification of students within the school and the system. My focus here is more microscopic: on the classroom-centred power and knowledge around assessment which are produced within such conditions. This will arise out of a reading of three pieces of student writing and the contexts of their production. Not included in this focus is the reception of these pieces: how the teachers graded them, what comments they wrote, what the writers felt and did with that feedback, how their writing contributed to the 'success' of the students. While that is a necessary part of the larger tale about class-room learning, it is an episode for another occasion.

In much critical literacy theorising about pedagogy there is a silence so resounding about matters of assessment that one could almost think it a scandal which must be hushed up. The scandal lies rather in the silence.

Teachers however know they are involved in the politics of representation when they assess their students, whether by means of a single letter or number, or a 'profile'. In the classrooms of critical literacy teachers who must work within that system, no less than in others, this practice is inevitably a form of normalisation – of determining the bounds between what is average or typical, what is exemplary and what is inadequate, and what is desirable as the outcome of teaching. Many teachers who have not read Foucault's *Discipline and Punish* (1979) still know a great deal about the workings of this instance of modern social regulation and control.

Such recognition can bring a persistent discomfiture. Some teachers may need to repress or rationalise their unease about branding students and their work with a symbol of worth (the two often being conflated in such expressions as 'she's an A'). Otherwise, their squeamishness might lessen the assuredness of their judgements. For paradoxically, while the practice of assessment is a source of power for teachers over students, many feel it as disempowering, in at least two ways. They are complicit with the system that constrains them as well as their students in their brokering students' life chances through such gatekeeping. And the practice diminishes their influence as teachers in their preferred, customary stance as trusted adult, honest guide and coach. However, the tension between this role and that of judge may be lessened in that the teacher is the best person to carry out such judgements based on knowledge of the students and what and how they have been taught. (This is of course preferable to the 'object-ivity' of public examinations which subject students to very 'thin' judgements.) Nonetheless, such tensions are an issue for those critical lit-eracy teachers who believe that good teacher–student relations depend on teachers' accepting the cultural knowledge and language skills (even if non-standard) which students bring into the classroom – while ultimately having to evaluate the success of those students' control over mainstream discourses.

This and other related concerns have to do ultimately with questions of power and value. If the aim of critical literacy teaching is for students to demonstrate mastery over dominant ideologies (by identifying the ways these are represented in texts) rather than being mastered by them, it is manifestly contradictory that students should have to submit to author-itative, even authoritarian, judgement within an ideologically suspect apparatus of state power. – That is the hardline view, at least. To take a more beneficent view of the matter, it could be argued that schooling inevitably involves subjecting students to disciplines and controls, includ-ing those of assessment tasks. At best this is based on a contractual understanding with students that their willing submission to tutelage will result in their greater freedom subsequently, when they have developed the capacities for independent performance they are now learning. In crit-ical literacy classrooms that capacity is eventually to take the form of wide-reaching social and political critique, as the meta-competence which mobilises those forms of linguistic competence which contribute to it. Meanwhile, even within that contract, one way to limit its possible oppressiveness is to give students the opportunity to critique the most immediate site of the production of power and knowledge: their own classrooms. Such critique may encompass the teacher's selection of texts, activities and forms of assessment. Just such an invitation has been taken up in three pieces of student writing examined below. (These will raise further concerns specific to teachers working within a critical literacy discourse.)

But even in such student critiques lies the risk, not always avoided, of their taking a politically correct line in order to satisfy the teacher. We heard Spiro in chapter four expressing his unease about the Year 12 student who announced that his story was 'politically correct'. The context for this writing was a unit on 'The Language of the Family', in which students were required to conform to the imperatives of social justice by producing a children's picture-book which overturned stereotypes they had found in other texts for children – representations of parents and children, family and social patterns. The point of this exercise was to have students inhabit the role of a writer concerned with social justice and so to imagine the world differently.

Lindsay cheerfully admits that this one instance is 'social engineering' – although in other cases students have plenty of opportunity not to toe the party line. But here, 'by forcing them to break the stereotypes . . . we're also forcing them to see that this concept of gender or race or whatever can be constructed differently.' He is unrepentant about such directiveness and its risk of legislating conformity, arguing that the opposition between freedom of thought and such overt shaping of attitudes is false: 'I *am* influencing students into thinking in particular ways, but they're already being influenced to think in particular ways that are quite restrictive. . . . What we're trying to do is open up the options.' For Lindsay also points out that the children's picture-book writing task, which is not the culminating task of the unit, becomes the means to a further end in that the experience enables the students to critique the notion of social justice.

Nonetheless, this paradox of 'options' being opened up through the constraints of critical literacy assessment requirements lies at the heart of a critical literacy classroom practice; it is just such issues that are raised here as we consider the concrete practicalities of teachers' work for student assessment.

READING CLASSROOM READINGS

English for the world of work: blind tasting no. 1

'When teachers begin to assess, they cease to read.' Like any exaggeration, this contains much truth. That is why the three students' work appears without any prior indication of the writers' backgrounds (the context of the units will be apparent from the writing itself), the tasks set and the stated criteria for assessment – though these are often the first things teacher-readers want to know, in order to know how to read. For English teachers, unlike wine-tasters, do not generally choose to go to their task without knowledge of maker and production processes. Readers are offered the chance of a (relatively) blind tasting here, however: to note their responses to each of the three pieces as they roll its phrases on their tongue, appreci-ate its colour and clarity, nose out any whiff of sulphur, and savour its length on the palate.

Talkback Radio

Host: Good morning to you all out there just dying to finish up your twelve-year Year 12 sentences. You are listening to 95PRFM, the station with the guru man himself, Rishaad Bader.

To get into your ears and overtake your consciousness, TZ and I will encapsulate you with your very own Top 40. Yes, over the last few weeks we have been jotting down the music which you most voted for.

But just before we start kicking your Top 40 we are going to have a little bit of a feedback session about this last term's new English unit, 'Language of Work'. For all of those would be workers who are going to brave it out in the '9-5 world' after grad-uation, this is your time to speak out and voice your opinion on the one and only compulsory subject of the school, English. So start dialling, 'cause we want to know just how it went – did you enjoy it? Do you really think it helped for when you leave? Teachers, did you enjoy teaching this new controversial way on how to look, act, and think within the workplace? Also did any of us really understand the concepts behind what was supposed to have been taught?

OK, here we have caller 1 on the line. Hello caller, say your piece.

Caller 1: Ah hello, my name is Anna Bolic and I'd just like to say that this unit that we've just completed was really interesting.

Host: Yes, OK and how so, Anna?

Caller 1: Interesting in the way of just how complicated and dog eat dog the workplace can be out there. You know. Everyone just thinks that once they finish school that you can just go out, get a job and work until you start moving up. It's just not like that and I think this unit really went into detail over the issues and complications within the workplace, particularly the 'Enterprise

Bargaining' and 'Maverick Managers' articles. I believe this unit told you a lot about the situations and issues we might face out there in the big wide world.

Host: OK, there you go, a very substantial point of view on the unit. Thank you Anna.

Caller 2, hello.

Caller 2: Yeh, hi Rishaad! I thought this unit was great.

Host: Yes, and why is that, person with no name?

Caller 2: Oh, my name is Gecko and I just thought the whole unit was a bludge, sometimes it got really boring. But like I said I could just fall asleep and let my group members do all the work. And yet still almost pass.

Host: OK, a very intelligent evaluation there Gecko.

Caller 3, shed some light on the subject.

Caller 3: Hello Bader. My name is Steve. Um, through the unit Mr Williams showed us a number of articles about management, systems and bargainings within the workplace. These concepts I felt were sometimes boring and yet also interesting because of what Anna said before.

Host: So Steve, you thought this unit will later on help you within the workforce?

Caller 3: Yes, but on another note we were told to be very critical of these situations within the workplace, not just to accept them as all good. This was good, in a way that we were taught to look at both sides of the situations and ask who was really the beneficiary. But again, what I'm trying to get at, was that we became *too* critically aware of the dangers within the workplace, almost paranoid if you like.

Host: I see, well thankyou, Steve. Time to wrap things up. So from pure interest, bludging, to paranoia. We've covered still only a little, but very different factors about 'Language of Work' today on this talkback session.

Remember though, whether you like or dislike, you have to understand that it's one of the first times this unit has been run in Queensland and subsequently bound to have hiccups.

And for students to come, fear not, for the unit can only get better . . . I think.

Now for the Top 40!

(Shaun McLaren, Year 12)

Producing readings

It has become a truism of English education that any text is conditioned by the context of its production – the writer's informing ideologies and discourses, the available genres, the writer's social purposes, the nature of the audience and the like. It is equally true of a text like Shaun's, produced within a curriculum unit on 'The Language of Work'. We already know something of Lindsay's intentions in constructing this. We have glimpsed the classroom activities he set up. And we have heard him modelling and coaxing students in the discourse of critical literacy. What needs to be added here is information about the task Shaun and his classmates were set.

For Lindsay the constraints in setting that task were of several overlapping kinds. Of two practical constraints, one had to do with the requirement by the Queensland Board of Senior Secondary School Studies that the folio on which students' 'exit achievements' are based should encompass a range of genres (narrative, procedural, transactional, reporting, analytical expository, and persuasive expository) produced in either written or oral mode, under a range of conditions, some in restricted conditions in which the student's authorship can be verified. The task set here was to fulfil the social purpose of persuasive exposition by means of a transcript or playscript, and it was to be done exclusively in class time during five lessons. This brings us to the second constraint: many students had not submitted sufficient (or sufficiently satisfactory) pieces to date, so both this task and its conditions had to encourage them to complete their work for Board requirements – at a time when their thoughts were preoccupied by the end-of-year formal. (Such are the gritty realities which are often in the forefront of teachers' minds when they set assessment tasks.)

A further set of conditions derives from the curriculum unit: what subject matter is to be the focus, what genre will be most appropriate, and what literacy competence is thereby to be demonstrated and assessed. Lindsay specified three similar alternatives in subject matter and genre, so that the students could pursue an issue of particular interest to them and might therefore be more likely to demonstrate their capacity for analysis and critique. Shaun chose as his genre a 'transcript of talkback radio program to express/debate opinions and critically evaluate work in the '90s'; the subject matter he selected was 'this unit and the way it's been taught'.

In Queensland, before students produce an assessment piece teachers are required to supply them with written statements about the task-specific criteria and the standards which will be used to determine the grade. This requirement is justified on the grounds of equity: it gives students a more equal chance of success, since all are alike informed about the kind of text to be produced and the ways to shape it appropriately and effectively. In this instance, Shaun was given information about the staging of the generic structure – welcome to listeners, introduction of programme, establishment of issue and background to issue, details on how to call in, introduction of callers, structure of caller's comments (thesis, reasons, supporting evidence, concluding comment), and conclusion to the programme. He was also given advice about grammar (the appropriate kind of verb tenses, mood and modality), cohesion, vocabulary and other matters of presentation.

Such specification of task and criteria is especially significant among the factors that frame the teacher's reading. By these directions teachers become the readers of texts that are 'already read' even before they are written. This gives an extraordinary power to the reader; it exceeds the wildest dreams of reader-response critics. But it can also lead to a limitation on teacher-readers. Unlike other readers they do not read an unknown text that gives them a reading position and aims to set up and fulfil their desire. Instead they read as assessors, checking how closely the text corresponds to their requirements of structure and substance. Such determined expectations are rather different from other readers' hopeful anticipations, and may be a source of disappointment, in that the scope for surprise is limited. Any interest may well be evoked only by how closely this piece matches, exceeds or falls short of previous work by the student. Or it may be occasioned by the occasional insightful comment as permitted within the specified framework of the task.

Against this general risk in criteria-based assessment some forms of modification are possible. Lindsay notes that he and his fellow teachers encourage students to move beyond the conventional features specified in criteria sheets, adding that 'I actually beg students to surprise me, especially in those genres where surprise is appropriate.' On many assessment tasks students are asked to write a brief explanation of what they hoped to achieve and how, in order to guide the teacher's reading. And in writing narrative, senior students are asked to write their own criteria, using the regular framework.

Nonetheless, in reading student work any teachers look for confirmation of what they value. (In Queensland this is in Year 12 conditioned by what teachers know Board assessment panels value.) For critical literacy teachers the value of any piece may have to do with a demonstration of political critique as much as – or even more than – a close knowledge of literary or other texts or correctness in expression. In this instance the invitation to critique the classroom as a site of sociopolitical relations and production of knowledge could be piquant, if the sharpness of critique (approved of and fostered by the teacher in general terms) were to result in a negative assessment of the unit and the teaching (which the teacher would find disappointing). But the tables are unlikely to be turned completely by a student's wholesale condemnation – even though Shaun knew this was his last unit and last piece of work at school, and though

Lindsay repeatedly asks for honest evaluations of his units. (As we have seen in chapter five, he shows openness and acceptance in the face of critical challenges from students – or colleagues and researcher.) When such critique is framed as a task through which the student is directly assessed as he assesses the teacher, it becomes a relatively 'safe' invitation for both Lindsay and Shaun, if the latter adheres to the decorum expected of students – even as he adopts the role of an educational critic 'free' to speak his 'own' mind.

Where we encourage students to be honest in setting forth what they 'genuinely' feel and think, will we not come to their work presuming their sincerity and wanting to find evidence of it? Will we value such signs rather than the text's rhetorical effectiveness according to the given purpose and genre? (Surely we will not sceptically suppose that the writer is calculated, even cynical in aiming to please the teacher-reader through the appearance of critique which nonetheless conforms and confirms?) In Shaun's case, the genre largely allows him to evade the issue of 'sincerity', while also permitting him to express views he might not feel able to in first person. Thus three speakers express different views, and the host is not required to do more than invite a range of viewpoints without evaluating any or taking a stand – only suggesting that things may well improve. (That Shaun chose not to have the host evaluate other speakers' comments had in Lindsay's view as much to do with Shaun's laid-back attitude as the genre.)

It would be possible to exploit the polyvocality of the form, so that the medium becomes the message about a multiplicity of views and values on the given topic, juxtaposed to expose the sharpness of their differences. Such mutually corrective ironies may be intended by a writer, but their effect depends on the willingness of a reader to elicit the fullness of those latent ironies. (It is a fundamental uncertainty about intention and effect which bothers many teacher-reader-assessors.) In this case, despite – or rather, because of – these subtleties of meaning and effect, the genre, as assessable outcome, is well matched to a major purpose of the unit as a whole, which was for students to develop the ability to weigh up any situation or issue from more than one viewpoint and ask about whose interests might be served by a particular textual representation of that issue.

Many voices, many views: recalling the sociability of that classroom, I am reminded how thin even this quartet of voices sounds as an outcome of the investigations and speculations, discussions and arguments which preceded it. Incidentally, this piece was only one of several tasks which contributed to the students' grades for this unit. The oral task was an assessment of students' participation in 'team work' (identified in the Mayer Report as a Key Competence in preparing school students for the workforce: *Putting General Education to Work*, Australian Education Council and Ministers for Vocational Education, Employment and Training 1992).

As the students took part in team work they were asked to reflect on it, through peer observation and the construction of guidelines for effective team work. Then they were asked to evaluate and critique this 'competence'. This written piece of Shaun's is therefore not so much a distillation as a partial representation of the content and processes of the unit. It is more direct as a demonstration of the competence which Lindsay rated as being the most valuable, of critique.

So what is the substance of the critique? And how in turn might this critical evaluation be evaluated by a critical literacy reader? (There are of course many such readers and readings, and I do not claim to speak for Lindsay here, only for myself.) The talk-show host proposes three criteria: interest, utility and understanding. The relevance of the information about work in the 1990s, hence its interest, is rated highly on balance, the credibility of Gecko's negative vote being undermined by his self-confessed self-interest, his readiness to have team mates do his work. The one substantial point of critique has to do with critique and its risk of paranoid suspicion. In the persona of caller 3 (as he had earlier in his own person – cf. chapter five) Shaun resists his teacher's relentlessly resistant reading of workplaces, while conceding the value of identifying who benefits from any workplace arrangement. The point is asserted but not substantiated, and a question remains. How shall we determine what is appropriately critical and what is hypercritical? The question is important (in chapter four we heard the Park Ridge teachers grappling with the same issue), but we are not given an answer. Presumably it depends on what the critical observer understands the 'reality' of any situation to be. In this way the student challenges the authority of the critical literacy teacher to know and name the source of oppression. However, the caller's point is evaluative but is not itself evaluated, and as noted previously, the genre permits such assertions of opinion to stand unelaborated, unchallenged.

The features of any genre are both enabling and limiting. Enabling here in that they allow for a variety of sometimes conflicting views to be held without the writer having to lay claim to any one of them exclusively. Productive also in demonstrating diversity and incompatibility of opinions so directly. Limiting by the same token, in that the talk-show genre does not expect participants to move beyond assertion and opinion, to reconcile different views or to argue for one over another. Remembering how much more forceful Shaun and others were in group interview, and how many more substantial points were argued through in shared talk, I identify a greater limitation in a form of assessment which can only very thinly represent on the page the sociality of knowledge production, argumentation and evaluation. (A further limitation is of course the focus here on one isolated piece of work withdrawn from a folio that makes up Shaun's profile as an English student.)

A canonical text for today: blind tasting no. 2

The purpose of our second example is also persuasive exposition, but this takes the form of a written submission to a committee and must therefore show more elaborated analysis and argumentation. The substance of its views will be our focus here and the questions these raise about conformity in critique.

Submission to the Park Ridge High School P & C

Background

The Queensland Curriculum Review has recently recommended that values start to be taught in all schools. The P & C Committee, here at Park Ridge State High, agrees with this recommendation. They have decided that the best way to achieve this aim would be through the reading of classic literature, which illustrates universal morals and values. It proposed, then, that it should be compulsory for all Year 10 students to study Shakespeare's *Romeo and Juliet*.

General comment

As a student who has studied Shakespeare's *Romeo and Juliet* in great detail, I feel that there would be a number of issues to be considered when introducing such a text into the compulsory curriculum. There are definitely some values present in this play which would be worth introducing to our youths, such as the sincerity of true love and loss due to battle, yet I also have some apprehensions about other aspects of the script. The main concerns I wish to address in my report are:

1   The portrayal of the genders
2   Roles played by family members
3   Courtship and love

Specific comments

Concern 1: The portrayal of the genders

Throughout the text of *Romeo and Juliet*, a reader can easily detect a certain distinction in the way characters of different genders are portrayed. I would like to discuss these in three separate categories. These are:

A   Higher class females
B   Lower class females
C   Males

A Higher class females   It seems that every upper class female in *Romeo and Juliet* is viewed very highly by all males. These women are practically worshipped and have the very best of everything. Romeo displays this procedure frequently throughout the play, as he worships Juliet. An example of this is where Romeo is talking to himself as he watches Juliet, through some bushes, on the balcony above him (II, 2, 15–22). Here Romeo is complimenting Juliet's beautiful eyes, to a great extent. If a boy was to compliment a girl today, he would probably just say, 'You have beautiful eyes,' and that would be the end of it. This scene also displays the way men used to put their loves up on pedestals. However, in the twentieth century, equity has become a major issue. Therefore, it is as important for girls to compliment boys as boys girls, and some compliments are now classed as sexual harassment.

B Lower class females   The females I refer to as 'lower class' are the women who are not royal or wealthy and usually have 'second-rate' positions. There are not many examples of these women in *Romeo and Juliet*, as the story is set around the feuding of two wealthy, powerful families and their children. However, Juliet's servant and foster-mother, the Nurse, displays how women of such a role within society are treated.

Ladies in these roles are usually the victims of practical jokes and remarks from males. It seems they are almost regarded as not being feminine in comparison with the upper class women. Although their behaviour evokes such responses from the males. Throughout the text, the Nurse seems to lack the elegance that Juliet and Lady Montague possess. An example of such unsophisticated behaviour is when Juliet sends the Nurse to deliver a message to Romeo for her (II, 4, 151–9). Here we see that Romeo's friends have just finished playing several practical jokes on the nurse. She then continues to tell Romeo that if he tries it again she will take him and twenty others like him on. She will make him feel inferior and if she can't, she will find others who can! This, to me, is hardly the behaviour of an elegant woman, and the whole situation would never have arrived had Juliet delivered the message herself, but such activities are not carried out by the higher class females.

C Males   The males in *Romeo and Juliet* are definitely the superior gender. Even within a marriage, the woman may be worshipped but she must obey every single rule laid down by her husband. You could even go to the extent of saying, the man owned the woman's life. However out of a marriage the men treat women with the utmost respect to their face. Throughout the play, men comment on women almost as though they were toys for their sexual pleasure. An illustration of this is when Gregory and Sampson, two members of the Capulet household, are talking in the street (I, 1, 16–28). Here we hear Sampson saying he is going to get revenge on the Montagues by fighting with them and then, what we would call as today, raping their women. He says he will 'thrust them to the wall' and take their heads or their maidenheads, meaning he will have sex with them and take their virginity or behead them. This is hardly having respect for the women themselves.

Another aspect of poor male behaviour in this book is their problem solving. Whenever any males have a disagreement or are simply bored, the first solution that enters their minds is physically fight. The sword fight in which Mercutio and Tybalt are killed, began by a mere harsh word. A simple statement ended two lives. However, today it takes much more than a harsh word for a fight to progress past the early verbal stages. I feel this is because the penalties for violence and physical or mental abuse these days are a lot harsher.

Concern 2: Roles played by family members

The characters in *Romeo and Juliet* have a very different family structure compared with the type of structure we have today. Different family members seem to be responsible for different duties, such as the raising of children, etc. I would once again like to address the characters in three separate sections. These are:
A   The roles of parents
B   The roles of children
C   The roles of servants

A The roles of parents   The only parents we know of in *Romeo and Juliet* are Montague and his Lady and Capulet and his Lady. The first thing that struck me as peculiar when reading the text is, never do the children call their parents Mum and Dad, only Sir and Madam as though addressing strangers. They only really talk to their parents when sent for!

Even then, the conversation is very restricted and some other servant or friend is usually present. The only real responsibility these parents take on is choosing their children's future marital parents. Therefore, I really don't see the parents as being parents, merely the source of their children's material requirements.

B The roles of children   I see the main role of children in this play to be the new generation who continues the wealth and blood lines of their families. They do not seem to have any goals, as in careers or means of support, as they have the family fortunes to live off and do not require employment. It seems the only main event in their lives is marriage which they don't have a say in anyway. Consequently, I feel these characters are incompatible role models for our generation.

C The roles of servants   To me, it is the servants who are the parents of the children. The Nurse is the only member of Juliet's family who knew of her love for Romeo, her hatred for Paris and of her marriage. It is the Nurse who comforts her in her time of need and performs whatever duties she has to, in order to keep her happy. So too in the Montague household. It is Benvolio and Balthasar who listen to Romeo's problems and offer advice from past experience. To me these figures seem to fit our definition of parents much better.

In our family structure today, the average family does not have servants and the parents are responsible for every aspect of their child's upbringing, financial, physical and emotional. The children are faced with the reality of high unemployment figures and therefore must strive to achieve their very best possible or basically the life they have ahead of them will be far from easy.

Concern 3: Courtship and love

The differences between the love in the Middle Ages and love today are numerous. Today everyone is entitled to fall in love with and marry whomever they choose. However, in the Middle Ages, the period in which *Romeo and Juliet* is set, there seemed to be a set of rules followed as far as love was concerned. A man should have fallen in love with a woman he could not have due to her status. Not only does this seem to be a boring waste of time but the fact he could not have her was supposed to make him more passionate!

As previously stated, the parents choose their children's marital partners. This decision was usually affected by the wealth and power the marriage would bring to the family, not for love. It was also common for girls to be married and having children at the tender age of fourteen and fifteen. Any girl of that age today is not considered old enough to look after themselves, let alone be responsible for someone else. I feel this is a good thing, as the child will not be able to lead a happy life if their mother is incapable of providing for them.

Recommendation

I feel that Shakespeare's *Romeo and Juliet* should remain an optional piece of literature in the Year 10 curriculum. I feel it does have some good morals but if a reader did not appreciate the era it is set in, they could focus on the wrong aspects of the play. However, I would definitely recommend *Romeo and Juliet* as a good piece of literature for students to use when trying to enhance their analytical skills, as it stimulates debate.

(Sarah Easton, Year 10)

Producing readings

The title of this chapter comes from another of Shakespeare's plays; it quotes Shylock from *The Merchant of Venice*, who praises Portia in these terms when her assessment of his written words – the bond – seems to be going in his favour. Teachers as judges would like a similar judgement of their impartiality and expertise, but that may be particularly difficult in a case like this, where the values imparted in the teaching have apparently been so faithfully reproduced.

Before coming to the substance of its argument, a word about Sarah's competence in deploying the textual features of the genre. Her control is impeccable, and that command could be equated with authority – the authority of writing that has rhetorical effectiveness. (This at least is the promise made by advocates of genre teaching.) Sarah's task, defined by the criteria sheet, was in part to demonstrate generic conformity; the generic conventions and their ways of legitimising certain kinds of knowledge are not the target of her critique. Indeed, these normative conventions have enabled her to produce her text and modulate her 'voice'. And thus she is shaped by them.

Adherence to generic conventions does not necessarily constitute persuasiveness. In this case Sarah's text does have a rhetorical effectiveness insofar as Sarah has her eye on her teacher as the 'real' (implied) audience rather than her ostensible hearers. She aims to please not the unknown many but the known, already persuaded, reader whose views will be confirmed by this demonstration of solidarity. Such targeting is not at all surprising in a first attempt at a critical piece of writing of this kind, based on Sarah's first formal exposure to critical literacy.

It should be emphasised that all class members were given the opportunity to mount whatever case they chose, including a straight canonical line. Despite this apparent freedom, Sarah and her classmates had no doubt been reading the classroom and the direction of Lindsay's teaching – some of which we have heard in the previous chapter. Sarah dismisses the play's positive values (the sincerity of love, the pathos of young death by duelling) in half a sentence before rolling up her sleeves for the main business of the submission. Not surprisingly therefore her evaluation in her recommendation commends the play only for the opportunity it provides students to develop their analytical skills.

In my belief Sarah has identified with her teacher's analyses and evaluations and she therefore rehearses in her writing the ideas she believes are right – and also most acceptable. Lindsay however needed to supplement my reading of this writing: in his view it did not do justice to the hours he knew Sarah had spent in going through the text, 'trying to interpret things for herself'. He added, quite rightly, that those who are inexperienced at some activity are likely to learn at first by emulating a more proficient practitioner, though they may later move beyond that model.

Nonetheless it is possible to see here the regulating and normalising of students. Lindsay would argue that he is merely offering a counter-discourse to the dominant mode of thinking about great literature. But while some class time was spent in examining the aesthetic argument, it was instead Lindsay's reading of the play, his emphases and interests, which demonstrated most forcefully to the students what counted as the preferable reading practice and how a literate person thinks and writes. This is no exception to the rule (it has always been thus in literature classes); the difference lies in the particular argument being validated through such an inevitably selective reading.

In this unit Sarah has been undertaking a particular kind of disciplinary exercise (broadly speaking, of ideological unmasking) set up and modelled by her teacher. Ultimately therefore Lindsay's role, in reading her work, is to assess how keen her X-ray vision is in penetrating seductive surfaces. In such cases we teachers hope – in vain – to put on hold our own attachment to certain ideologies, and to think that instead of evaluating the substance of students' arguments, we are assessing merely the protocols of argumentation. We insist for instance that students substantiate a point of interpretation by showing the portion of text which ostensibly grounds it. 'You can say anything you like,' we say, ' if you can prove it from the text.' We conveniently forget that a text can be made to say almost anything, given the partiality of any reading and the often peculiar version created by any paraphrase. And in this democratic spirit we are caught on the horns of a dilemma, since we judge that some readings are better – more attentive, more scrupulous, or more incisively critical – than others. And so too some readings will seem better because they echo in the resonating chambers of our hearts.

Sarah's paraphrase offers a particularly 'strong' or resistant reading. (What follows in this analysis is of course my paraphrase of hers.) Given the nature of the genre she emphasises logic rather than affect – though she is quickly moved to an indignation which motivates her argument. Throughout, her argument is intended to counter the assertion that Romeo and Juliet 'illustrates universal morals and values'. If one's opponents assume that the play itself does advocate certain values which are still admirable today, then the logical move is to demonstrate how different are our society's preferred views on the relations between men and women, parents and offspring, husbands and wives, employers and workers. Thus it can be concluded that Shakespeare's characters are inappropriate role models. The points that Sarah makes about gender relations are clear and substantial, and point to incompatible attitudes to women when the ideals of a courtly love tradition meet the realities of dynastic alliance. She also differentiates the kinds of respect accorded to upper-class and lower-class women. (She comes close to making another interesting point when she notes that the Nurse would not have had to endure the men's verbal and practical jokes had Juliet conveyed her own messages. That is, the difference between the classes functions to conceal a mutual dependence in service and patronage; women may not let solidarity with members of their gender carry greater weight than their alignments according to class difference.)

When Sarah comes to parent–child relations there seems to be a touch of envy, resentment and anxiety that those adolescents should have had wealth and security handed to them on the ancestral plate, unlike today's young people, who are 'faced with the reality of high unemployment figures and therefore must strive to achieve to their very best possible or basically, the life they have ahead of them will be far from easy.' Hence, it is suggested, those indolent 'golden lads and girls' deserve our contempt, rather than pity because 'all must, / like chimney sweepers, come to dust'. This is problematic if it suggests that one cannot or should not feel empathy through imagination. Sarah grants that we need an historical understanding, but her dismissal perhaps stems from her line of argument; to make any concessions of acceptance or approval might seem to weaken her case. When Sarah even more brusquely dismisses a centuries-long courtly love tradition as a 'boring waste of time', I am not sure, as a former medievalist, whether to be amused or appalled at this instance of a naive chronological snobbery – an assumption that modern ways must be superior. Her essay ends with an argument which counters this point: 'if a reader did not appreciate the era it was set in, they could focus on the wrong aspects of the play.'

Knowing much of what went on during lessons, it is clear to me that Sarah is rehearsing – in a highly competent manner – ideas that have already been established. The task does not require her to push onward to new knowledge, different thoughts, enhanced responses. (Indeed, some genre-based teachers would argue that it would be inherently inequitable to require students to be so inventive without benefit of a trial run staged in class.) The reading and writing demonstrated here are framed by principles of social justice for this world; the task did not ask Sarah to give full rein to her pleasurable engagement with an imaginative, dramatic narrative. (However, in another task for this unit students were encouraged to be more playful – to write their own script by either setting the story in the modern world or taking up the story some ten years later, assuming that Romeo and Juliet had faked their deaths, escaped Verona and married.)

In this task, but in a different way from Shaun's, what enables also constrains. The invitation to think otherwise than according to the premises of a cultural heritage discourse has been taken as an invitation to think like-wise, according to the counter-dominant norm of the classroom: Sarah seeks to strip the canonical text of its authority, and in so doing asserts the authority of a teacher's line. It would be regrettable if the move to critique has been so swift that it inhibits the development of those kinds of pleasure in reading and writing just mentioned – indeed, if it casts suspicion on them as somehow illicit.

All English teachers know how the heart sinks when our most earnestly imitative students produce a hideously distorted and smudged mirror of the brilliantly coloured and subtly detailed interpretations and arguments we offered them. So here Lindsay would not have modelled the faint car-icature of political correctness and the censure that might tip into censorship. Yet even the most sincere imitation is only a hair's breadth from parody, and whenever imitation becomes parroting, its very success is its failure. I do not believe that Sarah's essay should be so dismissed. It is not a garbled pastiche but the highly competent work of a fifteen year old whose understanding is still developing. The questions that this writ-ing poses for critical literacy teachers are these: what other forms of discipline would help Sarah to develop a more generous tolerance of the inhabitants of that imagined world? What taught practices of reading would encourage her to sustain a more scrupulous valuing before evalua-tion in writing? If we cannot find answers, then we are indeed setting up a hall of crazy mirrors rather than a palace of enlightenment.

A parable about assessment: blind tasting no. 3

In this third example a student offers a teacher a sketch of herself in rather unusual garb.

The literature class

Today's reading comes from the Book of Threats, chapter eleven, verses five to thirteen.

[5]In the beginning, Wendy said, 'Let the members of the class open their epistles to the twenty-seventh page.' And they did. The lord looked, and saw that it was good. The disciples turned to the task at hand and began their learning. On the eleventh minute, Wendy said, 'Truly I tell thee, those who believe in my word shall evermore be blessed. I am the teacher and the light, and I say this poem is good. For the poet's tongue speaks truly in the face of adversity.'

[6]But the crowd was dissatisfied, being slow to understand the word. They asked, 'But why is one good and one bad, that the most humble may become favoured by the Lord?' Again She spoke, and

the answer was this: 'Let not the right hand know what the left hand is doing. Let the words of truth be ever hidden in the language, and let it be enjoyable to all God's children. This is good poetry.'

[7]Once more disagreement arose amongst the crowd. Tobias, a prejudiced young boy, sought to sway the crowd against Her. 'Your words are false, Head of English. Is it not wrong to say and not to do? You tell us that good literature is enjoyable and may be hard to interpret, and yet when you mark our essays you do not take this into account. How are we to believe you?'

[8]Now Wendy loved her teaching, and therefore sought a way of showing her class the light. 'Is it not written in the scriptures that it is a sin to work on the sabbath? And yet I know of times when my Father will bless those who work on the sabbath.'

[9]'Blasphemy!' cried the crowd. But She went on to say: 'Let me tell you a story. There lived not far from here a shepherd named Daniel. Now Daniel was a pious man, who knew that it is easier for a camel to pass through the eye of a needle than a rich man to enter heaven. Consequently, he never attempted to live on more than was necessary. Now it came to pass that there came to the village where he lived a very cold winter, and all but one of his sheep died from the cold.

[10]'On one sabbath, his last remaining sheep fell down a pothole and would surely also have died if it had remained there all night. Now Daniel knew as well as any of you that on the seventh day we must rest, but knowing that his livelihood relied on this sheep, he prayed to the Lord for forgiveness and pulled the sheep from the hole, thus saving his family from sure starvation.

[11]'Thus to work on the sabbath is not always a sin. So too there are distinctions between good literature and good essays about literature.'

[12]And now those who saw the light fell to their knees and begged her blessing. She gave it to them gladly, saying, 'Let the little children come unto me, and my Father will receive you with open arms. Confess your sins, open your hearts, and you will be rewarded with everlasting life.'

[13]But then she turned to those still standing, and declaimed with a thunderous voice that echoed through the cloisters, 'Repent, sinners! It is said that those who take the good Lord's name in vain and call her Dr Spock, or those who do not believe I am the salt of the earth will be damned, and forever more doomed to suffer an eternal Friday night detention. This is the word of the Lord.'

Here endeth the lesson.

(Stephanie Reid, Year 11)

Producing readings

The joke of course is on me, and I was delighted to read it. The piece was produced in a year-long class which Year 11 students who had an interest in literature could opt to take in addition to their regular English lessons. The school I taught at in Victoria drew on a higher sociopolitical-economic group than does Park Ridge, and many of the students, including Stephanie, came from homes rich in literary resources and practices. A unit called 'Literature' might suggest it had nothing to do with critical literacy. Indeed, the term was unknown to Australian teachers in the mid-1980s, though some of us were working with poststructuralist ideas of the kind outlined in chapter two. In brief, my aim in that unit was to inquire into two aspects of regulation and judgement related to works categorised as 'literature'. One concerned conventions of form. So we read a variety of often unconventional literary texts – 'found poems', concrete and performance poems, experimental fictions and metafictions. These led to questions about 'the' form of 'the good short story' (as defined by Poe), or about 'poetic' language. They also brought to the surface for examination the students' reading practices and preferences and their assumptions about the bounds of the literary. The second, related aspect had to do with the production of literature, via publishing houses, magazines, literary prizes, reviewing, promotion and marketing. In this way too we were inquiring into how 'inherent' literary quality is, and how the 'value' of a literary work can be promoted.

As one of their pieces of assessment the students produced a folio of at least four creative writing experiments. These were in some way to be related to the texts read during the unit. For example, a topic that had come up in the course of reading one text might be explored by exploiting the form of another. Or a form might be parodied; or more than one genre combined in a collage; or a narrative point of view might be altered, and so on. That is, there was no one model form to be adhered to, as in much genre-based writing instruction; instead, there was to be play with and among a set of possibilities. (For more details and examples of student work see Morgan 1994f; for a sample of the unconventional Australian short fictions I used see Morgan 1987.)

In Victoria I was not obliged to specify the contextual and textual features of the genre in which students were to write – and given the individually experimental nature of the writing that would have been impossible in any but the most general terms. (This is the case when Park Ridge students also undertake unconventional writing.) Hence, though I had had some involvement with the students' planning and drafting, I did not know exactly what to expect when I came to read their writing, and in some cases, like Stephanie's, I had no prior knowledge of what I would find when I turned to a particular piece in a folio. Thus I needed to feel my way into each by careful reading, following intertextual and textual clues.

This does not mean that I did not have teacherly hopes, but these were of experimentation rather than predetermined expectations of form and substance. As the students knew, I wanted to be surprised, intrigued, delighted about textual play of the kind we had been exploring. What I valued in such writing – play based on understanding of the forms and language features of the texts they were working from – these were their only criteria and standards if they aimed to please me. This makes writing more risky for both students and teacher where so little is specified in advance. However, some framework had been provided for their writing in the given textual materials which offered structures and ideas. For students these may well be productive constraints that focus their freedom of choices, much as a window frame enables us to see a view.

Here is Stephanie explaining how she developed 'The literature class':

> Although this parody of the biblical style is directly related to the poem, 'News from Judaea' [by Bruce Dawe], I admit that my original idea for this piece came from a set of notes Fiona [a classmate] and I wrote to each other. That's where the 'Book of Threats' and 'Those who take the good Lord's name in vain . . .' ideas came from. The idea for writing this piece may have come from rereading those notes, but I think that the poem inspired the notes.
>
> The genre may have come from the poem, but the subject matter came from the 'good book' itself. [After considering other ideas] . . . I ended up choosing the teacher–class situation, as it was closer to the biblical situation of Jesus and his disciples.
>
> In order to get the right tone to this piece, I went through the New Testament, writing down phrases that seemed as if they would be applicable or appropriate to use. With this list in front of me, I was able to keep the tone more consistent and 'believable' than I think I would otherwise have been able to. Another thing I tried to incorporate into my writing was the fact that Jesus often used parables to teach. Since I was equating Dr Morgan with Jesus, she therefore needed to use the same technique.
>
> I don't think this piece was as much of a success as it perhaps should have been; the tone worked all right for some sections, but there seemed to be discrepancies in the style and the story. Oh well, at least I enjoyed writing it!

It is a fascinating insight into the complex, interwoven associations, deliberations and textual scrutiny involved in the creation of the piece. A number of points strike me afresh on rereading. First, to write in relation to other studied texts is to enter into a dialogue with them and with readers. This is rather different from Sarah's dialectic about a text by means of another text form faithfully followed. For while Stephanie's text also apparently conforms to the textual features of gospel narrative, in its form (as well as its intertextual references) it is a dialogue, with questions and answers including storytelling. In this it resembles Shaun's, and like his it is used to critique aspects of the classroom. The difference lies in the way Stephanie uses the form itself as a means of critique, through her biblical parody of Jesus and his disciples. (The substance of her points will be taken up shortly.)

Next, the possibilities of parody, so richly exemplified here, have perhaps been under-utilised by critical literacy teachers of a solemn persuasion. Yet it is a mode of thinking and writing that requires writers and readers to see otherwise than according to face value – and such a disposition to irony is congenial to the practice of critical literacy. For adolescents the invitation to parody can be particularly helpful, to engage them productively in very congenial ways. And by its means they may be able to mount a critique – often subtle and substantial – which they could not produce through 'straight' analytical exposition. The form itself can lead to a rich understanding of topic, textual effects and reading practices. Of course, it might instead be a kind of cop-out. It might be a case of having a bob each way – of holding acceptance and critique in balance and so refusing to make judgements about the matter being parodied. Or the parody might become an exercise in cynicism rather than in valuing something which the object of scrutiny falls short of. Or the reader may be left to complete the critique by reading it into or out of the text's ambiguous suggestions. (It is a duplicity that most perplexes teacher-readers as assessors. For they need to align the text's effect with the writer's intention and the text's features, so that their grading appears objective, based on qualities 'really' observable on the page, rather than subjective, depending on the subtlety of the teacher's reading.)

I do not read Stephanie's writing as a cop-out in either form or substance. But before we come to her analysis of my teaching and assessment practices, one last point about her last words: 'I enjoyed it!' We ought never to forget the pleasure of creating something new – of moving beyond what student and teacher have already rehearsed together. (That other work, of reiteration, can also have its own pleasures, of course.)

Stephanie takes a calculated risk in her critique, for unlike Shaun's it is not based on a teacher's invitation. But I was (and am) seduced by the wit and wry appropriateness of her parodic form – so she must have judged – and was therefore unlikely to take offence at this very shrewd and incisive analysis of authority in my literature classroom. This authority has several dimensions. One is the Book of Threats itself, which conjures up the system of school coercion that underwrites the activities of this exemplary classroom. The teacher's authority is (absurdly) messianic; student-disciples are required to believe in her word as dogma when she pronounces judgement on 'good' and 'bad' works of literature. Such authoritative judgements are necessary to guide followers when poetic truth is covert, 'hidden in the language'.

'Tobias' (Toby was a most outspoken and challenging member of class), leading the doubters, offers a subtle argument: granted that some poems are good and some bad; and granted that their interpretation is difficult. Nonetheless, such interpretative acts form the basis of one's judgements. Two questions arise therefore: why does the teacher not admit that students have such difficulty and take this into account when assessing their interpretations? And why will she not acknowledge that it may equally be difficult to differentiate between good and bad prose writing on poems and therefore show an equal provisionality in assessing student work? These questions make telling points about the professional expertise on which the teacher's authority in assessing poems or essays is founded. The speciously persuasive parable by which the Jesus-teacher seeks to answer these questions ultimately asserts that the rules can be changed and words do not always have the same force. 'So too,' Wendy concludes by a very wobbly step of logic, 'there are distinctions between good literature and good essays about literature.' With this fiat the teacher's judgemental powers remain undiminished: those who refuse to believe will be condemned to black marks – a Friday night detention being among the most feared punishments at that school and surely a symbolic substitution for fail grades on essays.

I need to continue to ask how close to my classroom authority this representation is. Was it as arbitrary, non-negotiable, absolute as Stephanie suggests? I would like to think not, remembering – I hope not inaccurately – that my discussions with students over texts and their written responses were more negotiated (but any of us must be most critical about what touches us most nearly). I would like to read this as a more general critique of the oppressiveness of teachers' power over knowledge and their control through assessment. It is certainly a useful reminder of how much students understand of the politics involved in this aspect of our work.

Before we return to those broad concerns, one last point needs to be made about Stephanie's critique. Hers is an act of 'spontaneous' rather than 'directed' critical literacy. It is made possible rather than mandated by the conditions of the curriculum and classroom activities, with their double focus on inquiry into the making of literary judgements and reputations and into the norms of 'proper' literature. I am too close to judge whether it may be the better for being unsolicited. Certainly no other class members made an equivalent move: they took their freedom within the constraints in other directions. What are the implications of this for further critical literacy practice?

A PANOPTICON, OR NEW SOUTH WALES?

These are the alternatives set up in the title of Jeremy Bentham's famous work on prison surveillance so famously used by Foucault (1979). To his twentieth-century eyes it looks a paradigm of many of the modern forms of 'biopower' – including schools – that work from beneath via the 'microtechniques' of examination. Like any poststructuralist I am suspicious of any tidy binary opposition between perfect prison and Australian penal settlement, between incarceration and exile, between the unimpeded gaze of the warder and the invisibility of the antipodes. So too I reject any simple alternatives between freedom (of an ideal critical literacy, in which activity and products should, like virtue, be their own reward) and constraints (of an oppressive system of assessments and ranking in current schooling). As the three tasks and the ensuing products have shown, what constrains or disciplines can enable, and what enables can also constrain or contain.

We have seen how teachers set constraints overtly relating to the assessment task itself with its topics, genres and conditions. They also frame students' work in ways which may be more or less covert, in the line they take in teaching and the values that underlie that. In turn teachers themselves are subject to constraints: there are watchers beyond the classroom and the school (principals, parents, system-wide assessment authorities) whose surveillance may be immediately directive or internalised as norms and expectations. And then of course there is surveillance from 'below', in the gaze of students alert to the signposts to success and to signs of injustice in distributing grades. And all are conditioned by discourses of education which set up a commonsense about the 'quality control' mechanisms of assessment. Critical literacy teachers may oppose such discourses but are still subject to them in their assessment practices.

Some of the tasks such teachers set are more productively constraining than others. The necessity of writing within the bounds of a genre may enable a student to produce a competent product, but this may be a rehearsal of what has already been established as correct. On the other hand, giving students greater freedom – of genre or approach – may free them up to make more inventive and critical play with generic conventions and to make moves in critique that have not already been choreographed. (However, this may not occur unless student writers already bring competencies and knowledge of forms and conventions and a critical understanding from previous learning.)

The Park Ridge teachers are examining such opportunities for more diverse and open assessment tasks. (A draft of this chapter, and our subsequent professional development discussions, is prompting them to carry out their own evaluations. Their critical literacy practice is still evolving.) These tasks are to include a balance between 'set', mainstream genres and those decided on by the students themselves as an appropriate means for persuading a particular audience. For example, in a Year 11 unit on the language of work, students might be developing a Home Page, a video, or a youth radio segment about out-work, or the effects of Australian consumer practices on workers in other countries, technology and work changes, or gender in workplaces. There will also be a better balance between more seriously analytical and more playful tasks such as satirical or parodic versions of texts like advertisements or fast food chain vouchers. For the assessment of such tasks students will increasingly write their own criteria based on group research of their chosen genre. And they will write or audiotape reflections in which they explain their choices of textual features and assess the effects they intended to achieve. Another way of breaking the mould will be to ensure that not all tasks are the culmination of the unit, but instead are designed to help students understand how particular genres work, in order to critique them. And even where tasks do conclude a unit, students are to be given opportunities to discuss and critique those tasks.

The writing we have examined in this chapter has certainly been limited, in that the product is expected to be the written work of isolated individuals, whatever class discussions or group conversations preceded it. That is only commonsense, according to any system of rank-ordering or profiling students. This individualism in practice may be close to the heart of the quarrel between critical literacy and normal schooling. It underplays the sociality of literacy in various ways. Certainly most English teachers allow for such collaboration in the classroom talk that is central to the processes of learning and in the preparation for the task itself. And many of them will pay at least lip-service to the cultural context of the writing and the social, communicative purposes that shape it. But when the actual audience of the writing is limited to the teacher alone, this curtails any effectiveness that such words might have in the world. There are of course examples of alternative kinds of tasks in which groups of students work together for some purpose they have defined for themselves, for an audience they deem most appropriate, in a form they have identified as most effective, and where the success of the endeavour consists not in a teacher's grade (or not exclusively) but in the responses from that audience the students were aiming at.

The Park Ridge teachers are keen to use such means to supplement the individualism of most assessment. More tasks will be undertaken by pairs or small groups. Some will be carried out in conjunction with the Social Education department in the school. And beyond the school, Lindsay is keen to link up with organisations involved in community action 'so that students can produce genuine texts that will perform genuinely critical functions'. He concedes that such liaisons may take time and work to establish – 'maybe, though, there's an opportunity to turn some responsibility over to students'.

Of themselves such 'sociable' alternatives are not the practice of critical literacy but might be especially congruent with it. Different viewpoints must be negotiated, tolerance of others shown, cooperation developed,

teams harnessed to a socially persuasive end, and so on. Such group pro-
ductions can be supplemented with individual written production logs or
reports where assessment requirements dictate – though, as Buckingham
and Sefton-Green (1994) demonstrate, such writing may come nowhere
near capturing the complexity of the conceptualising, decision making
and crafting embedded in the productive processes.

If this and other such modes of production are congruent with a critical
literacy, other questions still remain that emerged earlier in this chapter.
Can we, should we, work against our own partiality for a certain kind of
political and literary critique? We have seen how 'strong' teaching or
directive assignments may carry the risk of students' toeing the line (the
party line) or of rebelling against such non-conformist conformity. The
latter raises a related question for our partiality: how shall we deal with
political incorrectness (racism, sexism, heterosexism and the like) in students' reading and writing, especially when such an attitude has been
unconsciously assimilated? As our imagined scenario in chapter three suggested, it will not do simply to police it and rule it out in writing (with a
red pen) or gag it in speech: that is to substitute one dogma for another,
when both are deemed beyond debate. It will not do simply to accept this
as the student's 'personal' views or as evidence of a subcultural revolt
against any authority, any norms: that is to romanticise the individual or
the group. Sometimes it might be best by indirection to seek direction out.
We might have students transform a text by moving from one language
mode or genre to another, and from one ideological position to another in
role play. Such acts of transformation can also transform understanding:
they can be a way of students' acquiring metacognitive and discursive
understanding. And they might also therefore lead to some shifts of
attitude.

The matter of attitudes returns me to my question about partiality for a
certain line in political and literary critique. How one answers that question will depend on how one defines success for teachers and students. If
the aim of critical literacy is to develop students whose eyes are opened,
the success of their demonstrations of this capacity is the measure of the
teacher's success in demystification. Such products must be 'sincere':
'genuinely' thought and felt by the students themselves, for then the
efficacy of the teacher is certified. But if the aim of critical literacy is to
begin the always incomplete process of developing secondary students'
disposition for principled evaluation of cultural products, for metacognition and self-reflexivity, then the substance of any critiques and the
correctness of any line matter less than that attitude, for it is the latter that
indicates success in teaching and learning.

Most critical literacy teachers would argue that each outcome needs to
be complemented by the other: that the steam engine of disposition needs
the tracks of a line of sociopolitical critique to run along if it is to make

progress beyond the station of scepticism. Together in any individual these aspects amount to a kind of competence which is conceptually complex and affectively intricate – not at all easy to pin down for examination. And so educators and teachers may desire to legislate for something simpler, more definable as a critical literacy behaviour or product that can be assessed. My nightmare is that a critical literacy as educational orthodoxy might become a constraining and containing list of ideal or typical 'skills' or 'behaviours'. But if I fear a statement like this one I have just invented – 'students [will] critically analyse, evaluate and seek to influence the power and status of institutions which maintain the privilege of canonical texts' – I need to ask how different it is in intention and effect from the units described which led to Sarah's and Stephanie's writing. Perhaps only in specifying demonstrable outcomes which may all too readily become mandatory. It may become a hegemonic practice even as it legislates the form that critical resistance to hegemony is to take and the behaviours that will enact it. I do not want 'my' critical literacy to be quite so relentlessly directive in governing students' behaviour.

Lowering our sights somewhat from this cultural critique, the question of literacy skills, like matters of knowledge and attitude addressed above, must be addressed by critical literacy teachers. Most critical literacy teachers agree with critical sociolinguists (e.g. Fairclough 1989, Gee 1990) that 'literacy' in its fullest manifestation becomes nothing less than cultural critique. The kinds of competence required for such activity are highly complex. Meanwhile, for students like Shaun, Stephanie and Sarah and their schoolmates in earlier years of schooling, what interim 'skills' or capacities in reading, writing and orality are desirable and appropriate? (That is, what norms shall we establish as the aims of a critical literacy teaching within secondary English?) In many respects these may look rather like the reading and writing abilities more traditional teachers have long been fostering: rhetorical effectiveness in writing through full appreciation of the various resources of language, close attentiveness to nuance and implication in reading. The challenge is to satisfy our critics – including especially ourselves – that we can and do develop such competencies better, as well as through different means to different ends, by means of our disciplines; that we do encourage valuing and enjoying literary and other texts as well as evaluating and critiquing them. To balance the scales in this way, and not just rush to removing the scales from students' eyes: this requires of teachers the skill of a Daniel. In what matters ultimately, our students, in their dispositions, knowledge and skills, serve to assess us even as we assess them for those capacities.

CHAPTER 7

POSTMODERN CLASSROOMS ON THE BORDERS?

1 HOMEPAGE

In its original form this chapter was a hypertext. You will have to unbind this linear version by creating links from one segment to another, one phrase or concept or argument to another, as your imagination, memory or anticipation suggest. Give the text different colours, fonts, formats. Add pictures, sound, movies.

This digitised, hypermedia text-world is increasingly the home environment of young people across the globe. It brings new challenges and possibilities for critical literacy teachers and theorists. Some of them are gestured towards here. For example, the 'real' or fictional status of some of the teachers and students and events described here is deliberately kept uncertain, to raise questions about the authority of texts and of teachers whose own authority have depended on the apparent permanence and reliability of such texts. But this kind of text, like the new order it brings in, is always still in the making. Herein lie opportunities, to contribute to this world – as readers in a hypertext environment could 'write back' and so write onwards.

> The conceptual space of electronic writing . . . is characterised by fluidity and an interactive relationship between writer and reader.
>
> (Bolter 1991: 11)

2.1 GENTLE READER

Over to you, dear reader

A text is not so much an artifact as an event. It becomes what it is as you turn the pages one after another. Texts may also tell stories about events. This hypertext contains several such stories. Each story, each commentary on it, presents itself to you within the frames of the screen. You can shuffle story with argument with poem with image with voice with video with quotation, until the frames that separate them begin to dissolve.

The text shapes itself to your interest. Words yield to the pressure of your curiosity. Thus the text is what you perform as you amble down this alley or that and crisscross mall or park in the city of text.

2.2 TEXT CITY

I like to map the oral metaphor of the forum upon the topographic metaphor of the city of text. The city of text describes the new public space of the information age, including the electronic text itself. For the electronic text is always a forum even in isolation, teeming with multiple voices, surprising vistas, exotic sounds, or the possibilities of them.

(Joyce 1995: 125)

3.1 BOUNDARY RIDER 1

Saving, then quitting, Lucy glances at the time display on the computer. Half an hour to spare. Year 7 and the teachers are already piling on the homework.

'Mum. I've finished. Can I get on the MOO for a while?'

'Sure, Luce.'

With swift moves made automatic through long practice, Lucy first checks her Home Page on the Web to see how many people have read it. She'll have to change the order of names of her best friends after Carly was so mean to her at lunch. Then she goes into the Owl's Nest, goes east and north to the Discussion Den and joins the conversation as Rosey. . . .

'Your fingers are going to drop off, girl.'

Dad pats her shoulder in passing. Wow, been on for over an hour. Time for her shower. Tomorrow's a big day at school with the netball finals.

Do you want to know more about this student and her education? **Yes / No**

3.2 MOO

Sometimes called a MUD (a multi user domain). A MOO is a MUD which is Object Oriented; an electronically linked space for writing in which a number of participants interact by composing a conversation in real-time. Each player types in speech or descriptions which then appear on the other players' screen for them to respond to.

3.3 OWL'S NEST

The following is an extract from an online discussion held on 5.6.96

between Wendy Morgan (as Foxymoron) and Lucy (as Rosey). Here is where the conversation occurs:

The Foyer

The foyer is spartan, but clean. Benches are fixed to
each wall and a heavy door swings to the west.
Construction noises can be heard from nearby rooms.
To the north are some swing doors. Above, a holosign
flickers: The Discussion Den. Beside the far wall, an
old teachtec stands, broken and unused for some time.
It doesn't seem to be connected to the ComboBus
anymore. People often wonder why it's left there. To
the south a passageway leads to the Conference
Centre. A spiral staircase leads to the basement
below.

. . . Rosey pours a tall glass of lemonade with a
twist of lemon and fills another glass with
orangeade.
Foxymoron says, 'Cheers. Here's to your good health.'
Rosey clanks glasses.
Rosey says, 'I like Diversity University, the new MOO.
It's interesting because you can go to lots of places
and there are usually quite a few people online.
Programming does interest me, I have tried to program a
few things, so far I haven't had much success.'
Rosey sips quickly on the orangeade.
Foxymoron says, 'But you have got a Home Page,
haven't you?'
'Yes, I'm alright at HTML programming.'
Foxymoron says, 'So if I wanted to go look at your
Home Page, where would I
find it?'
'On the Owl server —
http://owl.qwut.edu.au/~visitor1.'
Foxymoron raises eyebrows in question.
'Oops sorry . . . owl.qut.'
Foxymoron says, 'I see. I'll certainly go look.'
Rosey says, 'Look at this trick I picked up. . . .
Rosey oO (wonders about . . .). It looks a little
like thought bubbles.'
Foxymoron smiles and frowns. Foxymoron says, 'I see
what you mean. Good trick!'

Rosey smiles.

Foxymoron says, 'On another subject, are your friends interested in computers, Moos and so on? Or do they mostly play computer games?'

Rosey says, 'There is only one person at school who has the Internet, Stephanie, but quite a few others have computers.'

'I guess you're lucky having a "teacher" at home to help you.'

Rosey smiles. 'Well, yeah, I am.'

Foxymoron says, 'Do your teachers know more than you about HTML, the Internet and so on, do you think?'

Rosey says, 'My teacher at school has practically never heard of the Web! Our librarian is more advanced but I don't think she knows more than me.'

Rosey yawns.

Foxymoron watches someone at the next table knock his drink with his elbow all over his nice white shirt, and says, 'Does that bother you, that you know more than your teachers?'

'No. I normally don't talk about it . . . but today I did an oral report on the Internet.'

Foxymoron says, 'Do you find stuff on the Net that you use for school projects?'

'Yes I do. Lots of my information is found on the Internet, Web mainly.'

Rosey fills a large metal cup up with thick milkshake!

Foxymoron says, 'OK. What do you do with the information you get from the Web? Download it, remember it, what? — I mean for school work.'

Rosey says, 'I print it out from the page and take it to school. Our printer is black + white but the text is good. Hmm . . . I might as well tell you what applications I use. Netscape for Web, Netscape Mail for Mail and QUTNet for Telnet . . . though I used to use something else, forgot the name.'

Foxymoron says, 'Sounds good. Do your mates at school wish they had that stuff too?'

Rosey says, 'Maybe they do wish that . . . they call me "square" for going and doing stuff for school work. Really annoying.'

Foxymoron says, 'Of course. They're envious, I guess.'

Rosey sucks her long straw definitely. Foxymoron
looks sideways at the milkshake. Rosey grins
toothily.
Foxymoron says, 'If you could have a wish come true,
what would you wish could be invented for computers?'
'I suppose sort of like . . . well I guess this is
already invented but just to talk into something and
somebody else could hear it from somewhere else . . .
sort of combination telephone and MOO. And perhaps
you could smile and someone could see your smiles.
That sort of thing.'
Foxymoron says, 'Agreed that would be good. Instant
television and telephone combined.'
Rosey nods, takes her straw out and puts her lips
onto the cold metal cup to spllurp the last drops of
milkshake. Foxymoron looks sideways: manners!
Foxymoron sips neatly to make the point about the
younger generation. Rosey orders a plate of fresh
imported strawberries and pops the first one into her
mouth neatly. Rosey offers one kindly to Foxymoron.
Foxymoron with exaggerated care takes the second
strawberry.
Rosey says, 'Dad came past just then and said my
fingers will drop off soon.'
Foxymoron says, 'OK, I've just looked at my watch
and seen how long we've
been in this place! Time flies like an owl when
you're having fun.'
Rosey smiles. 'Would you like me to show you some
other rooms and then we
can go?'
'Yes please!'
Rosey says, 'Let's go north.'

North
You walk onto the veranda. The view is superb, you
are surrounded by
mountains and blue sky. You inhale the fresh air and
you feel like lying down.

Veranda
There is a long chair to lie on here. Rosey sighs
with contentment. . . .

4.1 BOUNDARY RIDER 2

That same afternoon in his bedroom Jason was getting ready to go surfing. Old Mr Thommo had told them to find out what the ancient Greek hero Ulysses did in the Trojan War. Tomorrow they'd be getting stuck into the CD-ROM of some poem about him returning home. He could have checked out the info in the library after school, but he wanted to borrow a new computer game from a mate round the corner and he could find out what he needed about the old guy at home.

So now, he's scanning the multimedia encyclopedia CD. Yep: Greeks, Trojan War, Odysseus, Penelope. . . . Even some old vases under Art. Moving easily between the CD and his wordprocessing program, he enters notes about the key information.

He could knock the socks off old Thommo with this one. He hops onto the Internet, checks out a couple of library catalogues, does a quick search. Pretty boring. Time for a break: that site Nikko mentioned about the latest game catalogues: yep, here's the address on the back of his school diary.

. . . Hell. Where did the time go? He'll have to burn rubber to get this stuff done: he'd promised Billy the Kid Brother they'd throw a few baskets before dinner. Jase downloads the relevant documents and does a cut and paste job, imports a graphic of the map of Europe and a Greek-looking warrior from his Clip Art files, uses his design and layout program to create a newspaper page with banner ('Trojan Times'), headlines ('Greeks Offer Peace'; 'Huge Gift-Horse Ours, says Ulysses'), and brief copy, with a pen portrait of that trickiest Greek of them all, Ulysses, who came up with the idea of the horse. For good measure (and to balance the picture of the warrior) Jase inserts the map showing Ulysses' goal, the far western island of Ithaca. He prints it out in colour.

That'll do; better, probably, than what the rest of the Year 10s will hand in. Pity there wasn't time to turn it into a hypermedia event. Now to that computer game. Who was it Gazza said you had to be careful of: the hooded guy with the bazooka? Wait on, though: there was that address on the Net he'd bookmarked where you could get advice on the cheat codes. . . .

Do you want to know more about this student and his education? **Yes / No**

4.2 THERE'S NO SUCH THING AS A FREE LUNCH

Add Video Inserts from CD-ROM of IBM Illuminated Books 'Ulysses' as QuickTime Movies

5.1 THE PHANTOM OF THE OPUS, or, WILL THE REAL AUTHOR PLEASE STAND UP?

Notes while first 'reading' 'Ulysses' CD-ROM (Illuminated Book)

10th November

Began by refreshing my memory of the poem by Tennyson. Had meant to read right through, but soon I'm checking out different dramatised readings – for example, how Ulysses could say 'This is my son, mine own Telemachus' with pride, resignation, scorn etc. This leads me to see if I can find out information about Tennyson's family relations. Disappointment – as far as I can see, there's nothing in the hypertext about the author or the Victorian context at all. NB: in teaching, would need to supply this. Pity to have to go outside the text to books. After this hype those print materials would seem less interesting to students.

The makers of this hypertext seem to have their own rather narrow ideas of what counts as info. Whatever's included is therefore thrown into high relief, and other potentially useful materials are likely to be passed over.

. . . How much seepage there is between the lines of the poem and the information that's supposed to enrich it. I'm enjoying this kind of osmosis – but I'm not concentrating on the poem itself in a sustained, absorbed kind of way, as I would have done if I'd read it on the page of an anthology.

Colour and movement, sound and image: if this is the new (inter)face of old texts, let's have more of it, say I! My kids will certainly think so. The old fogeys in the staff room would be shocked down to their long white socks at this kind of (mis)treatment of a work of literature. This isn't a work of literature fenced off with warning signs that say: 'Literary Mansion', 'Trespassers will be prosecuted', 'Keep to the paths'. It's more like a house of cards made from a pack you can shuffle at random

. . . I've just got to where they've introduced Joseph Campbell. I can just hear my students saying, 'Who the hell is this old guy? Why should I listen to him mumbling about some hero with a thousand faces?' After all, these kids are living in a world where fame lasts fifteen minutes, not a world of eternal universal symbols of heroism. So they'll browse the hypertext for something more fun to focus on – the shots of Tiennanmen Square, I bet. And so they won't hear the argument about heroism that threads through those images of heroes, let alone be in a position to argue back about it.

One other problem too. The kids are likely to think this is all there is to be known about Ulysses – the hero and the poem – when there's such a wealth of information they can select from. If they're under the illusion that they can manipulate all the knowledge there is they may fall into the delusion that they have power over knowledge. And so ironically they come under the text's power to define that world for them. – Not if I can help it!

5.2 MINDFUL TEACHING OR MINDLESS TEACHING MATERIALS?

Our paradigm is to show students how language works. Ultimately, the idea was that someone could use these tools to get more out of literature – to see all these levels at which we read and understand. It's a higher-order literacy, if you will.

(Allen DeBevois (1991), Creative Director, IBM Illuminated Books)

5.3 BIG MACS: FAST FOOD FOR THE BRAIN

our engineers, not our poets, are the unacknowledged legislators of our time.

(Postman 1988: xiii)

Multimedia . . . gives you a direct pipeline into the brain. . . . The power of full-motion video combined with interactivity allows every person to discover knowledge in the pattern that fits their paradigm for learning – the way they learn best, individualised.

(James Dezell Jr, President, IBM Eduquest, quoted in Reeves 1993: 80)

Imagine a classroom with a window on all the world's knowledge. Imagine a teacher with the capability to bring to life any image, any sound, any event. Imagine a student with the power to visit any place on earth at any time in history.

(John Sculley, CEO, Apple Computers, quoted in Reeves 1993: 79)

Yes, I know this is supposed to be self-paced, 'permissive' learning, in which students can discover their own path through a database of reference materials via a network of choices. But I think this is inter-passivity rather than interactivity. Look at that metaphor, 'a direct pipeline into the brain'! – that's a computer nerd's view of education.

This is information as 'infotainment' (I like that word, it contains the suggestion of containment as well as entertainment). These piles of materials are mindless in themselves: they need the active minds of teachers sifting through them to help students learn from them. – That is, it's the pile, the collection that's mindless, not the materials themselves: they're certainly offering a viewpoint they want students to buy.

These computer company directors claim that hypermedia opens a window on the world, as if it's glass that gives a clear view of reality. How naive do they think we are? Any view offers a perspective on the 'reality' it depicts. They'd have us believe hypermedia is a classroom without walls – but the walls are still there, and all the more dangerous for appearing so transparent.

So it's all the more important that any such CD-ROMs are presented by mindful teachers who work with and against what's on offer, to extend and question it. If we don't, education becomes 'edutainment', and hypermedia merely 'hyperMTV', as McDaid puts it (1991: 457).

5.4 EDUTAINMENT

INTERVIEWER: How do you feel when you're playing computer games?

O: Oh, if I do something wrong and I get killed, I get angry. And that's why I don't play much with computers. 'Cos I don't get past levels and I get angry at myself. I feel excited because I'm going to get past it, but then I don't. [Year 5 student]

INTERVIEWER: How does it feel when you get to the end of a game?

N: You feel so relieved because if you've been at it for about a month you think, 'Finally I've finished!'

J: You feel, well I feel, well you get all hot in the room, you're holding your breath to finish the game.

INTERVIEWER: What do you think about these computer games?

K: They're dumb!

J: Yeah! [laughing]

I: But you still play them?

J: Well, it's not the story behind them that makes us want to play them. It's what the game is actually like when you play it.

K: If there was a game called Cinderella –

J: If there was a game called Cinderella it's probably be really boring.

J: There's always a really big bad guy at the end of the game and you've gotta beat him.

K: Yeah.

J: If you beat him, you've won. You've won the game. [Year 5]

(excerpts from Smith, *et al.* 1996)

5.5 CRITICAL LITERACY AT WORK WITH / AGAINST THE TEXT

1 Critique

Texts and their meanings are always historically, socially, and ideologically situated.

So I'm asking: Why did Tennyson choose Ulysses? – tensions between the masculine world of exploration and the feminine world of domesticity?

Why did the IBM Illuminated Books developers choose the poem 'Ulysses'? – much studied in the USA, hence rewarding to an educational publisher?

Texts and their meanings are always capable of multiple readings.

So I'll ask, How would a Vietnamese student read this, whose community had been destroyed by the 'protection' of American soldiers like those depicted as heroes here?

How would historians read this, who think that the Greeks launched their thousand ships not to rescue Helen but to break Trojan control of the grain trade routes through the Hellespont?

Texts and their meanings are always partial (interested and never final).

So I'm asking – Which aspects of the story that we know from Homer's poem aren't presented in Tennyson's or the CD-ROM version? (Like cloves of a garlic bulb, these other parts of the story might give a different flavour.)

Texts and their meanings are always political (privileging or marginalising someone's interests).

So I'll ask – What political interests seem to be at work in the ways heroism is being represented? And who might disagree with this view?

Consider these women who are singled out as heroes:
    Joan of Arc (a cross-dressing activist saintly in shining armour)
    Mother Teresa (the embodiment of motherly self-sacrifice)
    Marie Curie (the aseptic scientist)

2 From Critique to (Re)Construction

We have asked, How does this text construct a version of reality and knowledge? and
What is left out of this story?

So I'll be gathering additional stories and information to set alongside this version.

We have asked, How does this text represent the ideal or intended reader and set up a position for reading? and
What other position might there be for reading?

Therefore I'll be setting other viewpoints alongside those in the CD-ROM, to see how these alter our angle for viewing.

We have asked, How does this text set up its authority and encourage your belief? and
How can you deconstruct its authority?

So my students and I will need to examine the structures as well as the content of the hypertext. (We'll want to see how it encourages you to think this is all the knowledge that's relevant to the poem.)

And we'll be considering how we'd add links to other texts with divergent, even opposed viewpoints, so that the authority of any text wasn't absolute, but relative to other texts and their viewpoints.

That is . . . we would need to author a supplementary hypertext: 'Ulysses Unbound' or 'Ithaca Revisited'.

6.1 JASON OF THE CYBERNAUTS

'Snapshot': Case Study no. 1

Nicholas is twelve years old. He is a proficient touch keyboarder. There are both Apple and IBM-type computers in his home. He and his older siblings spend time on the home computers daily – in a range of activities including school work. By contrast, there is no permanent computer in his classroom. Rather, two classrooms and the library share a single computer of limited capacity and with limited software. The classroom houses the computer for one third of the school year. The students are rostered to use the computer, in pairs, for half an hour per week. The pairs go to the computer when it is their rostered time to do so, regardless of what is going on in class. Most students spend their weekly half hours playing educational games . . . or 'publishing' work they have already written in class, using a beginner level desktop publishing program. The teacher rarely intervenes, and when he does it is usually to restore discipline.

The episode in question sees Nicholas seated at the computer. He has to produce a short recount of Athletics Day for the school magazine. As a competent keyboarder and a proficient computer user since reaching school age, Nicholas' preferred mode is to compose directly onto a machine. . . . Nicholas tries to start his story. He quickly becomes frustrated and complains. 'I hate this computer,' he says, rolling his eyes. The program is too basic for his skills and knowledge. It is a lock-step, linear program which is not at all flexible. It begins with commands for inputting the heading, then for moving to the first paragraph, and so on. The default font on the screen is, for someone like Nicholas, insultingly large. He wants to go directly to composing text, and does so – only to find his text has gone into the heading space. He tries to select different functions, but cannot break easily out of the lock-step.

He gets frustrated – 'Can you believe this stuff?' – gives up on composing, and spends the next half hour keying 'Athletics Day' into the heading space, in an old English font, alternately enlarging and reducing it. . . . At the end of his half hour, with the story not written, Nicholas asks for an extension. The teacher is not impressed, but agrees. Nicholas takes the assignment home and produces it inside of fifteen minutes.

(Knobel and Lankshear 1995)

6.2 SUPERVISOR'S NOTES TO CH. 5 DRAFT 5TH MAY

Fascinating snapshot. I look forward to your analysis. Meanwhile, I'll just add a few comments, and let's discuss them when we meet next –

Nicholas and his friends – and parents and the wider community too – value the skilled use of computer technologies to inform and communicate, manipulate and control images and words. But these skills are increasingly not to be found in schools and teachers, books and libraries – those traditional sources of knowledge. So young people go elsewhere for their learning and recreation. And naturally enough, like Nicholas, they come to scorn the old-fashioned limitations of school. (I'm not blaming the teachers: they're often as frustrated as the students are by the lack of hardware, software and curricular opportunities.) As a result schools risk losing their status as the legitimate means of teaching the forms of literacy that society values. So computers become the covert teachers of the next generation.

. . . May become. . . . If teachers aren't able to take up the challenge. It seems to me that they can no longer operate in a medium and a language that are very different from their students'. They can't afford to rely on different ways of making sense (informing), different ways of making a case (persuading) and different ways of making an effect (moving) that simply don't apply in the world they're educating their students for. I don't mean educating for conformity with that world, but for critical use and transformation. What do you think?

W.

7.1 SHORING UP THE BULWARKS AGAINST THE SHIFTING SANDS

TUMAN: The immense retrieval powers of computers are subtly and irrevocably eroding the status of the independent, unified text – the basis of literary study and, by extension, reading instruction this century (1992a: 8).

MORGAN: If I may be blunt, your idea of the unified, independent text is a bit of fiction anyway, and one we no longer find so credible at the end of this century. You know as well as I do all the theories about intertextuality – how one text draws on, alludes to others. But what I really want to challenge is your metaphor of 'eroding'. I'm not interested in piling up the sandbags around fragile monumental works of literature. I'd rather think in terms of another metaphor. Suppose instead we're expanding the edifice: adding a lean-to here, a cantilevered balcony there, throwing out a wing to the south and a gazebo in the shrubbery. The work indeed may be enriched by such additions, for more uses, more inhabitants. And its status may also be enhanced. I don't see here an erosion of the ground of literary study.

TUMAN: Does your English involve immersion in literature or submersion in electronic culture? Students are drowning in a sea of infotainment; I want to preserve an island for the best of humanity.

7.2 THE CASE OF THE DISAPPEARING AUTHOR

Above all, hypertext challenges our sense that each book is a complete, separate, and unique expression of its author.

(Bolter 1992: 22)

Notes towards a new story
Character 1: the hypertext reader

Prime suspect for death of author as sole creator of text.

1   Identifying characteristics

1.1 Inter/active in making choices re direction of navigation. Such choices assemble the text as reader reads. Thus the reader 'authors' the text by affecting and effecting it. Reader may have power to record path taken for others, thus become author in turn.
1.2 May become aggressive – handle text without proper respect by ripping through it in pursuit of own ends.
1.3 Occasionally intrudes annotations, comments which become merged with author's text (fingerprints of style a clue to distinguish author-author from reader-author?).

2   Possible motives / gains

Reader pursues own desire for information and power it brings, or follows curiosity concerning narrative and how reader can manipulate this.

3   Circumstances favourable to crime against author

Introduction of digital technology.

4   Twists to story

4.1   Murder victim (author) found to be accessory before the fact
      – that is, hypertext author creates for reader links and pathways; to
      allow reader opportunity for re-composition, author must let go some
      control over sequence, content.
4.2   Author's revenge: the killer brought to justice –
      when reader becomes co-author in making choices that effect the
      text, reader cannot judge, even condemn, the text without judging his
      / her own choices / contributions.

7.3 THE DOCUVERSE

(Docuverse is a universe of linked documents.)

> In a fully hypertextual library, readers will be able to choose any of the
> existing paths, or define a new path, through the materials they are
> reading and perhaps leave that path for other readers to follow if they
> choose. What we get from this speculation is a vision of the library as an
> encompassing hypertextual book in which everyone can read and
> everyone can add his or her own writing.
>
> (Bolter 1992: 23)

7.4 A LIBRARIAN'S VIEW

```
Date: Wed. 06 Mar 1996 11:18:17 +1000 (EST)
From:
Subject: COMMENT ABOUT THE INTERNET
To: w.morgan@qut.edu.au
MIME-version: 1.0
--------------------------------------------------
```

I thought the following comment might have some
general interest.

   The net is like a huge vandalised library. Someone
   has destroyed the catalog and removed the front
   matter, indexes, etc., from hundreds of thousands
   of books and torn and scattered what remains . . .
   and the walls are covered with graffiti. 'Surfing'
   is the process of sifting through this disorganised
   mess in the hope of coming across some useful
   fragments of text and images that can be related to
   other fragments. The net is even worse than a

> vandalised library because thousands of additional
> unorganised fragments are added daily by the myriad
> cranks, sages, and persons with time on their hands
> who launch their unfiltered messages in cyberspace.
>
> Michael Gorman, quoted in Linkage: Newsletter of the
> QUT Library, 1996, 6,1: 11)

7.5 THE VIRTUAL SHOPPING MALL, or MANAGING THE KNOWLEDGE ECONOMY

Insert cartoon of woman with anguished face searching handbag. Caption reads, 'Oh no! I've left my technological skills at home!'

7.6 DRIFT NETTING

Just as a library void of intelligent, skilled teachers and students capable of utilising its resources is merely a warehouse, multimedia without the interpretative acts of learners is only a collection of textual, graphical and audio elements.

(Reeves 1993: 80)

Is it possible for the ascendancy of hypertext to do anything but push literacy in the direction of information management?

(Tuman 1992b: 78)

7.7 THE DISCRETE CHARM OF THE BOURGEOIS BOOK

The reader can now deconstruct the work even before reading it in a continuous manner, a practice some would recoil at, not only on the grounds of bourgeois taste but as an educational and political issue.

(Aronowitz 1992: 134)

Further notes on navigating with 'Ulysses' (the CD)

When I'm 'reading' a hypermedia document I move between reading the text (print, video, graphics, whatever) and reading the text's structure – its links. That is, I alternate between looking at it and looking through it. – 'Looking through' in two senses: seeing what's underneath or to one side of the screen, and browsing by means of those links. I wonder if this electronic environment also encourages a further kind of 'seeing through the text' – seeing how it works to persuade us to accept its view of the world. Or is it rather that a hypertext can so dazzle us with the speed of the connections it and we can make that we're blinded to the argument it carries?

8.1 ONLY CONNECT

Associative thinking is more difficult to follow than linear thinking. Linear thinking specifies the steps it has taken; associative thinking is discontinuous – a series of jumps like . . . the movements of the mind in creating metaphor.

(Slatin 1990: 874)

The emphasis upon linking materials in hypertext stimulates and encourages habits of relational thinking in the users.

(Landow 1989: 189)

Douglas Hofstadter has suggested that the perception of relatedness is a defining characteristic – perhaps the defining characteristic – of intelligent behaviour.

(Slatin 1990: 877)

A user may just glance over the surface of a body of knowledge without integrating it into a personal knowing.

(Barrett 1988: xx)

Hypertext is weakest when it comes to spelling out what these relationships entail.

(Slatin 1990: 881)

8.2 ARGUMENT

Hypertexts are, in more than a manner of speaking, three dimensional. Fuguelike, they can carry on an argument at several levels simultaneously. and if we cannot read them exactly simultaneously, we can switch back and forth with great rapidity.

(Lanham 1989: 283)

8.3 SCEPTIC [THINK] TANK

OBJECTION # 437

Their proposition

That hypertext with its associative links enhances the synthesising power of thinking.

Our doubts

That the medium itself does not provide a synthesis.
That the associations a reader makes may be merely haphazard.
That the habits of mind encouraged by this medium may detract from the development of
(a)   sustained argumentation in a text and
(b)   the reader's capacity to follow a logical argument.

See for example Tuman (1992a: 267): 'the very notion of critical thought may be tied to print technology and, thus, . . . new computer-based forms of litercy may well engender different and not necessarily better (or more "critical") modes of thought.'

Recommendations

That teachers develop students' capacities for argumentation by means of discussion and analysis of texts, including hypertexts.

That special attention be given to covert lines of argument in hypertext set up by texts juxtaposed by means of the authored links.

That teachers work with the tendency to irony already present in adolescents and fostered by hypertext juxtapositions as a way to encourage critical habits of thinking.

8.4 THINKING ELECTRONICALLY

I want to learn how to write and think electronically – in a way that supplements without replacing analytical reasoning.

(Ulmer 1989: x)

8.5 DANGEROUS LIAISONS

The following excerpt is taken from the print-out of part of an electronic discussion group on hypertext.

A: I'd like to ask if you people think that argumentation as we know it is likely to go the way of the dodo, in an age of electronic text. By argumentation I mean a logical sequence of propositions, with major and minor premises, super- and sub-ordinate points, all leading to a conclusion. Here's a quote from Ulmer (1992: 162) that might set us thinking:

> The most essential practice of print writing is argumentation — exploiting . . . expositional logic . . . and leading readers in a linear fashion through a body of information oriented by a problem to a univocal conclusion or solution. The most essential practice of hypermedia is to provide the whole set of possibilities . . . through which many different arguments or lines might be traced, or even by means of which alternative framings (other than that of 'problem') might be arranged.

B: For a start, just look at the irony of Ulmer arguing this point in book form, by the very kind of argumentative procedures he evidently thinks are going to be superseded. And you're inviting us to display the same kind of logical thinking in an electronic discussion space!

C: Tuman makes a point in some of his writing (e.g. 1992a, 1992b) that the kind of associative thinking (hence reading and writing) fostered by hypertext could lead to the demise of that disciplined kind of argumentation, carefully constructed by a writer and equally carefully followed by a reader. Schwartz too asks (1992: 106):

> Are the author's traditional rhetorical goals (informing, persuading, moving) achievable with the non-determinacy of order in hypertext and the loss of coherence when pearls of text can be strung in a variety of ways?

D: 'Informing' can still be done in an electronic text-world, even if the author doesn't control the body of information (and no author ever did). 'Moving' has always taken a variety of forms, depending on the cultural context (Roman forum, television advertisement), the immediate social situation (pillow talk, classroom) and the kinds of language that are most calculated to persuade. To 'persuade' — to convince your audience that you're right — you need not adopt formal or informal logic of the kind practised by Greek philosphers, medieval scholars, or barristers. Most of the world gets by pretty well without that developed kind of argumentation.

A: You might be right. I'm thinking that an individual point of argument (propositions and what supports them) is likely to be located in a text space (a node). In that case, the argumentation — that is, the movement from one point to another ('therefore it follows', 'on the other hand, however') will be located in the links. And here we come to the heart of the matter: since the reader activates the links, it's the reader who will generate the argumentation by inferring the nature of the connection.

C: Traditionally, argumentation has meant dialectic — investigating the truth of a proposition by logical means in order to arrive at a conclusion. This discussion group is dialogic — we're having a conversation in which viewpoints are shared and negotiated in a more democratic manner. Hypertext is polylogic — offering many voices, many views, many texts, none of them synthesised into one argument, one conversation.

8.6 A WISH LIST

From hypertext I want
the play of words and texts / the play
   of a phone wire strung between poles /
the fun and games texts play
   / snakes and ladders, mirror mazes /
the pleasure of sinuous moves
   / (dis)appearing
   sideways /
the sharp delight of corners
   / light and dark, image as ground /
the play of minds weaving with / alongside / against each other
give me wit for my wisdom

9.1 THE UNBOUNDED CLASSROOM

Here the new technologies will make possible new forms of communication and the new social relations that follow.

Here will be more 'writers' and 'readers', and more 'teachers': other students, teachers in other classrooms online, and adults – experts, informants – in the local or global community. The roles of 'teacher' and 'student' are more likely to be exchanged in this world of circulating information.

9.2 THE SHIFTING FRAME OF LITERACY

Technology (here the ability to integrate text and graphics and to work with screens in a non-linear fashion) is finally a driving force in how we communicate and in turn establish, through curriculum and elsewhere, the norms for proper communication – that is, what it means to be literate.

(Tuman 1992a: 266)

If this is what it means to be a literate adult in our society, what must a literacy curriculum look like, to educate today's students to become such adults tomorrow?

INDEX

- The virtual classroom and its teachers
- Cyborg students
- A new literacy: comprehending

- A new literacy: composing
- A curriculum example

9.3 CYBERSCHOOL: BY LEAPS AND BOUNDS

From Progress Report (March 1996), 'Technology and Language and Literacy Learning', Children's Literacy National Projects, Department of Education, Employment, Training and Youth Affairs

TECHNOLOGY PROGRAMS, QUEENSLAND SCHOOLS (excerpts)

Mosman High School

School has successfully developed a special course to cater for indigenous students, in conjunction with the nearby TAFE (technical and further education) college. Three days a week, indigenous secondary students join adult indigenous clients at TAFE where computers are used extensively for literacy and numeracy.

Monkland State School

Thirty-six students (intellectually handicapped, mild to moderate disability) are using sophisticated electronic communication and publishing e.g. World Wide Web. Each student is encouraged to follow an interest area with software such as CD-ROM and Internet.

Charleville Distance Education

Ten modems were distributed to students from pre-school to Year 10 on properties with a computer. Parents and students received a day's training each. Students then started sending messages to each other via Key-Link, an Information Access network database supported by the Queensland Education Department. Later email will be established, and Internet access. First joint project was a local newspaper. The Technical Advisor provides support to parents and children via weekly broadcasts on School of the Air Radio.

Atherton Tablelands Region

BushNet provides access to Internet to isolated small schools.

9.4 STUDENTS AS CYBORGS

> A cyborg is a . . . hybrid of [cybernetic – computer] machine and organism, a creature of social reality as well as a creature of fiction.
>
> (Haraway 1990: 191)

People are shaped by the language they speak and the texts they read, hear and view about themselves and others. Therefore different forms of communication will alter not just our social relations but also our sense of self – our psychological make-up. This includes our sense of ourselves as text users and text makers. This has consequences for ourselves as teachers and for our students, who, as Tuman puts it (1992a: 226–7), 'are likely to come to us deeply enculturated in the notion of "reading" as a kind of literal exploration of new territory and "writing" as a kind of pasting together of diverse materials.'

9.5 THE INTERFACE THAT LAUNCHED A THOUSAND SHIPS: READING IN A NEW MEDIUM

> Understanding of a text occurs when a reader acts purposefully on the given material: to adapt it, integrate it into understanding, hold a conversation – even argue – with it. . . . Understanding means that transformations occur in the reader. A hypertext encourages readers in that kind of interactive processing.

9.6 ALPHABET SOUP

BONHOEFFEN HIGH SCHOOL HANDBOOK: DRAFT NO. 4

Components of the Secondary School English Program

B COMPOSITION (GENRES AND GRAMMAR)

1 **Print texts**
   [as in previous draft]

2 **Electronic texts**

Effectiveness of structure

- control of the collection of materials in and across text nodes and their linking in accordance with purpose
- skill in facilitating readers' associative moves
- ability to control and to combine or transform a range of genres or text types (verbal, visual and auditory)
- ability to construct hypertexts marked by openness and dynamism in use of space

Control of textual features

- ability to manipulate language (words, signs, images, sounds) effectively and appropriately to suit a variety of purposes and audiences
- ability to make effective and economical use of composition spaces and links
- ability to deploy the features of hypertext to communicate meaning e.g. maps and overviews, layout and graphics and icons, links and pathways
- ability to mark up and publish texts in appropriate sites on the Internet

Memo
To English Staff
From Head of Department

So far so good. I think we might need to recognise these skills too –

- deciding the topic of a node
- writing succinctly and coherently within a text space
- providing a transition for the reader between the end of one text and the beginning of another
- organising the writing spaces by setting up links for readers
- providing maps, overviews.

In general I think we're still using writing in a print medium as the 'default mode'. But when we enter the field of electronic composition, we've got to include music, visual art, animation and graphics, diagrams and charts, if we're to help our students communicate in this new environment that integrates all of these forms.

As a result, I believe, we'll need to teach a new kind of structuring, which will be very different from those we currently teach and evaluate – stories and essays. I think it will be more like collage. This kind of composition involves more than throwing a miscellaneous armful of bric-a-brac into a box and letting every passer by make a lucky dip. I'm hoping the Art staff can help us understand more about the aesthetics of collage. (I've got an article by Ulmer (1992) if anyone's interested in following this up.)

Another point: we're still thinking in terms of what individuals do. But computers and electronic networks encourage collaborative composition, and we need to allow for that and assess it as a valid means of producing text.

Please bring along ideas to next meeting. I've invited the Art, Music and Media staff to join us, with their curricular statements in hand, to help us plan for a new literacy across the curriculum.

10.1 WRITES OF PASSAGE

Quotes and notes towards a discussion of composition in a digital age

> Learning these complex, integrated skills [of authoring hypermedia] may in fact be easier for many students than the literacy we now teach. Today we teach students to write in a single medium, one that is remote and artificial relative to their daily experience, and for many of them, alien to their personal communicative dispositions.
>
> (Lemke 1996: 8–9)

I grant that collage is a mode of communication that works by setting one text alongside another, so that the reader works out the connections and the line of argument there in the links the author has set up. I grant that this topographic writing, this spatial kind of composition is dominant in the world of today's students, as Lemke argues. Does this mean we can or should dispense with teaching other forms of composition that give us other ways of making sense of our social world such as narrative, exposition or argumentation? Surely students will still be telling stories, recounting events, reporting matters and arguing a case online?

> We may profit more, at this juncture, by investigating and composing hypertexts with aesthetic rather than purely functional objectives. Not to exclude expository hypertexts; rather, exposition in hypertext becomes even more artistic – the linking and building of webs is a highly complex, aesthetic process.
>
> (McDaid 1991: 453)

Does this mean that narrative and poetry, argument and exposition, can no longer be thought of and taught as separate genres? If this 'hyper-genre' is developing conventions of its own, what are they and how do we teach them? And what are the aesthetics of composing and constructing in this new kind of multi-generic environment?

> To the extent that hypertext challenges traditional intellectual structures, it may be that this cardinal technology, like others before it, will threaten

too much to unhinge us. We may perhaps, in the short term at least, lack the vision to appropriate these tools to the new tasks they suggest.

(Joyce 1995: 49)

We need to ask, 'What does this technology ask you to become to use it fully? Are we prepared to break out of the frames of our present work, our present selves? Break into what spaces for what and who do not yet exist?

10.2 AUTHORSHIP

At present we think of plagiarism as theft of private property – the ideas as expressed by an individual author. And yet we've accepted that texts are written and read, spoken and heard, in relation to other texts, that meanings drift, fragments are woven together, frames yield. This is all the more so when texts occupy the same reading-writing space. So instead of resisting this electronic shiftiness of texts, we could accept the dynamics: here is information interacting with other information to produce new understanding in a text world where voices blend or quarrel.

10.3 INTERVENING

From an email reply from Mark Bernstein of Eastgate Systems (Storyspace)

```
To Wendy Morgan:
Mark Bernstein:
------------------------------------------------
You note that

>When 'reading' some stand-alone Storyreader texts in
>Windows, I was able to insert writing spaces and
>text within those into the original program, and
>create links with the original text, then save it as
>another document. While I'm happy with this level of
>readerly intervention, I'm not sure that the
>original authors would be.

This openess to intervention and inscription is, as
you might expect, an intentional design decision.
Storyspace's designers are deeply interested in
reader intervention, and Michael Joyce in particular
has written extensively on 'constructive hypertext'
```

that invites the reader to rewrite a text that 'is
constantly in the process of becoming'. Both Joyce's
Of Two Minds and Jay David Bolter's Writing Space
discuss this in some detail; Bolter introduces the
hypertext Writing Space with a Copyright Notice that
suggests that the Copyright Notice might itself have
been altered by a previous reader!

The issue of forgery — creation of a modified
hypertext that masquerades as the original — is at
heart a matter of ethical and archival practice.

10.4 NOTE

As one who's just read the stuff on authorship, I'd like to throw a bit of
cold water on the romantic notion about writers and readers being equal
in an electronic world. We'll keep on bowing the knee before the big
names and the big names will keep on big noting themselves on the
global networks. The medium can work to exclude as well as include, to
create hierarchies as well as democracies of writers. That's why we students have to be apprenticed to the trade. We've got to learn to 'speak
the language' (whatever that involves) like a native if we're going to be
read and noticed. For that we still need teachers – those who can help us
make our way in the world – of the World Wide Web.

J. Farmer
Student no: 0987456

10.5 AND ANOTHER

Not being accepted as a fully fledged author? – that's cool. My main
worry is that someone will rip off my work and use it to beef up their
own. Or else they'll simply download something from the Net and pass
it off entire as their own, and so inflate their grades, possibly at the
expense of mine. If this is the new economy of a global village, give me
the suburbs any day and private property I can fence off as my own!

F. Naysmith
Student no: 09865574

10.6 FINGERING THE RED HANDED WRITER

As an example of that stuff on plagiarism I'd just like to dob in the unidentified voice in the node 'Writes of Passage'. S/he uses a phrase, 'topographic writing' without acknowledging that it comes from Jay Bolter, *Writing Space: The Computer, Hypertext, and the History of Writing*, Hillsdale, NJ: Erlbaum.

C. Bentley
Student no: 09854386

11.1 TOURISM WITHOUT TEARS: A CASE STUDY IN NAVIGATING AN ONLINE CURRICULUM

1 Project development
1.1 Curriculum

'Mighty oaks from little acorns grow.' This cross-school, cross-age project using online technologies began when a little seed was planted in the mind of one of our English teachers in the region. Three years ago she was on a bus in North Queensland, taking students on a school excursion to the wet tropical rainforests of the Daintree region, a World Heritage Listed Area. The coach driver mentioned, as part of his usual tourist patter, that Trinity Bay was named by Captain Cook on Trinity Sunday. But when a student asked him which Sunday that was, and why a Sunday should have been named after a trinity, and what was a trinity anyway, the driver couldn't help. This got Ms Vari thinking. First, about mapping and naming: about how Cook assumed he had a right to impose a name on the area that was meant to recall a faraway time and a religion that was alien to the inhabitants of the area. Yet surely the Aboriginal people had already given it a name that evoked their stories about the land and their spiritual relation to it? – A name which is no longer recorded in 'official', non-Aboriginal histories, and a view of the world to which most students in the area have no access.

Ms Vari's next thought was that this could well be the basis of an English unit investigating the first and later names for local places. Cases where she and her students could not retrieve the original names would lead to questions about colonisation. So they would begin to explore the role of language in this, and the right of the powerful to name the world and know it in a way that made it open to exploitation.

But why should the knowledge she and her students gained stay only with them? Why not share it with the tour companies, to enrich the information drivers and guides passed on to travellers? But then – why limit its availability to tourists who opted for guided tours? And why downplay the critical perspectives, by offering just what would be taken as 'information'? And so the seed began to sprout. Ms Vari began to talk with other teachers in her school and to email other teachers linked on the region's network.

At this stage we called the project 'Mapping Stories'. It took the form of an ever-growing database of information, to be made available via a Web site, about the names of places: their origins, their alternatives, and some stories associated with those places. Oral histories recorded with Aboriginal people in the area were central to that Mapping. The planning teachers decided from the outset that such 'information' could never be neutral and should not be presented as if it were: diverse and contradictory materials should be linked in that hypertextual environment. Students in Studies of Society and Environment joined those in English to carry out investigations.

They were soon joined by others. As part of their marketing course, students from Business Studies conducted surveys and interviews to find out what unanswered questions tourists had.

The librarians and information technology advisers were crucial in helping students to locate information, conduct searches on the Net, send email inquiries to experts and discussion groups and to link up with other classrooms in the region. And so they began putting together some of the jigsaw pieces and discussing the emerging fragments of the picture. As the cluster of materials grew, the Art staff enrolled students to design a Home Page for the Web site, while Music students were called on to find or create music for the hypermedia documents being developed as stand-alone texts.

This initiative quickly attracted favourable attention from tour companies, travellers, local businesses, as well as from teachers and students in other subjects. For example, the Legal Studies teachers developed a unit on land tenure in the Daintree region – which includes a peculiar mix of crown land, leasehold and freehold even in the World Heritage listed area. The study also investigated native title, pastoral leases, and mining rights issues. The students' reports on various aspects were subsequently published and linked to other materials on the site.

The Science Department also adapted a number of units. In biology there were two contributing projects. One was a computer-based simulation exercise designed to show graphically the effects of pesticides, herbicides and fertilisers on the biodiversity of the Great Barrier Reef. This joint project with the Science Education School of the University was developed in hypercard form and will next year be available as a CD-ROM.

In the second project, students with the help of the North Queensland Conservation Council compiled a list of rare and endangered species, with a description and picture, and information about their habits and habitat and ways to encourage the preservation of such species. Members of this and other conservation groups were encouraged to use the Web site to post information about possible sightings, seasonal patterns and the like.

Mathematics teachers collaborated with Science and Economics teachers in teaching their students how to develop statistical tables in graphical forms via computer, to be available on the Web. These were used in various projects across the curriculum.

Not to be outdone, the Film and Media Studies teachers in the area joined forces to develop a unit called 'Gone Troppo: Images of Forest and Reef'. Students analysed the construction of the region as a tourist venue through the images presented in promotional films and brochures. They then developed a hypermedia stack to analyse these representations critically and to offer other ways of being a visitor that were environmentally and culturally more sensitive. Much of this has been added to the Web site and linked to materials already there.

Concurrently the primary schools have been pioneering a new development with BushMOO, a virtual bush town designed to share information about our local environment with people overseas. This is a text space environment: as participants 'walk around' in the space they see a description in words of this place or that. In their science lessons the students researched aspects of the environment, and in Language Arts they wrote the descriptions that have created a virtual rainforest. The wealth of material assembled by the secondary students is currently being linked with this site. BushMOO was developed with assistance from the University and an Honours graphics student. And with programming by Guy Carpenter, the systems administrator, Web pages have been linked to the MOO. This innovation is the first of its kind in Australia, and we believe it is a significant curriculum venture into an electronic realm.

11.2 THE URL-Y BIRD CATCHES THE WORM

Transcript from ABC radio programme, 'Click On', 12.5.96 5 p.m.

INTERVIEWER: Was it hard to learn to put that information up on the Internet?

STUDENT: Not really. It's just like doing a project. There's a thing that's called HTML, a special language that tells the computer what to write. And HTML stands for hypertext mark up language.

INTERVIEWER: Do all the children learn HTML? Is there a band of people teach them all that?

TEACHER: Basically most schools are at the early stages, but with my children here at school we've been learning it in its pure form, how to learn the tags and that. It's really important that they learn what they're for. And they develop their Home Pages. They're very simple; there's nothing flash about them at all at the moment. But we're getting there and they're understanding what we're doing, and that's probably better than trying to create them a wonderful flashy page when they don't understand how it works.

RADIO COMMENTATOR: There are lots of programs run by the BushNet. As well as individual students' Home Pages, there's an online athletics competition, and my favourite is the VP Page, run by the ladies of the local Historical Society who attended the school during the Second World War, when it was an army camp. The style and the graphics are very colourful and evocative. When you visit the BushNet pages, you know you're in Far North Queensland. Now there's even a virtual rainforest under construction. . . .

TEACHER: BushMOO is a virtual bush town. It's a text space environment, so as you walk around you don't actually see the room, you see a description. These students are using their Language Arts time to work on the descriptions. It's going across curriculum. In science they're researching the environment. And we have an enrichment and extension project in Mareeba that happened out of our Gifted and Talented Program. It's allowing these students to be more creative. So they're creating this rainforest to share information about our local environment with people overseas. We've got assistance from James Cook University, we've got an Honours graphics student who's working with us so that we will be able to use a piece of programming by Guy Carpenter, our systems administrator, to actually link Web pages to the MOO. So, as you walk through and look at these things, we'll have Web pages up that will be working on such programs as Netscape behind the scenes. This is a big If, but if we do do it this will be a first at least for Australia.

INTERVIEWER: You obviously think the Internet is a very important educational tool.

TEACHER: I feel it's really broadened my horizons. My support network was fairly limited. It takes just over an hour to travel to Cairns . . . and there aren't really too many special needs teachers around, and to get us together is a bit hard. But by using email I've been able to contact hundreds of special educators daily. If I have a problem I can email a special list I'm on with special needs teachers around the world and there's usually someone there who's had that same problem, so I don't need to reinvent the wheel over and over again. And likewise I can help them solve problems I've come across.

INTERVIEWER: So what are you hoping to achieve by allowing all the students access to the Internet?

TEACHER: The future of education is really going to change. . . . So it's really important to help students to learn how to learn rather than what to learn. Using the Internet to do research projects puts them in touch with a wider range of resources than we could ever hope to provide in one school. It allows them to get a window on the world.

11.3 CURRICULUM EVALUATION

Preliminary report (for discussion only)

At the outset we would like to convey our thanks for the invitation to evaluate the Curriculum Project and to advise on further developments.

In general we have been very impressed by every aspect of its development to date. Some members of our team however have raised questions or voiced concerns, which will need to be addressed during our further Working Party sessions. The points that follow are intended to provide a focus for those discussions. They are grouped under the following headings:
1 A cross-disciplinary curriculum
2 Communication with wider communities
3 Effects on teachers and students
4 Technological tools
5 A socially critical practice

11.3.1 A CROSS-DISCIPLINARY CURRICULUM

In our multi-media, technologised society the predominant forms of literacy are changing. This requires a similar change in the kinds of literacy taught and practised in schools. The project is exemplary in this regard. It has thereby revealed a number of considerations for curriculum developers.
1 Teachers across the curriculum areas have needed prompt and expert advice and and support in helping students develop
   • appropriate multimedia reading and writing practices
   • control of the genres dominant in each discipline which may differ markedly from one to another.
2 This new technologised environment gives access to a world of linked knowledge and thus encourages the reframing of the subject disciplines.

Certainly each of these disciplines may help learners to produce knowledge in a way specific to the subject. But our students, in that newly connected world, must also be helped to cross and to challenge the boundaries between those disciplines if they are to produce different, creative ways of thinking and knowing.

3   Critics of such a cross-curricular approach are concerned that it will dilute students' developing expertise in any one area. Our surveys have shown no evidence of this in the region's schools to date.

4   Conversely, it will be crucial to ensure that such an inter-disciplinary curriculum does not become fragmented, linked only by a vaguely 'thematic' focus across the subject boundaries.

5   As we have seen here, a cross-curricular initiative can encourage a positive learning community. In our society beyond school, different individuals and groups develop different kinds of knowledge and skills, which they contribute to that society. A similar kind of contribution to group knowledge and expertise is being modelled here by the students in their collaborations.

6   From the foregoing points a crucial question arises: how are students to develop a multimedia, multi-disciplinary critical literacy? – That is, to understand how partial and 'interested' those ways are of 'reading' and 'writing' the world; to critique them; and to supplement them with others that allow for different voices and viewpoints.

11.3.2 COMMUNICATION WITH WIDER COMMUNITIES

Classrooms, curricula and schools are usually spaces that enclose teachers and learners and forms of knowledge and keep them separate from each other. The social practices developed there are quite different from social practices beyond the school gates.

This project is exemplary in opening up those enclosures by setting up links with local and global communities and their knowledge. We were particularly impressed by the schools' moves to involve parents and local business, community and environmental groups.

However, these opportunities for wider 'conversations' raise a question: how are students being equipped to evaluate the various ideas, 'facts' and viewpoints which each of the communities offers as truth? For example, how would students be helped to differentiate between the truth claims in statements made by a lobbyist for a mining company wanting to extract uranium from a national park area, a scientist weighing up the environmental and economic consequences of mining, and a far left Green campaigner? Our team believes that teachers will need to help students develop the attitudes and skills needed for such critique. This must be undertaken within and also across the curriculum areas. In our information-saturated world such critique is too important to be left to chance or uneven coverage in schools.

11.3.3 EFFECTS ON TEACHERS AND STUDENTS

In the team's view, one of the most obvious benefits has been a shift in the relationships between students and teachers, among students and among teachers. In most curricula the focus is on what teachers teach for students to learn. Here however the teachers have been learners alongside students. Some students have at times taught their teachers and their peers. In such a situation of shared learning about new information and new ways of presenting and critiquing it, the focus has been on what all the learners are doing as they learn, assemble and present their learning in ways that allow others to learn according to their interests and needs.

In a technologised curriculum a particular group of students may become the experts and insiders – the 'nerds' and hackers. We have found no evidence of this here, we believe because of the diversity of curriculum areas, knowledge and skills drawn into the project. The teachers have also avoided this risk in two ways: they have set up a range of productive tasks that contributed to a whole class or team project; and they have supported students according to their abilities and interests. By these means all have felt that their contributions counted.

It is evident too that those younger students who have been involved from the beginning, and who are already more familiar with online communication, will be able to carry the project further as they reach the higher levels of schooling, so that they will be able to handle routine management of and development of the Web site.

11.3.4 TECHNOLOGICAL TOOLS

While our brief does not include matters of technological hardware and software and the mechanics of networking, we would note in passing that the success of the project has relied on cooperation among various experts:

- technical experts, who repaired breakdowns and minimised frustrations; over time they also taught others to become experts
- curriculum experts, who had a cross-curricular, cross-school, cross-community vision
- teaching experts, who understood that students learn differently today in

a multi-media world saturated with information from many sources in which they move selectively
- students, as expert users of multimedia texts, and as peer-teachers.

The benefits of incorporating electronic technologies have clearly out-weighed the significant costs in time and teachers' energies. Some of our team were initially sceptical about such benefits: they wondered how this project would really differ from a similar project accomplished without such elaborate technologies. The answers, we now believe, are to be found in all the areas we have surveyed.

11.3.5 A SOCIALLY CRITICAL PRACTICE

> In asking what computers can do, we are drawn into asking what people can do with them, and in the end addressing the fundamental question of what it means to be human.
>
> (Winograd and Flores 1986: 7)

No technology can be a neutral 'tool'. These computer-mediated tech-nologies carry ideologies – not only in the information they present, but also in the ways they encourage users to act and think, communicate and be as social creatures. Thus computers may be used to support a retrograde status quo, in schools and universities, communities, government and industry. Or they may be used to subvert more repressive forms of power and open up more of life's chances for those who have traditionally been marginalised by the exercise of power in the hands of the few.

First however it must be said that we should not direct all our critique at others' practices while turning our gaze away from our own back yard. For example, the 'Tourism without Tears' Project is a particular package that encourages people to come by particular paths to particular kinds of under-standing, and hence to interact in particular ways with others and with the environment. That is, while the information in the Web site and the hyper-texts may supplement and critique other prevailing forms of knowledge, it is important that students should also be encouraged to critique the texts they themselves have created. Indeed, the critique of their own and others' texts should be mutually informing.

Three suggestions follow for investigating some of the politics of these technologies. All of them pertain in some way to students' immediate con-texts. We would not wish these to be imposed on the curriculum but rather to provide starting points for teachers' discussions about such issues as they arise in the various discipline areas. It is for the teachers to decide the best ways of bringing students to understand any such issues.

Computer mediated communications: enhancing capacities and magnifying differences

First, in a 'webbed' world differences among people may take on new dimensions. To those more familiar forms of difference – region and nation, race and ethnicity, gender, class, generation and the like – we must add another: between those who are wired and those who are not, between those who are plugged into the circuits of the local and global information marketplace and those who are not. In such a situation, how could the democratic potential of electronic information technologies be enhanced?

Second, youth entertainment is increasingly becoming a computerised, digitised, world-wide 'culture industry'. When great profits on a global scale can be made from young people, capitalists in this industry have a correspondingly great motivation to increase their share of the market. However, the technologies also enable easier access to production and distribution. How could this be used to encourage the production and consumption of local talents and to encourage cultural diversity?

Third, schools themselves are sites of difference around computers: professional class students often have very different access at home and school from those of blue-collar class; students identified as less able may be set more routine tasks via computer drills, while the more able are further enabled by being given opportunities for more creative tasks; students of a certain culture, ethnicity and gender may have different learning styles and values from those often encouraged in a computer environment which has tended to favour white males.

How can the norms be altered?

12 DIGITOPIA: UTOPIA OR DYSTOPIA?

The revolution most important to me will be the revolution in access to ideas: a grand open hypertext system that will let anyone explore all the ideas there are in the world, as expounded by those who believe in them.

(Theodor Holm Nelson, cited in Tuman 1992a: 51)

As people concerned with the potential of computer-mediated discourse, we must push for a vision of hypermedia as decentred and democratic, as a read-write rather than read-only medium, and as a way of telling new stories rather than repackaging and repurposing the old.

(McDaid 1991: 456)

Computers are an evolving technology like any other, shaped within particular social relations, and responsive to the needs of those with the power to direct that evolution.

(Ohmann 1985: 680)

Digital data of various kinds is already flowing into our places of work, study and leisure. But the nature of the data and its delivery is part of a huge, evolving transnational marketplace. From the time the term 'information highway' came into common use in the United States, the 'flows of bytes' along cable were seen as potential 'flows of capital'. . . . In September 1993 the White House, presenting its National Information Infrastructure, described the information highway as a means 'to enable US firms to compete and win in the global economy' and to give the domestic economy a 'competitive edge internationally'.

(Nixon 1996: 22)

To us falls the task of breaking a frame many of us are deeply attached to. But we have no choice: we must act, now, to shape a digital culture of empowerment and difference, or we will be swept, wordless, into the matrix where the future may well be a DataBoot – stamping on the human interface, forever.

(McDaid 1991: 457)

13 CHOREOGRAPHY

If I could explain it, I wouldn't have to dance it.

(Isadora Duncan)

What serpentine dance – wreathing sideways, leaves shuffling at your passage – brings you to this point? You may be done with your reading and hoped to find a conclusion here. (Such foolishness: the world serpent bites its own tail.) Or you may just have made your first move and expected to see a forecast, a predigested (book)worm cast. But the text you read has no beginning or end, so how can it be known in advance of your dance across its spaces?

Coda

The end of the previous chapter indicated that there was no ending. So too this book can have no tidy conclusion, no QED. That is why this section is entitled a coda – a passage that passes again over previous tunes. And the practice of an evolving critical literacy goes on, when the book is closed. But at this point, before the last page is turned, it may be useful to gather together some of those tunes and hum a note or phrase again, even with modulations.

There is productive work in the writing here – in two senses. The book is about the ways in which teachers and students, texts and knowledge, procedures and practices are produced in critical literacy classrooms. And this text also produces an account, a version which it promotes through critique of some practices and approval of others.

Classrooms are at the centre of this book, in their diversity as well as in their regularities. The constraints peculiar to such classrooms and schools, to the discourses of English education and teaching practice (some of which we have seen here), need to be acknowledged if critical literacy is to be subtly flexible and answerable – both responsive to and responsible about students' learning, in these conditions.

But here too is a place of possibility: classrooms are a central site of social practice and social relations for teachers and students. A politics is practised here too, of course, and as we have seen classroom politics may itself be the object of critique, for such scrutiny should not concern just what happens elsewhere. It is not just or mostly elsewhere that change occurs.

It could be argued that the kind of critical literacy represented here is concerned more with the politics of representation in texts than with politics *per se*; that changing the range or meaning of texts studied and created does not change the material conditions of our lives. There is some truth in this charge, but it risks setting up a false dichotomy:

> The fact that reality is constructed thus through social and discursive representations does not make 'reality' any less real. But it does mean that 'reality' can be seen differently and difference can be seen in

'reality'. This is a task which can only be carried out through changing our social practices, including the practice of education – a practice which itself plays a significant part in bringing about change.

(Usher and Edwards 1994: 28)

So here is a third sense in which critical literacy can be productive work: it is the means available to critical literacy teachers for helping students use language for change. And through language and practice our subjectivities might also change.

Those teachers we have heard and glimpsed in these pages – their subjectivities are surely changing, as they (re)invent themselves in developing a version of critical literacy that is workable in their environment. They show an admirably stubborn pragmatism and a principled eclecticism as they theorise their practice and practise their theory. They show a principled commitment to social justice even when principles and absolutes can be doubted.

If the teachers produce themselves, and are also produced, in this site, the same is true of their students. They too are 'produced', and 'normalised', within this practice of critical literacy. But as we have seen, they too are continually negotiating a position: of consensus, (partial) conformity, reciprocal critique, resistance, irony and parody. By such interactions communities are constituted. Communities are built on affinity, affection, tolerance, disagreement and difference, and pleasure in company. They depend on desire – to be pleasing to ourselves and to others; desire for the realisation of certain kinds of possible community. And that may entail struggle, conflict.

The kind of teaching argued for here is a practice that supplements the rigour of contestation and critique with the play of enactment, the pleasure of embodiment and engagement of the imagination. These are complementary and can be mutually enhancing. A generous imagination is needed if teachers are to ask how students (and also but not only teachers) are 'right', how they might come to desire to be 'more right', and what part teachers might play in this. Such speculation is demanded in these new times, when new forms of electronic, computer-mediated communication create new texts, new representations of power and desire, and call forth new practices, new subjectivities for teachers and students. These in turn may require new forms of critical literacy. What these may be we do not yet know: the evolving, thoughtful, theorised practice of teachers in company with students will show.

And therefore this conclusion must remain inconclusive: after all, the game of critical literacy is about unsettling certainties. So while some of the issues raised in chapter one (of voice, empowerment, enlightenment, paternalism and the like) remain as issues, this is because they are not problems with a solution but problematics: matters always in question, always in need of questioning, especially when they touch our dearest certainties.

In these pages is one story, told with a conviction that promotes the views summarised here. It follows therefore that these last words must invite critique from others about the certainties offered here, in order to continue the conversations about critical literacy and keep their problematics in play.

Bibliography

Althusser, L. (1971) 'Ideology and ideological state apparatuses', in *Lenin and Philosophy, and Other Essays*, trans. B. Brewster, New York: Monthly Review Press.

Anderson, G. and Irvine, P. (1993) 'Informing critical literacy with ethnography', in C. Lankshear and P. McLaren (eds) *Critical Literacy: Politics, Praxis, and the Postmodern*, Albany, NY: State University of New York Press.

Argyris, C. and Schon, D. (1974) *Theory into Practice*, San Francisco, CA: Jossey-Bass.

Aronowitz, S. (1992) 'Looking out: The impact of computers on the lives of professionals', in M. Tuman (ed.) *Literacy Online: The Promise (and Peril) of Writing with Computers*, Pittsburgh, PA and London: Pittsburgh University Press.

Aronowitz, S. and Giroux, H. (1985) *Education Under Siege*, South Hadley, MA: Bergin and Garvey.

——(1991) *Postmodern Education: Politics, Culture, and Social Criticism*, Minneapolis: University of Minnesota Press.

Australian Education Council and Curriculum Corporation (1994a) *English: A Curriculum Profile for Australian Schools*, Carlton, Vic.

——(1994b) *Statement on English for Australian Schools*, Carlton, Vic.

Australian Education Council and Ministers for Vocational Education, Employment and Training (1992) *Putting General Education to Work: The Key Competencies Report*, Canberra.

Baker, C. (1991) 'Literacy practices and social relations in classroom reading events', in C. Baker and A. Luke (eds) *Towards a Critical Sociology of Reading Pedagogy*, Amsterdam and Philadelphia, PA: John Benjamins.

Baker, C. and Freebody, P. (1989) 'Talk around text: Constructions of textual and teacher authority in classroom discourse', in S. De Castell, A. Luke and C. Luke (eds) *Language, Authority and Criticism: Readings on the School Textbook*, London: Falmer Press.

Barnes, D. (1976) *From Communication to Curriculum*, Harmondsworth: Penguin.

Barnes, D. and Todd, F. (1977) *Communication and Learning in Small Groups*, London: Routledge and Kegan Paul.

Barnes, D., Britton, J. and Rosen, H. (1969) *Language, the Learner and the School*, Harmondsworth: Penguin.

Barrett, E. (1988) 'A new paradigm for writing *with* and *for* the computer', in E. Barrett (ed.) *Text, Context, and Hypertext: Writing with and for the Computer*, Cambridge, MA: MIT Press.

Bauer, M. (ed.) (1994) *Am I Blue? Coming Out from the Silence*, New York: HarperCollins.

Beach, R. (1992) 'Adopting multiple stances in conducting literacy research', in R.

Beach, J. Green, M. Kamil and T. Shanahan (eds) *Multidisciplinary Perspectives on Literacy Research*, Urbana, IL: National Council of Teachers of English.

Berlin, J. (1993) 'Literacy, pedagogy, and English studies: Postmodern connections', in C. Lankshear and P. McLaren (eds) *Critical Literacy: Politics, Praxis, and the Postmodern*, Albany, NY: State University of New York Press.

Board of Senior Secondary School Studies, Queensland (1996) *Senior Syllabus in English*, Brisbane.

Bolter, D.J. (1991) *Writing Space: The Computer, Hypertext, and the History of Writing*, Hillsdale, NJ: Erlbaum.

——(1992) 'Literature in the electronic writing space', in M. Tuman (ed.) *Literacy Online: The Promise (and Peril) of Reading and Writing with Computers*, Pittsburgh, PA: University of Pittsburgh Press.

Bourdieu, P. and Passeron, J.-C. (1977) *Reproduction in Education, Society and Culture*, trans. R. Nice, London: Sage.

Bowles, S. and Gintis, H. (1976) *Schooling in Capitalist America*, New York: Basic Books.

Brice Heath, S. (1983) *Ways with Words: Language, Life and Work in Communities and Classrooms*, Cambridge: Cambridge University Press.

Brice Heath, S. and Mangiola, L. (1991) *Children of Promise: Literate Activity in Linguistically and Culturally Diverse Classrooms*, Washington, DC: National Education Association of the United States.

Brown, M. (1948) *Australian Son: The Story of Ned Kelly*, Melbourne: Georgian House.

Bruner, J. (1988) 'Life as narrative', *Language Arts* 65, 6: 574–83.

Buckingham, D. and Sefton-Green, J. (1994) *Cultural Studies Goes to School: Reading and Teaching Popular Media*, London: Taylor and Francis.

Butler, J. (1991) 'Imitation and gender insubordination', in D. Fuss (ed.) *Inside / Out*, New York: Routledge.

——(1993) 'Critically queer', *CLQ: A Journal of Lesbian and Gay Studies* 1: 17–32.

Cave, C. (ed.) (1968) *Ned Kelly: Man and Myth*, North Ryde, NSW: Cassell.

Cherryholmes, C. (1988) *Power and Criticism: Poststructural Investigations in Education*, New York: Teachers College Press.

Christie, F., Devlin, B., Freebody, P., Luke, A., Martin, J.R., Threadgold, T. and Walton, C. (1991) *Teaching English Literacy: A Project of National Significance on the Preservice Preparation of Teachers for Teaching English Literacy*, Canberra: Department of Employment, Education and Training.

Colmer, J. and Colmer, D. (1987) *Australian Autobiography*, Ringwood, Vic: Penguin.

Corcoran, B. (1994) 'Balancing reader response and cultural theory and practice', in B. Corcoran, M. Hayhoe and G. Pradl (eds) *Knowledge in the Making: Challenging the Text in the Classroom*, Portsmouth, NH: Boynton/Cook Heinemann.

Cox, B. (1991) *Cox on Cox: An English Curriculum for the 1990s*, London: Hodder and Stoughton.

Crawford, J. with Kippax, S., Onyx, J., Gault, U. and Benton, P. (1992) *Emotion and Gender: Constructing Meaning from Memory*, London: Sage.

Davies, B. (1995) 'What about the boys? The parable of the bear and the rabbit', *Interpretations* 28, 2: 1–17.

Department of Education, Queensland (1994a) *A Guide to Using English Syllabus Materials*, Brisbane.

——(1994b) *Syllabus: English for Years 1–10*, Brisbane.

——(1994c) *The Departmental Standard for Inclusive Curriculum*, Brisbane.

Dillon, J.T. (1988) *Questioning and Teaching*, London: Croom Helm.

Dixon, J. (1967) *Growth through English*, London: National Association for the Teaching of English and Oxford University Press.

Doyle, B. (1989) *English and Englishness*, London and New York: Routledge.

Dyson, M. (1994) 'Be like Mike? Michael Jordan and the pedagogy of desire', in H. Giroux and P. McLaren (eds) *Between Borders: Pedagogy and the Politics of Cultural Studies*, New York and London: Routledge.

Eagleton, T. (1983) *Literary Theory: An Introduction*, Oxford: Blackwell.

——(1985) 'The subject of literature', *The English Magazine* 15: 4–7.

Ebert, T. (1991) 'Political semiosis in / of American Cultural Studies', *American Journal of Semiotics* 8: 113-35.

Edwards, A.D. (1981) 'Analysing classroom talk', in P. French and M. MacLure (eds) *School Experience: Explorations in the Sociology of Education*, London: Croom Helm.

Edwards, A.D. and Mercer, N. (1978) *Common Knowledge: The Development of Understanding in the Classroom*, London: Methuen.

Edwards, A.D. and Westgate, D.P.G. (1994) *Investigating Classroom Talk* (revised edition), London: Falmer Press.

Elbow, P. (1990) *What is English?*, New York: Modern Language Association of America, and Urbana, IL: National Council of Teachers of English.

Ellsworth, E. (1989) 'Why doesn't this feel empowering? Working through the repressive myths of critical pedagogy', *Harvard Educational Review* 59, 3: 297-324.

Fairclough, N. (1989) *Language and Power*, London: Longman.

——(ed.) (1992a) *Critical Language Awareness*, London: Longman.

——(1992b) *Discourse and Social Change*, Oxford: Polity Press.

Farwell, G. (1970) *What a Life! Ned Kelly*, Melbourne: Cheshire.

Foucault, M. (1970) *The Order of Things*, New York: Random House.

——(1972) *The Archaeology of Knowledge*, London: Tavistock.

——(1979) *Discipline and Punish: The Birth of the Prison*, New York: Vintage Books.

——(1980) *Power/Knowledge: Selected Interviews and Other Writings*, ed. C. Gordon, New York: Pantheon.

Freedman, A. and Medway, P. (1994) *Learning and Teaching Genre*, Portsmouth, NH: Heinemann / Boynton Cook.

Freire, P. (1970) *Pedagogy of the Oppressed*, New York: Seabury Press.

——(1985) *The Politics of Education: Culture, Power, and Liberation*, trans. D. Macedo, South Hadley, MA: Bergin and Garvey.

Freire, P. and Macedo, D. (1987) *Literacy: Reading the Word and the World*, South Hadley, MA: Bergin and Garvey.

Gee, J.P. (1990) *Social Linguistics and Literacies: Ideology in Discourses*, London: Falmer Press.

——(1991) 'What is literacy?', in C. Mitchell and K. Weiler (eds) *Rewriting Literacy: Culture and the Discourse of the Other*, New York: Bergin and Garvey.

Gee, J.P. and Lankshear, C. (1995) 'The new work order: Critical language awareness and "fast capitalism" texts', *Discourse: Studies in the Cultural Politics of Education* 16, 1: 5–19.

Gilbert, P. (1989) *Writing, Schooling and Deconstruction: From Voice to Text in the Classroom*, London: Routledge.

——(1994) *Divided by a Common Language? Gender and the English Curriculum*, Carlton, Vic: Curriculum Corporation.

Giroux, H. (1983) *Schooling and the Struggle for Public Life: Critical Pedagogy in the Modern Age*, Minneapolis: University of Minnesota Press.

——(1988) *Teachers as Intellectuals: Towards a Critical Pedagogy of Learning*, New York: Bergin and Garvey.

——(1991) 'Literacy, difference, and the politics of border crossing', in C. Mitchell and K. Weiler (eds) *Rewriting Literacy: Culture and the Discourse of the Other*, New York: Bergin and Garvey.

——(1992) *Border Crossings: Cultural Workers and the Politics of Education*, New York and London: Routledge.

Giroux, H. and McLaren, P. (eds) (1994) *Between Borders: Pedagogy and the Politics of Cultural Studies*, New York and London: Routledge.

Gleitzman, M. (1990) *Two Weeks with the Queen*, Sydney: Pan.

Goodson, I. and Medway, P. (eds) (1990) *Bringing English to Order: History and Politics of a School Subject*, London: Falmer Press.

Graff, G. (1992) *Beyond the Culture Wars: How Teaching the Conflicts Can Revitalise American Education*, New York: Norton.

Green, B. (ed.) (1993) *The Insistence of the Letter: Literacy Studies and Curriculum Theorising*, London: Falmer Press.

Green, B. and Beavis, C. (eds) (1996) *Teaching the English Subjects: Essays on English Curriculum*, Geelong, Vic: Deakin University Press.

Green, J. (1988) 'Differing views of the academic and social texts of lessons: An introduction', in J. Green and J. Harker (eds) *Multiple Perspective Analyses of Classroom Discourse*, Norwood, NJ: Ablex.

Green, J. and Harker, J. (eds) (1988) *Multiple Perspective Analyses of Classroom Discourse*, Norwood, NJ: Ablex.

Grossberg, L. (1986) 'Teaching the popular', in C. Nelson (ed.) *Theory in the Classroom*, Urbana and Chicago: University of Chicago Press.

——(1994) 'Bringin' it all back home: Pedagogy and cultural studies', in H. Giroux and P. McLaren (eds) *Between Borders: Pedagogy and the Politics of Cultural Studies*, New York and London: Routledge.

Halliday, M. (1985) *An Introduction to Functional Grammar*, London: Edward Arnold.

Hammett, R. (1992) 'A rationale and unit plan for introducing gay and lesbian literature into the grade 12 curriculum', in P. Shannon (ed.) *Becoming Political: Readings and Writings in the Politics of Literacy Education*, Portsmouth, NH: Heinemann.

Hanrahan, B. (1973) *The Scent of Eucalyptus*, London: Chatto and Windus.

Haraway, D. (1990) 'A manifesto for cyborgs: Science, technology, and socialist feminism in the 1980s', in L. Nicholson (ed.) *Feminism / Postmodernism*, New York and London: Routledge.

Haug, F. with collective researchers (1987) *Female Sexualisation: A Collective Work of Memory*, trans. from the German by Erica Carter, London: Verso.

Hooton, J. (1990) *Stories of Herself When Young: Autobiographies of Childhood by Australian Women*, Melbourne: Oxford University Press.

Hunter, I. (1988) *Culture and Government: The Emergence of Literary Education*, London: Macmillan.

Janks, H. (1993a) *Language and Position* (Critical Language Awareness Series), Johannesburg: Witwatersrand University Press, and Randburg, South Africa: Hodder and Stoughton Educational.

——(1993b) *Language, Identity and Power* (Critical Language Awareness Series), Johannesburg: Witwatersrand University Press and Randburg, South Africa: Hodder and Stoughton Educational.

Jay, G. (1994) 'Taking multiculturalism personally: Ethnos and ethos in the classroom', *American Literary History* 6, 4: 613–31.

Joyce, M. (1995) *Of Two Minds: Hypertext Pedagogy and Poetics*, Ann Arbor: University of Michigan Press.

Kamler, B. and Woods, C. (1987) *Two Pathways to Literacy*, Norwood, SA: Australian Association for the Teaching of English.

Knobel, M. and Lankshear, C. (1995) 'Literacies, texts and difference in the electronic age', in J. Murray (ed.) *Celebrating Difference, Confronting Literacies*, Conference Papers, Australian Reading Association National Conference,

Sydney.

Knoblauch, C. and Brannon, L. (1993) *Critical Teaching and the Idea of Literacy*, Portsmouth, NH: Boynton/Cook Heinemann.

Kress, G. (1985) *Linguistic Processes in Sociocultural Practice*, Geelong, Vic: Deakin University Press.

LaMar, M. and Schnee, E. (1991) *Excerpts from 'The Global Factory' (Activities 1–15)*, New York: International Ladies Garment Workers Union.

Landow, G.P. (1989) 'Hypertext in literary education, criticism and scholarship', *Computers and the Humanities* 23: 173–98.

Lanham, R. (1989) 'The electronic word: Literary study and the digital revolution', *New Literary History* 20, 2: 265–90.

Lankshear, C. (1994) *Critical Literacy*, Canberra: Australian Curriculum Studies Association.

Lankshear, C. and McLaren, P. (eds) (1993) *Critical Literacy: Politics, Praxis, and the Postmodern*, Albany, NY: State University of New York Press.

Lankshear, C. and Williams, L. (1996) 'Discourse, grammar and critical literacy', in W. Morgan (ed.) *Critical Literacy: Readings and Resources*, Norwood, SA: Australian Association for the Teaching of English.

Last Outlaw, The (1980) A Pegasus Television Production in association with the Channel Seven Network, Sydney.

Lather, P. (1992) 'Post-critical pedagogies: A feminist reading', in C. Luke and J. Gore (eds) *Feminisms and Critical Pedagogy*, London: Routledge.

Lemke, J. (1995) *Textual Politics: Discourse and Social Dynamics*, London: Taylor and Francis.

——(1996) 'Critical literacy for the multimedia future', *Interpretations* 29, 2: 1–18.

Luke, A. (1993) 'Genres of power? Literacy education and the production of capital', in R. Hasan and G. Williams (eds) *Literacy in Society*, London: Longman.

Luke, C. (1992) 'Feminist politics in radical pedagogy', in C. Luke and J. Gore (eds) *Feminisms and Critical Pedagogy*, London: Routledge.

Lurie, M. (1987) *Whole Life: An Autobiography*, Melbourne: McPhee Gribble.

Lusted, D. (1986) 'Why pedagogy?', *Screen* 27, 5: 2–14.

Lyotard, J.-F. (1984) *The Postmodern Condition: A Report on Knowledge*, trans. G. Bennington and B. Massumi, Minneapolis: University of Minnesota Press.

Mac an Ghaill, M. (1994) *The Making of Men: Masculinities, Sexualities and Schooling*, Buckingham: Open University Press.

McDaid, J. (1991) 'Breaking frames: Hyper-mass media', in E. Berk and J. Devlin (eds) *Hypertext-Hypermedia Handbook*, New York: McGraw-Hill.

Macdonell, D. (1986) *Theories of Discourse: An Introduction*, Oxford: Blackwell.

McHoul, A. (1978) 'The organisation of turns of formal talk in the classroom', *Language in Society* 7: 183–213.

McLaren, P. (1995) *Critical Pedagogy and Predatory Culture: Oppositional Politics in a Postmodern Era*, London and New York: Routledge.

Macleod, M. (1996) *Ready or Not: Stories of Young Adult Sexuality*, Sydney: Random House.

McNeil, L. (1988) *Contradictions of Control: School Structure and School Knowledge*, London and New York: Routledge.

Martin, J. (1985) *Factual Writing*, Geelong, Vic: Deakin University Press.

Martino, W. (1994) 'Masculinity and learning: Exploring boys' under-achievement and under-representation in subject English', *Interpretations* 27, 2: 22–57.

Martino, W. with Mellor, B. (1995) *Gendered Fictions*, Cottesloe, WA: Chalkface Press.

Meek, M. and Miller, J. (eds) (1984) *Changing English: Essays for Harold Rosen*, London: Heinemann Educational.

Mehan, H. (1979) *Learning Lessons: Social Organisation in the Classroom*, Cambridge, MA: Harvard University Press.

Mellor, B., Hemming, J. and Leggett, J. (1984) *Changing Stories*, London: ILEA Centre, and Scarborough, WA: Chalkface Press.

Mellor, B., Patterson, A. and O'Neill, M. (1991) *Reading Fictions*, Scarborough, WA: Chalkface.

Meredith, J. and Scott, B. (1980) *Ned Kelly: After a Century of Acrimony*, Melbourne: Lansdowne Press.

Merod, J. (1992) 'Blues and the art of critical teaching', in M. Kecht (ed.) *Pedagogy is Politics: Literary Theory and Critical Teaching*, Urbana and Chicago: University of Illinois Press.

Misson, R. (1994) *A Brief Introduction to Literary Theory*, Carlton, Vic: Victorian Association for the Teaching of English.

——(1995) 'Dangerous lessons: Sexuality issues in the English classroom', *English in Australia* 112: 25–32.

——(1996) 'What's in it for me? Teaching against homophobic discourse', in L. Laskey and C. Beavis (eds) *Schooling and Sexualities: Teaching for a Positive Sexuality*, Geelong, Vic: Deakin University Press.

Morgan, W. (ed.) (1987) *Border Territory: An Anthology of Unorthodox Australian Writing*, Melbourne: Thomas Nelson.

——(1992a) 'Changing the face of the body of literature: Deviant writing in the secondary classroom', in *Reconstructing English Teaching*, Norwood, SA: Australian Association for the Teaching of English.

——(1992b) *A Post-Structuralist English Classroom: The Example of Ned Kelly*, Carlton, Vic: Victorian Association for the Teaching of English.

——(1993a) 'Self as text', in *Exploring and Connecting Texts*, Adelaide: Education Department of South Australia.

——(1993b) 'Talking like a book: Confessions of a course book writer', *Words'Worth* 26, 1: 28–32.

——(1994a) '"Clothes wear out, learning doesn't": Realising past and future in today's critical literacy curriculum', Perth, WA: Papers of the Australian Association for the Teaching of English National Conference.

——(1994b) 'Critical literacy: More than sceptical distrust or political correctness?', Keynote Address for the Australian Association for the Teaching of English Seminar (National Professional Development Program), Brisbane, Qld.

——(ed.) (1994c) *Figures in a Landscape: Writing from Australia*, Cambridge: Cambridge University Press.

——(1994d) *Ned Kelly Reconstructed*, Melbourne: Cambridge University Press.

——(1994e) 'The play of texts in contexts', *Literacy Learning: Secondary Thoughts* 2, 2: 8–24.

——(1994f) 'Works of literature or the play of texts? Unconventional writing in the secondary classroom', in B. Corcoran, M. Hayhoe and G. Pradl (eds) *Knowledge in the Making: Challenging the Text in the Classroom*, Portsmouth, NH: Boynton/Cook Heinemann.

Morgan, W., Williams, L., Werba, S., Cameron, L. and Moodley, P. (1995) *A World of Texts: Global Understanding in the English Classroom*, Brisbane: Global Learning Centre.

Morgan, W., Gilbert, P., Lankshear, C., Werba, S. and Williams, L. (1996) *Critical Literacy*, Norwood, SA: Australian Association for the Teaching of English, sponsored by the Commonwealth Department of Employment, Education and Training as part of the National Professional Development Program.

Morton, D. and Zavarzadeh, M. (eds) (1991) *Theory, Pedagogy, Politics: Texts for Change*, Urbana: University of Illinois Press.

Nixon, H. (1996) '"In plain English and without the snake oil": Educating the non-wired generation', *Interpretations* 29, 2: 19–37.

Ohmann, R. (1985) 'Literacy, technology, and monopoly capital', *College English* 47, 7: 675–89.

Orner, M. (1992) 'Interrupting the calls for student voice in "liberatory" education: A feminist poststructuralist perspective', in C. Luke and J.Gore (eds) *Feminisms and Critical Pedagogy*, London: Routledge.

Otte, G. (1995) 'In-voicing: Beyond the voice debate', pp. 147–55 in J. Gallop (ed.) *Pedagogy: The Question of Impersonation*, Bloomington and Indianapolis: Indiana University Press.

Pallotta-Chiarolli, M. (1995) '"Only your labels split me": Interweaving ethnicity and sexuality in English studies', *English in Australia* 112: 33–44.

Pausacker, J. (ed.) (1996) *Hide and Seek: Stories about being Young and Gay/Lesbian*, Melbourne: Reed.

Pennycook, A. (1994) 'Incommensurable discourses?', *Applied Linguistics* 15, 2: 115–38.

Plumarom, A. (1993) 'What's wrong with mass ecotourism?', *Contours* 6, 3/4: 15–21.

Postman, N. (1988) *Conscientious Objections*, New York: Knopf.

Poynton, C. (1985) *Language and Gender: Making the Difference*, Geelong, Vic: Deakin University Press.

Reeves, T. (1993) 'Research support for interactive multimedia: Existing foundations and new directions', in C. Latchem, J. Williamson and L. Henderson-Lancett (eds) *Interactive Multimedia*, London: Kogan Page.

Reid, I. (ed.) (1987) *The Place of Genre in Learning: Current Debates*, Geelong, Vic: Deakin University Centre for Studies in Literary Education.

Richardson, P. (1994) 'Language as personal resource and as social construct: Competing views of literacy pedagogy in Australia', in A. Freedman and P. Medway (1994) *Learning and Teaching Genre*, Portsmouth, NH: Heinemann / Boynton Cook.

Rockhill, K. (1993) 'Dis/connecting literacy and sexuality: Speaking the unspeakable in the classroom', in C. Lankshear and P. McLaren (eds) *Critical Literacy: Politics, Praxis, and the Postmodern*, Albany, NY: State University of New York Press.

Salvatori, M. (1994) 'Pedagogy and the academy: "The divine skill of the born teacher's instincts"', in P. Sullivan and D. Qualley (eds) *Pedagogy in the Age of Politics: Writing and Reading (in) the Academy*, Urbana, IL: National Council of Teachers of English.

Schwartz, H.J. (1992) '"Dominion everywhere": Computers as cultural artifacts', in M. Tuman (ed.) *Literacy Online: The Promise (and Peril) of Reading and Writing with Computers*, Pittsburgh, PA and London: Pittsburgh University Press.

Seal, G. (1980) *Ned Kelly in Popular Tradition*, Melbourne: Hyland House.

Sholle, D. and Denski, S. (1993) 'Reading and writing the media: Critical media literacy and postmodernism', in C. Lankshear and P. McLaren (eds) *Critical Literacy: Politics, Praxis, and the Postmodern*, Albany, NY: State University of New York Press.

Shor, I. (1980) *Critical Teaching and Everyday Life*, Chicago: University of Chicago Press.

——(ed.) (1987) *Freire for the Classroom: A Sourcebook for Liberatory Teaching*, Portsmouth, NH: Heinemann / Boynton-Cook.

Simon, R. (1992) *Teaching Against the Grain: Texts for a Pedagogy of Possibility*, New York: Bergin and Garvey.

——(1995) 'Face to face with alterity: Postmodern Jewish identity and the question of pedagogy', in J. Gallop (ed.) *Pedagogy: The Question of Impersonation*,

Bloomington and Indianapolis: Indiana University Press.

Simpson, R. (1977) *The Trial of Ned Kelly*, Melbourne: Heinemann Educational.

Sinclair, J.McH. and Coulthard, R.M. (1975) *Towards an Analysis of Discourse: The English Used by Teachers and Pupils*, London: Oxford University Press.

Singh, M. Garbutcheon (1989) 'A counter-hegemonic orientation to literacy in Australia', *Journal of Education* 171, 2.

Slatin, J.M. (1990) 'Reading hypertext: Order and coherence in a new medium', *College English* 52, 8: 870–83.

Smith, R., Curtin, P. and Newman, L. (1996) 'Kids in the kitchen: The educational implications of computer and computer games use by young children', Presentation at the Australian Association for Research in Education Annual Conference, Newcastle, NSW.

Stewart, D. (1943) *Ned Kelly*, Sydney: Angus and Robertson, reprinted in *Three Australian Plays* (1963), Ringwood, Vic: Penguin.

Strickland, R. (1991) 'Confrontational pedagogy and the introductory literature course', in J. Cahalan and D. Downing (eds) *Practicing Theory in Introductory College Literature Courses*, Urbana, IL: National Council of Teachers of English.

Thorburn, K. (1995) 'Critical literacy', *Words'Worth* 28,1: 51–9.

Thredgold, T. (ed.) (1987) *Semiotics, Ideology, Language*, Sydney: Sydney Association for Studies in Society and Culture.

Tuman, M. (ed.) (1992a) *Literacy Online: The Promise (and Peril) of Reading and Writing with Computers*, Pittsburgh, PA and London: Pittsburgh University Press.

——(1992b) *Word Perfect: Literacy in the Computer Age*, London: Falmer Press.

Ulmer, G. (1989) *Teletheory: Grammatology in the Age of Video*, London: Routledge.

——(1992) 'Grammatology (in the stacks) of hypermedia: A simulation', in M. Tuman (ed.) *Literacy Online: The Promise (and Peril) of Reading and Writing with Computers*, Pittsburgh, PA and London: Pittsburgh University Press.

Usher, R. and Edwards, R. (1994) *Postmodernism and Education*, London: Routledge.

Utemorrah, D. (1990) *Do Not Go Around the Edges*, Broome, WA: Magabala Books.

Wallace, C. (1992) 'Critical literacy awareness in the EFL classroom', in N. Fairclough (ed.) *Critical Language Awareness*, London: Longman.

Warnock, J. (1996) 'What we talk about when we talk about politics', in J. Slevin and A. Young (eds) *Critical Theory and the Teaching of Literature: Politics, Curriculum, Pedagogy*, Urbana, IL: National Council of Teachers of English.

Weedon, C. (1987) *Feminist Practice and Poststructuralist Theory*, Oxford: Blackwell.

Williams, L. (1995) 'Planet teenager', in W. Morgan, L. Williams, S. Werba, L. Cameron and P. Moodley, *A World of Texts: Global Understanding in the English Classroom*, Brisbane: Global Learning Centre.

Williams, R. (1989) 'Adult education and social change', in *What I Came to Say*, London: Hutchinson–Radus.

Willinsky, J. (1990) *The New Literacy*, New York and London: Routledge.

Winograd, T. and Flores, F. (1986) *Understanding Computers and Cognition: A New Foundation for Design*, Reading, MA: Addison-Wesley.

Young, R.E. (1984) 'Teaching equals indoctrination: The dominant epistemic practices of our schools', *British Journal of Educational Studies* 32, 3: 220–38.

Zavarzadeh, M. (1992) 'Theory as resistance', in M. Kecht (ed.) *Pedagogy is Politics: Literary Theory and Critical Teaching*, Urbana and Chicago: University of Illinois Press.

Index

aesthetics, in relation to critical literacy 90–2
agency 16–17; *see also* subjectivity
Althusser 7
Anderson 35
Aronowitz 5, 9, 24, 182
assessment tasks 87, 95; conditions and criteria for 146–7, 159, 163; in critical literacy 88, 141–3, 163–4; as folios 146, 159; individualism in 164–5; teachers' reading of 147–8, 159–60, 161
authority: of readers and readings 97, 98–101; of researcher 81–2; in student writing 154; of teacher in relation to student 88–9, 92, 101–4, 156, 161–2; *see also* freedom
authorship, in electronic text environment 180–1, 192–3
autobiography: in biography unit 76; childhood, reconstructed in 63, 66–7; curriculum unit in 62–71; forms of 65, 68; identity in 63–4, 69, 70; as life textually constructed 64–5, 68, 70; narrative in 63–4, 68; post-structuralist theories of 63–4; reading of 65–8; student writing of 68, 70

Baker 102, 109, 134
Barnes 109, 112
Barrett 182
Bauer 56
Beavis 1
Berlin 8
Bernstein 192
binary oppositions 26, 47, 125, 163
biography: collective 76; curriculum unit in 71–7; interviewing for 75; rationale for teaching 72–3
Bolter 180, 181, 193, 194
'borders' and critical pedagogy 5
Bothwell, V. ch. 4 (pp. 79–105) *passim*
Bourdieu 7, 51
Bowen 67–8
Bowles 7
Brannon 9, 10, 13, 29, 33, 100, 138
Brice Heath 35
Bruner 65
Buckingham 11, 12, 20, 32, 33
BushMOO 196, 197
BushNet 188, 197
Butler 52–3

Campbell 173
catechism in teacher discussion 109
CD-ROM, evaluation of 174–5, 176–7
Cherryholmes 44, 137
Christie *et al.* 2, 17, 109
Colmer 63
community, links with in electronically based curriculum 199–200
composition: ch. 6 (pp. 141–66) *passim*; in age of electronic text 189–91; *see also* assessment, autobiography, biography
computer games 175–6
conflicts, debate about 52
conscientisation, Freirean 9, 10
Corcoran 23, 62
Coulthard 109
Cox 17
Crawford 76
critical literacy: and aesthetics 90–2; assessment tasks 165–6, ch. 6 (pp. 141–66) *passim*; classroom discussion in 109–10; and composition

instruction 58, 62, 93–6; concepts
and pedagogy 137; curricular units
32–51; defined 1–2, 6; discourse of,
in English teaching 20, 83; in
educational policy 22; in electronic
environment 176–7, 199–200, 201–2;
metaphors of 84–7; as orthodoxy in
Australia 21–5, 79, 105; postmodern
25–8, 82; as social practice 28, 140;
students' responses to 103, ch. 6 (pp.
141–66) *passim*; success in 165–6; *see
also* curriculum planning, pedagogy,
critical
cultural heritage, in English teaching
18, 20; and composition instruction
60; in teachers' discussion 90–2
cultural studies 23
curriculum development in Australian
schools 22
curriculum planning for critical
literacy 29, 114; for academic literacy
115; critique of 43–5; in electronic
environment 194–6, 198–202; foci in
32–5; theories of texts on which
based 39–43; for workplace 115–16;
see also chs 3 (pp. 57–78) and 4 (pp.
79–105), *passim*
cyborg 187

Davis 23, 47
DeBevois 172
decentring 69, 73, 74
deconstructive critique 27
Denski 16
desire 27, 44–5; in curriculum 45–51,
52, 55
Dezell 173
dialogue: democratic 15; emancipatory
15–16
Dickens 91, 115
discourse: in biography unit 72–8; in
sociolinguistic theories 2–5, 81; in
texts 39–40, 42, 94
discourses of English education 1, 2; in
Australia 17–21; in teachers'
discussion ch. 4 (pp. 79–105) *passim*
Dixon 1
docuverse 180
Doyle 1
Dyson 31

Eagleton 50, 90
Ebert 27

'ecstasy', pedagogy of 55
education, aims of 16; *see also*
schooling
Edwards 11, 14, 27, 55, 109, 110, 114,
124, 138, 203
Elbow 1
Ellsworth 12, 15, 16
emancipation 14, 15, 27; *see also* critical
literacy, metaphors of
embodiment 53
empowerment 13–15
English: A Curriculum Profile 22
English Syllabus, Queensland 17, 19,
23–4, 72, 91, 95
enlightenment, critical 11–13, 26, 27,
86; *see also* critical literacy,
metaphors of
enterprise bargaining 123–4, 125
ethics 51, 89; *see also* social justice
ethnography, by students 35

Fairclough 2, 5, 110, 166
Farwell 39
Flores 201
Foucault 2, 10, 25, 79, 142, 162
Freebody 102, 109, 134
Freedman 95
freedom: of readers and readings 86,
92, 97, 98–101; in student–teacher
relations 101–4, 163; *see also*
authority
Freire 5–6, 8–9, 12–13, 25, 33, 71
functional literacy 59–60, 93–4

Gee 2, 5, 62, 110, 116, 135, 139,
166
gender issues 29, 30, 47; in student
critique of *Romeo and Juliet* 117–19,
121–2, 126–7, 150–2, 153, 156
genres: in assessment tasks 146–7, 159,
163; in composition instruction 59,
61; in electronic text environment
189–92; in English teaching 19,
20–21; parodied 160–1; in student
writing 149, 154–6; in teachers'
discussion 93–6
Gilbert 23, 24, 48
Gintis 7
Giroux 5, 6, 9, 10, 11, 12, 13, 15, 24,
30
Gleitzman 49
Goodson 1
Gorman 180

Graff 52
grammar, as tool of critical analysis
      94–5, 117–19
Green, B. 1
Green, J. 109
Grossberg 32, 33–34

Halliday 19, 94, 113
hamburger, in critical pedagogy 9–10,
      12
Hammett 45
handwriting 57–8
Hanrahan 65, 66, 67–8, 71
Haraway 189
Harker 109
Harlen 49
Haug 76
hegemony 7
homophobia 47, 49–50
Hooton 63, 64
Hunter 1
hypermedia 183; see also CD-ROM, ch.
      7 (pp. 167–203) passim
hypertext: argumentation in 183–7;
      associative links in 183; see also ch. 7
      (pp. 167–203) passim

identity 46, 53, 72; in autobiographical
      writing 64, 69, 70–1; see also
      subjectivity
ideology 7, 8, 42, 46, 47, 48, 51, 94, 137;
      analysed in biography unit 76; of
      'maverick managers' 119–21
imagination, in critical literacy 48, 55,
      74, 156; see also sociological
      imagination
Irvine 35

Janks 138
Jovic, S. ch. 4 (pp. 79–105) passim
Joyce 168, 190, 191

Kamler 23
Kelly, Ned, in curriculum unit 35–6, 38,
      39, 40, 42
Key Competencies 116
Knobel 178
Knoblauch 9, 10, 13, 29, 33, 100, 138
knowledge: constituted through
      classroom talk 132–9 and ch. 5 (pp.
      105–140) passim; in research 112;
      'schooled' 71, 73, 113
Kress 23, 110

LaMar 33
Landow 182
language: of critique and possibility
      7
Lanham 182
Lankshear 2, 6, 8, 9, 10, 11, 16, 23, 24,
      37, 94, 116, 135, 138, 178
Lather 26
Lemke 2, 52, 53, 189
literacy: in biography unit 74, 77; in
      critical literacy curriculum 34–5, 166;
      in electronic text environment 187–8,
      189, 198–9
literary criticism, value of 67, 90
literature study 71, 115, 159; threatened
      by computers 179–80
Luke, A. 2, 23, 24
Luke, C. 7
Lurie 41, 64
Lusted 111
Lyotard 7

Mac an Ghaill 47
McDaid 175, 191, 202, 203
Macdonnell 2
Macedo 12–13
McHoul 117, 124
McLaren 2, 5, 6, 8, 9, 10, 11, 16, 24, 32
Macleod 48
McNeil 133
Mangiola 35
Manning Clark 36
Martin 4
Martino 23, 48
masculinity 47
'maverick managers' 119–20
Mayer Report 148
Meday 1, 95
Meek 1
Mehan 117
Mellor 23
Mercer 124
Meredith 42
Merod 33
Miller 1
Misson 23, 45, 47, 100
models of English teaching 2
Monteiro, I. ch. 4 (pp. 79–105) passim
MOO 168–71
Morgan 23, 36, 41, 43, 62, 63, 74, 159,
      160
Morgan et al. 20, 29, 37, 42
Morton 31

multiculturalism, policy of 22
multimedia: *see* hypermedia

Nelson 202
Nixon 203

Ohmann 203
oppression 14
Orner 15
Ortega 51
Otte 54

Pallotta-Chiarolli 45
Park Ridge State High School 72;
    classroom talk in ch. 5 (pp. 106–140)
    passim; teachers on critical literacy
    ch. 4 (pp. 79–105) *passim*
parody 160–1
Passeron 7, 51
Patterson 23
Pausacker 56
pedagogy, critical/radical 6–7, 8, 10;
    conflict between means and ends
    137; critiques of 10–17; talk in 111;
    and teaching practice 30–2, 79
Pennycook 94
performative approaches to English
    teaching 51–4
'personal growth', in English teaching
    18, 20, 86, 96; and composition 58–9,
    60; *see also* writing, process of
pleasure 27, 48; in texts 44, 92; *see also*
    desire
Plumarom 40
political correctness 87, 143, 165
popular music, in critical literacy 33–4
Postman 173
postmodernism, ludic or resistant 23,
    27
poststructuralism: critiques of critical
    pedagogy 10–17; theory of texts 8,
    100–1, 159
power 14–15, 26; in classroom talk ch.
    5 (pp. 106–140) *passim*; in research
    112; student discussion of 128–9, 135;
    teachers' assessments as means of
    142–3
Poynton 71
practice: *see* theory and practice
praxis 8-9; in Australian critical
    literacy 24; critiques of 16–17

racism in texts 42–3

rationality, critiques of 12, 26
readers' responses 96–7, 98–101, 155; to
    hypertext 180–1, 182–3
Reeves 181
Reid 19
representation, textual 7, 23, 204–5; *see
    also* chs. 2 and 3 (pp. 29–78) for
    curriculum units on topic
research: data in 82, 112; discourse
    analysis methods 113; theory laden
    111
'resistant reading' 62, 74, 155
Richardson 95
Rockhill 45
role play 54

Salvatori 80
Schnee 33
schooling: aims of 16; in electronic text
    environment 177–8, 185; and social
    reproduction 7, 51, 141
Schwartz 186
Scott 42
Sculley 174
Seal 41
Sefton-Green 11, 12, 20, 32, 33
Senior Syllabus in English, Queensland
    20
sexuality 45, 47, 48; *see also* gender
    issues
Shakespeare 90, 91, 108, 115; *Merchant
    of Venice, The* 154; *Romeo and Juliet*
    117, 121–2, 126–7, 137, 138, 150–7
shirt manufacture, as topic of critical
    pedagogy 33
Sholle 16
Shor 6, 9, 10, 12
Simon 31, 53
Sinclair 109
Singh 35
Slatin 183
social justice: discourse of 87–9; policy
    of 22, 25, 80; student conformity to
    88, 143, 156
socioeconomic class, issues of 121–2,
    151, 153, 156
sociolinguistics 23–4
sociological imagination 67
Statement on English 17, 22
Stewart 36, 40–1, 42
Strickland 13
students, first world 14–15, 16,
    71

subjectivity 26, 52, 53; in autobiography 63–4, 78; *see also* identity

talk: in classroom relations 111, 139–40; in group work 117–24; IRE sequence of 113, 119, 124–30; in lesson phases 114–15; in producing knowledge 132–8; student evaluations of 130–2; student interrogation of teacher 123–4, 128–9
teachers: as agents of emancipation 14, 26; in electronic text environment 200; as transformative intellectuals 13
technology: programs in schools 188, 200–1
Tennyson 173, 176
texts: defined 29; in hypertext 167–8; juxtaposition of 39–43; as repository of meaning 97
theory and practice 28; *see also* ch. 4 (pp. 79–105) *passim*
Thomson 23
Thorburn 24
Thredgold 23
Todd 112
tourism in curriculum unit 37–8, 38–40, 41, 42, 194–6
Trojan War: *see Ulysses*
truth, scepticism about 10–11, 26

Tuman 179–80, 182, 184, 185, 187, 189, 202
Turner 23

Ulmer 185, 191
Ulysses (CD-ROM) 172–4, 176–7
Usher 11, 14, 27, 55, 205
Utemorrah 88

vanguardism 11–12

Wallace 34, 62, 138
Weedon 2, 4, 78
Westgate 109, 110, 114, 124, 138
Whole Language Movement 18
Williams, L 33, 37, 46, 72, 74–8, ch. 4 (pp. 79–105) and ch. 5 (pp. 106–140) *passim*
Williams, R. 31
Willinsky 1
Winograd 201
Woods 23
World Wide Web 170, 172, 181–2, 194–6, 196–8
writing, *see* composition
writing, process of 60–1

Young 113, 124

Zavarzadeh 31, 109